Aristotle's Critique of Political Economy

This book presents a positive account of Aristotle's theory of political economy, arguing that it contains elements that may help us better understand and resolve contemporary social and economic problems.

The book considers how Aristotle's work has been utilized by scholars including Marx, Polanyi, Rawls, Nussbaum and Sen to develop solutions to the problem of injustice. It then goes on to present a new Social Welfare Function (SWF) as an application of Aristotle's theory. In exploring how Aristotle's theories can be applied to contemporary social welfare analysis, the book offers a study that will be of relevance to scholars of the history of economic thought, political theory and the philosophy of economics.

Robert L. Gallagher is Director of the Eudemian Institute and Honorary Research Associate at the Institute for Philosophy and Social Theory, University of Belgrade, Serbia. Dr Gallagher lives in Lebanon.

T0383117

Routledge Studies in the History of Economics

For a full list of titles in this series, please visit www.routledge.com/series/SE0341

Aristotle's Critique of Political Economy

With a Contemporary Application

Robert L. Gallagher

Routledge
Taylor & Francis Group

LONDON AND NEW YORK

First published 2018
by Routledge

2 Park Square, Milton Park, Abingdon, Oxfordshire OX14 4RN
52 Vanderbilt Avenue, New York, NY 10017

Routledge is an imprint of the Taylor & Francis Group, an informa business

First issued in paperback 2020

British Library Cataloguing-in-Publication Data
A catalogue record for this book is available from the British Library

Library of Congress Cataloging-in-Publication Data
A catalog record has been requested for this book

ISBN: 978-1-138-64471-7 (hbk)
ISBN: 978-0-367-66656-9 (pbk)

Typeset in Bembo
by Swales & Willis Ltd, Exeter, Devon, UK

To Catherine

Contents

Figures

Tables

Foreword

David Konstan

New York University

What has Aristotle to do with modern life, and more especially, with modern economic life, with its industrialized production, global range, finance capital, and mysterious laws of supply and demand? Thomas Jefferson affirmed: "The introduction of this principle of representative democracy has rendered useless almost everything written before on the structure of government; and in great measure, relieves our regret, if the political writings of Aristotle, or of any other ancient, have been lost, or are unfaithfully rendered or explained."[1] Is this critical distance from antiquity not even more true for the structure of the economy? Aristotle's view of economics has been taken to be moral rather than strictly speaking economic. Rather than providing an objective description of how exchange works, he seems to seek fairness as the governing principle. Although Karl Marx acknowledged Aristotle's discussion of use value and exchange value as a major moment in the development of economic theory, he assumed that his own analysis entirely superseded that of his ancient Greek predecessor.

In the remarkable book you hold in your hands, Robert Gallagher has challenged the notion that Aristotle's economic thought is in any respect antiquated. Surveying with magisterial authority the views of Marx, John Rawls, Amartya Sen, Martha Nussbaum, Karl Polanyi, and other major economic theorists, Gallagher shows how Aristotle's interpretation of exchange is both mathematically sophisticated and socially positive. To be sure, Aristotle is not indifferent to the ethical dimension of exchange; as Gallagher points out, "The relationship through which superior members of a community benefit the more needy ones, characterizes for Aristotle a special sort of civic friendship, the aim of which is to maintain the existence, the being, of the lesser party . . . Aristotle's proposal encourages superior parties to practice the virtue of generosity, which *for them* is essential to the good life as a life of virtue." Despite the vogue of virtue ethics these days, Aristotle's insistence on the relationship between economic exchange and the good life may seem archaic. Yet modern approaches from those of Sen and Nussbaum also insist that the economy should promote the development of capacities and the "flourishing" of all members of society. But Aristotle has more to say on the topic: for him, reciprocity in exchange and justice share crucial properties. As Gallagher writes, when a shoemaker is in the business of purchasing a house, "under Aristotle's account of reciprocity in a community, the shoemaker deserves to receive the house because he is a member of such and such a community in which it is his function to practice the *techne* of shoemaking, just as it is the house builder's function to practice that of house building. To deny his need of a house, the community would have to deny its own need for his function. It can no more do that than it can get along with a two-legged stool." In contrast to modern views, according to which we are all equal because we are all the same, Aristotle recognizes the essential differences between one individual, or rather, one social function, and another. As Gallagher astutely observes, "surprisingly, it is through inequality that the rights of the individual are protected."

Gallagher's interpretations of Aristotle's ethical and metaphysical commitments and the way they contribute to his economic insights would be valuable enough in themselves, as would his comparisons with modern heirs to Aristotle's value-oriented critique of economy such as Sen and Nussbaum. But Gallagher offers much more, in the form of an original, consistent, and compelling reconstruction of the mathematical premises of Aristotle's arguments. Some of these pages make for hard going for those not familiar with mathematical economics, but please do not be daunted or put off by the symbols, fractions, and equations. What we learn is that mathematical modelling and coherence in the interpretation of exchange were as important for Aristotle as they are in modern theories. Yes, you will see formulas like $N_\delta \approx \frac{\alpha}{\beta} N_\gamma$ (and still more complicated ones), but Gallagher is careful to explain: "That means that party α is materially rewarded through the transaction due to possessing a higher status. That higher relative status skews the exchange ratio." Professional economists and mathematicians will want to examine the formulas, but we can all understand the narrative, and what it shows is that there is a solid, and still relevant, basis to Aristotle's economic ethics.

Gallagher's book is a major contribution to the understanding of Aristotle's political, ethical, and economic thought, but it is also more than that. For behind the scholarly analysis of Aristotle's texts there is a deep commitment on Gallagher's part to a different way of viewing economics, fully adumbrated in Aristotle's treatment but obscured by centuries of misinterpretation or indifference, when it was assumed that economics had no relation to justice. Gallagher has enlisted Aristotle as an ally – a most powerful one – in his argument, gracefully presented, for an economic vision that can have meaning today as well as in classical Greece. In a world of growing inequality and exploitation, Gallagher's argument deserves our most careful consideration.

Note

1 Thomas Jefferson to Isaac H. Tiffany, 26 August 1816; available online at https://founders. archives.gov/documents/Jefferson/03-10-02-0234 (accessed 24 October 2017).

Preface

I first became aware of the need for this book in my early twenties struggling to understand Marx's *Capital*, one of the works discussed in these pages. I was surprised to see that Marx uses the same model of exchange as Adam Smith and other modern economists. But the clue in Marx's text, in his criticism of Aristotle, to an alternative to the "classical" exchange model escaped my youthful attention. After some years, the project came to lay dormant. Suddenly it was revived decades later, after studying Aristotle's metaphysics and ethics. Here, Aristotle's alternative theory of political economy receives, I believe, its first accurate and sympathetic treatment. I cannot say that this book finishes the task set out so many years ago, but at least it's a start.

Robert L. Gallagher, Beirut, 2017

Acknowledgements

First and foremost, I thank David Konstan for his support and critical eye during the composition of this book. Professor Konstan read all the chapters as they were written and recommended needed revisions.

I thank Alan Code and Christopher Shields for introducing me to Aristotle's metaphysical writings, the study of which was crucial to developing the theses upon which the argument of this book rests. The reader will see the influence of Shields' *Order in Multiplicity* throughout Part II.

I thank the anonymous referee for the *British Journal for the History of Philosophy* who rejected an article submission with the taunt that I could never express my argument in mathematical formulae. Out of that rejection was born the set of formulae in the section "Quantifying Aristotle's incommensurables" in Chapter 8, which became the basis of the Social Welfare Function presented in Parts III and IV. That referee truly caused this book to come into existence, for he challenged me to make my theory, expressed in the draft article, mathematical. I thank my colleague, Kamal Khuri-Makdisi, of the mathematics department at American University of Beirut, for sitting with me in several sessions in which I worked out the necessary formulae. The revised text, greaved with those formulae, was subsequently accepted. After reading that article, Leo Michelis, of the economics department at Ryerson University, suggested that Aristotle's formula A "looks like Rawls" and recommended that I develop an Aristotelian Social Welfare Function. So began Parts III and IV of this book, and Chapter 3.

I am grateful to my research assistants for their efforts, first and foremost: Bisher Al-Makhlouf (now at University of Chicago), and Gabriella Gallagher (now at Université Saint Joseph), and Dalia Akhras, Marya Salman, and Mira Zorkot (now at Oxford). Al-Makhlouf pioneered the work on the figures in Chapter 14; he developed the first versions of Figures 14.1, 14.5, 14.6 and 14.10, and Gallagher developed the final versions of all figures in that chapter.

I thank Pavlos Kontos for his constant support and his brilliant *Aristotle's Moral Realism Reconsidered* (Routledge, 2011), which has helped me understand Aristotle's theory of community. I also thank Scott Meikle, whose *Aristotle's Economic Thought* is to be praised for beginning to uncover the philosophic issues at the heart of *EN* v.5. Meikle inspired me to defend Aristotle from his numerous, erroneous criticisms. I thank Kari Polanyi Levitt for sending me Karl Polanyi's lecture, "Aristotle and Galbraith on Affluence," from the Karl Polanyi archive, Concordia University, Montréal, Canada, and for her encouragement. I thank Fred Block for comments on Chapter 2. I thank Winfried Held for advice on archaeological issues relevant to Chapter 10. I thank Kostas Kalimtgis, Coralie Hindawi, Peter Bornedal, and Patrick Lewtas.

Although almost all the translations from Aristotle printed in this book are mine, I acknowledge the helpfulness of the translations of Terry Irwin of the *Nicomachean Ethics* and of C. D. C. Reeve of the *Politics*.

I thank the participants at the Conference "Ancient Ideas in the Contemporary World," sponsored by Instituto de Estudios Clásicos "Lucio Anneo Séneca," Universidad Carlos III de Madrid, 14–16 November 2013, and at the Conference "Ideals and Reality in Social Ethics," held at the University of South Wales, April 2014, and at the 2nd International Conference "Economic Philosophy," University of Strasbourg, 9–10 Oct 2014, organized by Bureau d'Economie Théorique et Appliquée (BETA) of CNRS, for their comments on earlier drafts of Parts III and IV. Some of the ideas in Chapter 10 were presented at the conference of the Classical Association of Canada in May 2006 in a paper entitled, "The Temple of Graces in Aristotle's Social Thought." I thank the Association for a travel grant that enabled me to attend that conference and present the paper.

I thank Harvard University Press for permission to reproduce Figure 6, from p. 66, and text from pp. 9, 87, 88, 90, 157, 374, 375 and 379 of A THEORY OF JUSTICE: REVISED EDITION by John Rawls, Cambridge, Mass.: The Belknap Press of Harvard University Press, Copyright © 1971, 1999 by the President and Fellows of Harvard College, and for permission to reproduce text from pp. 3, 142 and 143 from JUSTICE AS FAIRNESS: A RESTATEMENT by John Rawls, Cambridge, Mass.: The Belknap Press of Harvard University Press, Copyright © 2001 by the President and Fellows of Harvard College. I thank Beacon Press for permission to reproduce text from pp. 56, 96, 148, and 257 of "The Great Transformation" by Karl Polanyi Copyright © 1944, 1957, 2001 by Karl Polanyi reprinted by permission of Beacon Press, Boston.

I thank Franz Steiner Verlag for permission to reproduce portions of my "An Aristotelian Social Welfare Function," which appeared in: *Archiv für Rechts- und Sozialphilosophie* 104: 1 (2018), in Chapters 11, 12, 13 and 14, and of my "In defense of moral economy: Marx's criticisms of Aristotle's theory of value," which appeared in: *Archiv für Rechts- und Sozialphilosophie*, 100:1 (2014), 112–129. I thank Methexis for permission to reproduce portions of my "The role of grace in Aristotle's theory of exchange," which appeared in *Methexis* 26 (2013), 143–161, in Chapter 10. I thank Taylor and Francis for permission to reproduce portions of my "Aristotle on eidei diapherontes," *British Journal for the History of Philosophy* 19(3): 363–384, in Chapter 6, and of my "Incommensurability in Aristotle's theory of reciprocal justice," *British Journal for the History of Philosophy* 20(4): 667–701 in Chapters 8 and 9.

I acknowledge support from an American University of Beirut University Research Board multiyear grant, "A Neo-Aristotelian Evaluation of the Assumptions of Political Economy," 2011–2014, to fund the student research assistants named above, and a summer grant from the Center for American Studies and Research of the American University of Beirut in 2011.

Abbreviations

An.	*Aristotelis De Anima.*
Ath. Res.	*Aristotelis Atheniensium Respublica.*
EE	*Aristotelis Ethica Eudemia.*
EN	*Aristotelis Ethica Nicomachea.*
Gorg.	*Gorgias.* In *Platonis Opera.*
Lys.	Lysias, *Speeches.*
Met.	*Aristotelis Metaphysica.*
Od.	*Odyssiae Libros.* In *Homeri Opera.*
Oecon.	*Oeconomicus*
PA	Aristotle. *Parts of Animals.*
Phys.	*Aristotelis Physica.*
Pol.	*Aristotelis Politica.*
Rep.	*Platonis Rempublicam.*
Thuc.	*Thucydidis Historiae.*
Xen.	Xenophon

< > In translated passages, surround text supplied by translator in accordance with sense of the passage.

General introduction

It is strange in our current age, in which we have experienced the rise of extreme inequality in our societies and in the world at large, that Aristotle's critique of inequality and his theory of its role in exchange transactions are largely ignored or rejected. It is also peculiar that those very scholars who reject Aristotle's critique admit that they do not understand it.[1] Contemporary social scientists document the inequality that exists in our contemporary world, but ignore or put aside Aristotle's analysis and recommendations, which provide a basis for understanding how inequality works in an economy and how inequality is created and perpetuated. As we shall see, Aristotle is the first theorist of inequality, the first to develop and publish the very "inequality ratios" that are studied today. Yet, his groundbreaking work in the study of inequality is ignored. As a result, today, we lack scientific answer to the question, What is producing inequality in the world? That is a question that Aristotle attempts to answer, and this book offers his answer to its reader.

By political economy I mean the study of the interaction and interrelationships of social and political processes and the process of producing and consuming goods.[2] Insofar as Aristotle's critique of political economy is a critique of the social origin of exchange and of the role that social inequality plays in exchange, it satisfies the definition of political economy. In contrast, modern and contemporary models of exchange that neglect the role of inequality, are, as a result, less general than Aristotle's theory and are *reducible* to Aristotle's theory. To say that modern theories are "reducible" to Aristotle's means that they can be "brought back" to Aristotle's theory, that they can be derived from his theory, and that they are a simplified version of his theory, a version that leaves out at least one important parameter: inequality. That fact also makes those theories less general than Aristotle's, since they do not encompass the phenomenon of inequality. This result is unusual: Usually older theories are reducible to newer ones, but not here. Aristotle's theory of exchange is prior to those of modern political economy in the scope of its analysis.[3] As we shall see, Aristotle's theory employs more parameters than modern theories. That means that Aristotle's theory describes more dimensions of variability than conventional theories, namely, the dimensions he uses to represent the relative inequality of the exchangers. One can derive the modern theory of exchange from Aristotle's by eliminating those additional degrees of freedom. Therefore, those theories are reducible to Aristotle's.

In addition to arguing that the parties to an exchange are unequal, Aristotle also argues that those parties and their products are incommensurable and differ in kind (*eîdos*) (cf. Chapters 6 and 8). The humans involved in exchange relations are unequal, incommensurable and different in kind, that is in nature. This is heresy. The inclusion of human inequality in the terms of exchange and the proposition that people differ in kind both contradict the Enlightenment belief in the equality of all participants in exchange and in the other social relations of civil society. Aristotle's claim that people do not enter into an exchange as equals is a very difficult concept for the modern reader to grasp. We are educated to believe in the idea of equality. We are so inculcated with that idea that it blinds us to alternative concepts. I studied certain texts of Aristotle for several years before it dawned on me that he was arguing that people differ in kind and are unequal. I was therefore not surprised when I saw how many scholars misunderstand and reject Aristotle's view. For example, Meikle regards the extra degrees of freedom that Aristotle includes in his theory of exchange and their role in that theory to be "absurd." "Private property could not conceivably be exchanged in anything like this way," says Meikle. His point is, I believe, that people prefer to believe that they are being treated as equals when they are involved in a transaction, even when they are losing out to a more powerful exchange partner (e.g. Apple, Inc.). Meikle's point is that they would not tolerate being consciously and openly treated as unequal to the more powerful party.[4] They prefer the illusion of equality. But Aristotle is not concerned to defend illusion. Rather, he seeks to represent scientifically the actual process at work in exchange. As I show in the section on Marx at the end of Chapter 8, even in an exchange presented *as if* it were between equal exchange partners, the action of inequality is concealed.

Because Aristotle's theory contradicts post-Enlightenment belief, modernists, from Marx on, reject it. Marx claims that Aristotle's theory of exchange suffers from "the absence of any concept of value,"[5] a thesis echoed by Meikle.[6] (Marx's error is explained in Chapter 8.) More honest, Schumpeter says that Aristotle must be wrong because his theory is at odds with modern ones.[7]

The moderns' disputes over Aristotle, however, is not the topic of this book. Rather, this book presents Aristotle's critique of political economy based on Aristotle's writings, and then demonstrates the efficacy of Aristotle's theory by applying it to a contemporary problem, social welfare analysis. The book presents a three-part argument for the thesis that Aristotle advances a theory of political economy.

(1) Part I (Chapters 1 to 5) is devoted to the work of five modern thinkers who develop their own theories of political economy, at least in part, out of Aristotle's. These are Marx, Polanyi, Rawls, Sen and Nussbaum. It is generally acknowledged that these writers have made a contribution to political economy theory. If that is so, then so has the person who influenced and shaped their theories: Aristotle.

The chapters in Part I are independent of each other and may be read in any order. Together they constitute an extended Introduction to the book. They show that Aristotle's theory of inequality and his controversial exchange proportion (Proportion A presented in Chapter 8) are debated by Marx, defended by Polanyi, made the core of Rawls' Difference Principle and expressed in a new form in Sen's capabilities approach. Readers who do not need to be convinced that Aristotle may have contributed something valuable to political economy may start reading at Part II.

(2) Part II (Chapters 6 to 10) presents Aristotle's critique of political economy, including his Theory of Value. Part II proves that Aristotle advances a theory of political economy by documenting that theory in his writings. Part II refutes the notion that "Aristotle did no economics of any kind."[8]

I borrow the notion that Aristotle's economic writings are a critique from Marx and from Karl Polanyi, but it was David Konstan who coined the title of this book. Marx, of course, subtitled his masterpiece, *A Critique of Political Economy*, as his method was to criticize the economic thought of his contemporaries as Kant in his *Critiques* criticized the philosophers of his time. Polanyi says of Aristotle's economic writings that "their purpose is *economic criticism*."[9] By that, Polanyi means that Aristotle criticizes the economic behaviour and thought of his contemporaries from the standpoint that the purpose of the economy of a community is to support the good life for its citizens.[10] (That concept is elaborated in Chapters 2 and 7.) Part II begins with a presentation of Aristotle's theory of community (Chapter 6). It then moves on to present Aristotle's theory of living well (*eû zên*) and Aristotle's critique of the origin of commerce (Chapter 7). Chapter 8 presents Aristotle's theory of value, while Chapter 9 presents his theory of reciprocal justice, that is how to achieve justice in a community in which citizen exchange goods (or goods and money) with each other. Chapter 10 concludes Part II with a discussion of Aristotle's theory of the role of grace (*charis*) in exchange transactions.

(3) Part III (Chapters 11 and 12) presents the theoretical grounds for advancing an Aristotelian Social Welfare Function (SWF). It applies Aristotle's critique to answer the question, how ought we measure social welfare?

Chapter 11 evaluates contemporary social welfare analysis. Chapter 12 presents case studies documenting the role of inequality in exchange, and derives the Social Welfare Function.

(4) Part IV (Chapters 13 and 14) of *Aristotle's Critique of Political Economy* presents a method for estimating values of the Aristotelian Social Welfare Function and reports on data of the estimated function for several countries.

Chapter 14 argues that if the SWF for a country is increasing, then its economy is improving; and if the SWF is decreasing, the economy is declining.

The chapter shows that GDP per capita is not a reliable measure of economic growth, but must be studied together with values of the SWF presented here. The chapter advances the SWF as an ethical measure of economic growth.

In offering a credible solution to a contemporary problem in welfare economics, Parts III and IV constitute a third argument showing that Aristotle advances a theory of political economy. Part III is written independently of the other parts. As such, it provides a concise review of Aristotle's theory of value as relevant to social welfare analysis.

This book presents an argument for the total revision of the modern theory of exchange from an Aristotelian perspective. Nonetheless, the book is introductory and elementary. It presents the basics of an Aristotelian theory and sketches out one application. Future work will elaborate the theory and its uses. The book does not aim to produce a survey of the literature on Aristotle's theory of political economy, or even to produce a complete commentary on Aristotle's writings on that topic, and certainly does not provide a history of the ancient Greek economy. Rather, my aim is to construct a theory of political economy from Aristotle's work in the hope that this will have a positive influence on contemporary economics and ethics.[11] We begin by looking at those thinkers most influenced by Aristotle in modernity, so that the reader can get his bearings in this ancient terrain with the help of some modern landmarks.

Finally, to regard this book as somehow "finished" would be a mistake, for endless elaborations, explanations and citations may be added. Yet within a certain compass, the point has been made, and that lies before you.

Notes

1 Joachim, in Aristotle (1951), 150, for example, states, "How exactly the values of the producers are to be determined, and what the ratio between them can mean, is, I must confess, in the end unintelligible to me." Finley (1977): "I do not understand what the ratios between the producers can mean." Meikle (1997), 60: Diagonal pairing "remains a mystery." Much of what scholars say reflects their poor understanding of mathematics.

2 Cf. Gilpin (2001), Chapter 2.

3 On scientific reduction, cf. van Riel and van Gulick (2014), Nagel (1961).

4 Meikle's views are discussed in Chapters 8 and 9.

5 Marx (1962), 74. Translations are mine.

6 Cf. Meikle (1997), 26, 35, 41.

7 Cf. Schumpeter (1954), 54–62; Meikle (1997), 111–112.

8 Meikle (1997), 196, describing the view of Finley.

9 Cf. Polanyi (1959), 2; emphasis in original. The essay is in a review of Galbraith's *Affluent Society*.

10 Cf. Polanyi (1959), 2.

11 This is not a Marxist analysis, for Marx rejects Aristotle's critique of the role of inequality in exchange; cf. last section of Chapter 8.

Part I

Post–Enlightenment Aristotelian theorists of political economy

1   Karl Marx

"The Aristotle of the nineteenth century"[1]

Readers should note that the purpose of this chapter is not to praise the inde-fatigable Dr Marx, but rather to show how much Aristotle influenced him, by showing that Marx incorporated much of Aristotle's theory of political economy into his own.

Marx, more than other political economists, takes Aristotle's critique of political economy seriously, for he calls Aristotle "the great thinker who was the first to analyze . . . the form of value."[2] Marx openly acknowledges his debt to Aristotle in several places in *Capital* and in other works, such as in *A Contribution to the Critique of Political Economy*.[3] One such place is the chapters of *Capital* in which Marx develops his thesis that there are contradictions in the capitalist mode of production and distribution, a rather fundamental portion of his theory of political economy. He develops his argument out of Aristotle's analysis in the *Politics* that there exist two types of property acquisition (*ktētikē*), one in accord with nature, the other contrary to it.[4] Marx made that thesis of contradiction the core of his theory of political economy. Though Marx was influenced in his study of philosophy by Hegel, in his development of his theory of political economy it was Aristotle he rather turned to.

Much of the first two parts of *Capital* (Chapters 1 to 4[5]) can be understood as a commentary on Aristotle, *Politics*, Book i, Chapters 8, 9 and 10. Chapter 1 of *Capital*, "The Commodity," starts with a discussion of the distinction between use-value and exchange-value for which Marx credits Aristotle, even quoting in Greek from *Politics* i.9.[6] Later in Chapter 1, Marx praises Aristotle for first developing a theory of value and critiques Aristotle's theory while quoting from *Nicomachean Ethics* v.5.[7] In Chapter 2, in discussing exchange, Marx again cites Aristotle as an authority on exchange-value.[8] Here, how-ever, we are interested in discussing Part II of Volume I, Chapter 4, "The Transformation of Money into Capital." There Marx presents sections on "The General Formula of Capital" and on "Contradictions in the General Formula" (*Widersprüche der allgemeinen Formel*).[9] The first section presents the model for circulation of commodities (which he represents with the schema C—M—C), and the model for the accumulation of capital or "chrematistics"[10] (which he represents with M—C—M'). For several pages with multiple exam-ples he explains over and over again the differences between the two models.

He concludes: "The movement of capital is unlimited."[11] In a long footnote Marx credits Aristotle as being, in *Politics* i.8–10, the first to notice that "the craft of money-making" (*chrēmatistikē*) has no limit, and the first one to see that capitalists follow the M—C—M' model of circulation, not the C—M—C followed by ordinary citizens who enter into exchange in order to obtain goods for their households.[12] As Natali and Meikle each point out, Aristotle's *Politics* i.9 is often analysed using the schema of symbols first advanced by Marx.[13] Of course, Aristotle did not call those who practised "the craft of money-making" "capitalists," but rather *kapēloi*, meaning "merchants," "retail traders," or, as Polanyi likes to call them, "hucksters."[14] Marx summarizes his debt to Aristotle:

> Aristotle contrasts *oikonomia* with chrematistics . . . So far as <*oikonomia*> is the art of acquisition, it is limited to procuring the articles necessary to existence and useful either to a household or the state.

Marx continues with his own translation of a relevant text from the *Politics*:

> "True wealth (*ho alēthinos ploûtos*) consists in such use-values; for the amount of property which is needed for the good life is not unlimited . . . There is, however, a second mode of acquiring things, to which we may by preference and with correctness give the name of chrematistics, and in this case there appear to be no limits to riches or property."[15]

Continuing with his commentary, Marx says:

> As he [Aristotle] goes on to show, the original form of trade was barter, but with the extension of the latter there arose the necessity of money. With the discovery of money, barter of necessity developed into *kapēlikē*, into trading in commodities, and this again, in contradiction (*Widerspruch*) with its original tendency, into chrematistics, the art of making money (*zur Kunst, Geld zu machen*).

"Chrematistics" (*chrēmatistikē*) is in contradiction with the "original tendency" of barter and trading in commodities, for these were initiated for the purpose of completing the self-sufficiency of the household or city-state, while the purpose of chrematistics is to make a money profit. Marx continues his commentary:

> Now chrematistics can be distinguished from *oikonomia* in that [he translates Aristotle again] "for chrematistics, circulation (*poiētikē chrēmatōn . . . dia chrēmatōn metabolēs*) is the source of riches. And it appears to revolve around money, for money is the beginning and the end of this kind of exchange (*to gar nomisma stoikeîon kai peras tês allagês estin*). Therefore also riches such as chrematistics strives for are unlimited . . . with chrematistics there are no bounds to its aims, these aims being absolute wealth."[16]

Marx with Aristotle sees a contradiction between trading goods in order to "procure the articles necessary to existence and useful either to a household or the state" and trading goods to make a money profit. The first is a practice of *oikonomia* and is represented by the schema for circulation of goods, C—M—C; the second is what Marx calls "chrematistics" and is represented by the schema for the circulation of money, M—C—M'. Marx recognizes that Aristotle regarded there to be two forms of *chrēmatistikē*: One is part of *oikonomia* when money must be acquired for use in future exchanges to obtain goods for the household or city-state, and the second is trading in goods solely to make a money profit.[17] Natali calls these *chrematistique*[1] and *chrematistique*[2].[18] The contradiction between *oikonomia* and chrematistics (*chrematistique*[2]) is that in chrematistics the *kapēlos* draws value out of *oikonomia* by reselling goods he has purchased at a price higher than that at which he obtained them. The difference in value is extracted from "the commons," as Aristotle says, that is from the households (*oikoi*) of other citizens.[19]

In the passage above, Marx compactly translates Aristotle's Greek *poiētikē chrēmatōn . . . dia chrēmatōn metabolēs* with the one word "circulation"; that is Marx finds the modern political-economic concept of circulation in Aristotle's *Politics*.[20] Marx took the Greek phrase to mean "productive of money through the exchange of goods,"[21] that is circulation, the schema M—C—M' where the merchant exchanges money for commodities and then those commodities for more money, as explained below. In the passage, Marx refers to the contrast that Aristotle draws between two types of crafts of property acquisition (*ktētikē*) and the two types of crafts of making money (*chrēmatistikē*). Of these, as mentioned, one makes use of simple commodity exchange, mediated by money, to acquire goods necessary for the self-sufficiency of a household or polis. To more fully explain, Marx represents such exchange with the symbols C—M—C, that is goods are sold for money (C—M) and that money is used to purchase goods of equal value that a household or *polis* needs (M—C). That form of property acquisition "exists by nature" (*esti d' hē men phusei*),[22] says Aristotle, "because domestic economy (*oikonomia*) must either possess or acquire a storehouse of goods necessary for life and useful for the community of the household or city-state,"[23] a clause that Marx paraphrases above. But the other sort of property acquisition – called *chrēmatistikē* by Aristotle at *Politics* i.9 and which is transcribed "chrematistics" by Marx – is merchandising: buying commodities at one price and reselling them at a higher price. Marx represents that by M—C—M', that is a merchant buys goods C with capital M, in a transaction represented by M—C, and resells them at a total price M' > M, in a transaction represented by C—M'. Aristotle says that form of property acquisition "does not exist by nature" (*hē d' ou phusei autōn*).[24] Marx says that that chrematistics is "in contradiction with [the] original tendency" of *ktētikē*, because originally in *ktētikē* money served to make the exchange of goods easier by standing as a substitute for goods; the end of exchange is the satisfaction of human needs. But in chrematistics – which Marx translates above as "the craft of money-making" (*zur Kunst, Geld zu machen*)[25] – the end of exchange is money itself, that is as Marx would say, the accumulation of capital.

Marx restates this explicitly at the outset of the next section of *Capital,* "Contradictions in the General Formula." He advances the thesis of contradiction. He says: "The form of circulation within which money is transformed into capital" – the one which Aristotle says "does not exist by nature" – "contradicts all the previously developed laws bearing on the nature of commodities, value, money and even circulation itself."[26] That is it contradicts the laws governing the circulation of goods for the purpose of satisfying the needs of household or polis so that each is self-sufficient. Under those laws – discussed earlier in *Capital* – commodities are use-values bought and sold for the purpose of meeting human needs, the value of a commodity is the cost of producing it, money is simply a means of exchange and circulation is the activity of buying and selling commodities that meet human needs. But in the M—C—M' form of circulation, the C—M—C form is "inverted" (*umgekehrte*), says Marx, and now what had been simply a means of circulation, money, is reified into an end-product as capital and becomes the end or purpose of circulation, as Aristotle also notes.[27] In contrast, in the C—M—C form of circulation, the end is goods required for self-sufficiency and living well (*eû zên*). Moreover, in the C—M—C form of circulation, there is no change in value through circulation. Marx represents this by using the same symbol C for the commodities at the beginning of the phase when they are sold and for the different commodities that are purchased at the end of the phase. In contrast, in the M—C—M' form of circulation, if the entrepreneur succeeds at chrematistics, there is a difference between the money laid out in the beginning (M) and that drawn out at the end (M'): The latter is greater. Marx represents this by using a different symbol M' for the funds extracted. Aristotle refers to this difference M' – M as profit (*kerdos*), and in the *Eudemian Ethics*, he says "If someone makes a profit, we can refer it to no other vice than injustice."[28] The value of goods is fixed and if someone extracts a profit, she or he must have shortchanged someone else or charged them an unfair price. As Marx writes in his chapter on "Contradictions in the General Formula," "Circulation, or the exchange of commodities [which constitutes commerce], creates no value."[29] The nature of chrematistics is represented by both Marx and Aristotle in "usurer's capital," where, Marx says,

> The form M—C—M' is cut down to the unmediated extremes M—M', money which exchanges itself for more money, a form [of circulation] contradicting the nature of money and inexplicable from the standpoint of commodity exchange,[30]

that is inexplicable from the standpoint of the C—M—C form of circulation. Usury contradicts the nature of money, because money came into existence to facilitate the exchange of goods, but in usury goods are not exchanged. Therefore, M—M' is "inexplicable from the standpoint of commodity exchange." Marx quotes Aristotle's remark that the usurer's interest is "most contrary to nature" (*malista para phusin*).[31]

Aristotle's denunciations of profit-making and usury and his view that circulation produces no value are ideas difficult to swallow for modern scholars who have accepted the capitalist system. Through nineteenth-century industry, however, surplus value was created, argues Marx in subsequent chapters of *Capital,* so that there was produced in real goods a basis for the result M' > M and for profit (*kerdos*) M' − M. The evident production of surplus value is made possible by the existence of free labour, individuals who are free to sell their *Arbeitskraft* (work-power or labour-power) to employers who need workers. Those individuals who owe no work-obligations to a feudal estate or master craftsman or anyone else, a condition, frankly, not entirely to their benefit, since it obliges them to provide for themselves as free workers, whereas under feudalism they were supported by the feudal system. The evident basis of surplus value, which both the industrial employer and Marx were able to perceive, is that such labour paid for its own cost of reproduction; that is its wage is recovered by the capitalist in a fraction of the working day, with the result that in the remainder of the day that labour produced surplus value. Accordingly, Marx analysed M in the industrial case into capital advanced $C = c + v$, that is constant capital c, the cost of machinery and materials consumed, plus variable capital v, the cost of the reproduction of the worker's household, and analysed M' into capital extracted $C' = c + v + s$, where s represents surplus value, that is profit M' − M, the value created in the hours after the worker has expended the work necessary for her/his own reproduction.[32] Marx calls the process of producing value beyond the cost of materials and labour (M' − M), *Der Verwertungsprozeß*, translated perhaps as "process of producing surplus value."[33] One result of this development through nineteenth-century industry is that Aristotle's maxim − "If someone makes a profit, we can refer it to no other vice than injustice"[34] − was no longer true, for nineteenth-century industry shows that a just profit is possible. Whether the worker receives a living wage, or that profit is expended justly are another matter. Nonetheless, the contradiction of which Marx and Aristotle write, continues to exist, for now production is for the end of surplus value and not for the purpose of satisfying needs, and when that profit is threatened by circumstances, for example, a financial crisis, production itself is at risk as well the satisfaction of needs.

In addition to crediting Aristotle for understanding contradictions in the general formula of the circulation of capital, Marx also credits him for explaining the "antithesis" between use-value and exchange-value.[35] Marx opens both *A Contribution to the Critique of Political Economy* and *Capital* by contrasting use-value and exchange-value, which he says form an "antithesis." At the beginning of Chapter 1 of *A Contribution to the Critique of Political Economy* Marx quotes a relevant passage in Greek from the *Politics.*[36] He credits Aristotle for having first made the distinction between the proper or intrinsic use (*hē men oikeia chrēsis*) of a good, that is for consumption − out of which Marx develops the notion "use" or "intrinsic" value (*Gebrauchswert*) − and an improper or, rather, extrinsic use (*hē d' ouk oikeia*), that is its use as an article of exchange (*hē metablētikē*), from which it acquires an exchange value (*Tauschwert*) relative to other goods.[37]

The merchant exploits the extrinsic use to develop chrematistics, "the craft of money-making." Thus, the distinction between use value and exchange value underlies the distinction between the two types of wealth accumulation, for the latter distinction rests on the former.

Moreover, Marx's own theory of value is based on Aristotle's metaphysics of form and matter, I claim. In Aristotle's metaphysics, all things are composites of form and matter. In the *Ethics*, in the case of artifacts, it is human work (*ergon*) that forms matter into those products (*erga*).[38] A blacksmith forges iron into a plow: he transforms the iron: he imposes the form of plow onto the iron. The plow is his product (*ergon*). To form such things is his work (*ergon*) and his function (*ergon*) in the community. Such also is work (*Arbeit*) in Marx's sense. To argue this, I discuss two passages. In the first, Marx says:

> The bodies of commodities are unions of two elements, matter and work. If we take away the useful work expended upon them [and therefore their form − RG], a material substratum is always left, which is furnished by nature without the help of man. Man in his production can act only as nature itself does, i.e., he can alter only the form of matter.[39]

In another passage, he says:

> In the work-process, man's activity, by means of the instruments of work, effects an alteration, intended from the commencement, in the object of work. The process terminates in the product, the latter is a use-value, nature's material adapted to the wants of man by a change of form. Work has bound itself together with its object: the former is concretized, the latter worked (*verarbeiten*). What in the worker was made manifest in the form of motion, now appears in the product as a motionless quality in the form of its being. He has forged and the product is a forging.[40]

In these passages, Marx utilizes several concepts from Aristotle's metaphysics:

1) That artifacts, such as commodities, are composites, not solely of material components, but of matter and form, which Marx expresses by referring to what informs the matter, namely, human work.
2) That artifacts have a "material substratum" (*hupokeimenon* in Aristotle's Greek).
3) That humans "can alter only the form of matter."
4) That the work (*ergon*) of a worker forms matter into a product (*ergon*).

In his claim that commodities are composites of matter and work, rather than only of physical materials, Marx is Aristotelian, for when he says that commodities contain work, he explains that they are composed of matter and a form into which work has transformed that matter.[41] For that reason, his theory is correctly called "metaphysical,"[42] that is it is based on the action carried out in forming matter into commodities, not just on the physical ingredients of those commodities, for it is human work that shapes those ingredients into a useful good.

The metaphysics of goods that we have discussed is the philosophical foundation of Marx's theory of surplus value, for if it is the work (*ergon, Arbeit*) of workers that shapes the various material inputs into products (*erga, Arbeit*), and those products are sold so as to yield a surplus of value over and above the wages paid and the cost of material inputs, then that surplus value is produced, as is all the value of the products, out of the work that forms that matter into those products. Anyone who accepts that is thereby a Marxian thinker, aside from whether s/he regards as perfect Marx's specific formulations of that principle.

In conclusion, Marx credits Aristotle with a theory of contradiction in the circulation of money and goods, for Marx shows that Aristotle holds that merchants practising chrematistics draw wealth out of the ordinary circulation of goods within a community and that causes strife in the community. Moreover, Marx credits Aristotle with the concepts of use-value and exchange value, and he himself makes use of Aristotle's metaphysics of form and matter in his own, different theory of value. That all supports the view that Aristotle advances, at the very least, the rudiments of a theory of political economy.

But Marx also criticizes Aristotle's theory of value in *Capital*. The fact that he does again confirms that Aristotle has a theory of political economy, since his views are systematic enough to warrant criticism from members of another school of thought, in this case, Classical Political Economy. We will discuss those criticisms in Chapter 8, after we present Aristotle's theory of value.

Notes

1 So H.M. Hyndman, founder of the Social Democratic Federation in England, called Marx in *Record of an Adventurous Life*, p. 271, cited in McLellan (1973), 446.
2 Marx (1962), 100. Notwithstanding Aristotle's influence upon Smith; cf. Pact (2010), Part II. Among classical political economists, I consider primarily Smith, Ricardo and Marx.
3 Cf. Marx (1904), 19, 41, 53, 78–79, 153–154, 184.
4 Cf. *Pol.* i.8.1256b26–9.1257a5; Marx (1962), 167n6. References to Aristotle's works name a work by its abbreviation (for example, "Pol." here) and cite the text by book and chapter number and/or Bekker page number as used in the Oxford Classical Texts.
5 As numbered in the German edition, for example, Marx (1962).
6 Marx so credits Aristotle in Marx (1962), 100, 100n39; Marx (1904), 19.
7 Cf. Marx (1962), 73–74, where he quotes Aristotles' Greek from *EN* v.5 without actually naming the chapter; cf. Chapter 8 for discussion.
8 Marx (1962), 100, 100n39.
9 In the German edition (Marx, 1962), these are sections 1 and 2 of Chapter 4. In English editions (Marx, 1967 and 1976), they are Chapters 4 and 5.
10 With this interesting word Marx transcribes Aristotle's Greek χρηματιστική, which is formed from χρηματ-, meaning "goods" or "money."
11 Marx (1962), 167.
12 Marx (1962), 167n6, which is note 2 to page 150 in Marx (1967); note 6 to p. 253 in Marx (1976).

13 Concerning *Pol.* i.9.1257b1–5 where Aristotle contrasts necessary exchange with commercial exchange, Natali (1990), 313 says that the schema "on invoque normalement pour interpréter ce passage." Meikle (1997), 52n7 also notes that Marx develops his models of circulation from Aristotle, and adds that Defourney (1914) uses a version of Marx's notation in interpreting Aristotle's text.

14 These synonymous meanings appear in Liddell and Scott (1897), *kapēlos.* Cf. Polanyi (1957a).

15 Fowkes's translation in Marx (1976), 253n6 of Marx's translation of *Pol.* i.8.1256b30–57a1 into German. I correct this translation on pp. 90–92.

16 Marx (1976), I, 253n6; second quoted section from Aristotle is from *Pol.*i. 9.1257b20–30. I have replaced Fowkes' *economy* with Aristotle's term *oikonomia.* Otherwise, Marx uses Aristotle's Greek terms (e.g., *kapēlikē*) or transcribes them (e.g., "chrematistic" for χρηματιστική).

17 Marx (1962), 179 translates *Pol.* i.10.1258a38–b2.

18 Natali (1990), 314 says *chrematistique*[1] is "la bonne chrematistique" and *chrematistique*[2] "la mauvaise chrematistique."

19 Cf. *EN* viii.14.

20 Cf. Fowkes note on Marx's translation in Marx (1976).

21 That requires understanding *chrēmata* in two different ways in the same phrase, which is rather problematic. More accurately the phrase means "productive of goods through exchange of goods." The text is discussed in Chapters 2 and 7.

22 *Pol.* i.9.1257a4.

23 On the translation of *oikonomia* as "domestic economy," cf. Chapter 7; cf. also Leshem (2016).

24 The continuation of ἔστι δ' ἡ μὲν φύσει in *Pol.* i.9.1257a4. Aristotle emphasizes the "exists by nature, not by nature" distinction repeatedly; cf. 1257a17, a29, b19–21.

25 "Money-making" is the first meaning for *chrēmatistikos* given by Liddell and Scott (1897).

26 Marx (1962), 170; translation from Marx (1976), 258.

27 Marx (1962), 170; *Pol.* 1257b1–40.

28 Cf. *EN* 1130a32. Here Aristotle speaks about a profit from merchandising. In Aristotle's time there was no concept of producing a surplus value, that did not previously exist, through economic activity.

29 Marx (1962, 177–178; transl. from Marx (1976), 266. Marx quotes Say and Wayland to support his paragraph.

30 Marx (1962), 179; my translation; cf. *Pol.* 1258b1–7.

31 Cf. *Pol.* 1258b7, Marx (1962), 179.

32 Cf. Marx (1962).

33 By Moore and Aveling in Marx (1967), 181f. Ben Fawkes in Marx (1976), 293, 302 renders the phrase "valorization process."

34 Cf. *EN* 1130a32.

35 As noted by McCarthy, McLellan and Meikle, but not Miller. Smith (1904), I.iv.13 also distinguishes between "value in use" and "value in exchange."

36 ἑκάστου γὰρ κτήματος διττὴ ἡ χρῆσίς ἐστιν, ἀμφότεραι δὲ καθ' αὑτὸ μὲν ἀλλ' οὐχ ὁμοίως καθ' αὑτό, ἀλλ' ἡ μὲν οἰκεία ἡ δ' οὐκ οἰκεία τοῦ πράγματος, οἷον ὑποδήματος ἥ τε ὑπόδεσις καὶ ἡ μεταβλητική. ἀμφότεραι γὰρ ὑποδήματος χρήσεις· καὶ γὰρ ὁ ἀλλαττόμενος τῷ δεομένῳ ὑποδήματος ἀντὶ νομίσματος ἢ τροφῆς χρῆται τῷ ὑποδήματι ἢ ὑπόδημα, ἀλλ' οὐ τὴν οἰκείαν χρῆσιν· οὐ γὰρ ἀλλαγῆς ἕνεκεν γέγονε. τὸν αὐτὸν δὲ τρόπον ἔχει καὶ περὶ τῶν ἄλλων κτημάτων, as in Marx (1904), 19.

37 Cf. *Pol.* i.9.1257a6–9; Marx (1962), 73, 100n39; Marx (1904), 19.

38 Cf. Chapter 8 for discussion of the homonymy of *ergon* as signifying "work," "product" and "function."

39 Marx (1962), 57

40 Marx (1962), 195. Or, more literally, for the last sentence: "he has spun, and the product is spun yarn." Similarly, Hegel (1977), §195. Says: "work forms and shapes the thing. The negative relation to the object becomes its form and something permanent . . . This negative middle term or the formative activity is at the same time the individuality or pure being-for-self of consciousness which now in the work outside of it, acquires an element of permanence. It is in this way that consciousness, qua worker, comes to see in the independent being [of the object] its own independence."

41 This understanding of the Aristotelian nature of Marx's theory of value is stated for the first time in Gallagher (2014a), 113–114. M. Dobbs (1973), Robinson (1947), Becker (1977), Meikle (1985) and many others have failed to grasp Marx's debt to Aristotle.

42 Cf. Wartofsky (1983), esp. 728–730.

2   Karl Polanyi

Karl Polanyi dismissed Classical Political Economy, because, he argued, the Classical Political Economists (Smith, Ricardo, Marx) analysed a capitalism without a labour market, for they conducted their researches and laid down the foundation of their theories during the period when wages in England were determined by the level of poor relief under the Speenhamland policies.[1] Polanyi, though a socialist, rejected Marxian economics as "an essentially unsuccessful attempt" to reintegrate civil society into the human world, "a failure due to a Marx's too close adherence to Ricardo and the traditions of liberal economics," Polanyi explained.[2]

Instead, Polanyi studied Aristotle's critique of political economy, and anthropological research, in an effort to formulate the principles of a viable society that would be an alternative to both capitalism and communism, both of which he rejected. Polanyi developed an historic analysis of the causes of World War I and the 1930s Great Depression in the collapse of the nineteenth-century "self-regulating free market economy." He advanced a theory of 100 years of history that he used to justify efforts by governments to protect their citizens from the effects of a free-market, as in the "New Deal" of US President Franklin Delano Roosevelt, or collectivism in the Soviet Union.[3] Beyond that, Polanyi founded the "substantive" school of political economy as an alternative to the neo-Classical or Viennese school of political economy.[4]

Polanyi credits Aristotle's critique of political economy with many concepts that contributed to his own theories, including those regarding the nature of human communities, the development of modern capitalism and the substantive theory of political economy. Studying Polanyi may very well be helpful for understanding the current state of the world economy and contemporary globalism, which in large measure result from US President Ronald Reagan's dismemberment of Roosevelt's programmes and attempt to establish a free market through deregulation of the financial sector and other measures. Polanyi's work has come to public attention as a potential source for understanding contemporary affairs.[5]

Polanyi says that in the *Politics* and *Nicomachean Ethics* Aristotle engages in "economic criticism."[6] From his close reading of Aristotle's economic criticism, Polanyi drew considerable material:

First, Polanyi articulated several principles of social and economic integration: In his *The Great Transformation*, three of them are reciprocity, redistribution and *oikonomia*, which he translates as householding.[7] He later added the principle of market exchange. He drew and justified the principles of *oikonomia* and market exchange from Aristotle's work.[8]

Second, from Aristotle's theory of *oikonomia*, Polanyi also drew his principle of "self-sufficiency." Polanyi said, "Man, like any other animal, was presented by [Aristotle] as naturally self-sufficient."[9] From that standpoint, Polanyi developed his criticism of the emphasis on scarcity in contemporary economic theory.

Third, Polanyi adopted and developed Aristotle's core concept of *eû zên* – translated as the "good life" or "living well" – which is dependent on self-sufficiency. Living well in the Greek city-state means that citizens experience a life of culture and involvement in civic affairs. Polanyi extended Aristotle's concept into an outline for "the good life in an industrial society."[10] Polanyi applied Aristotle's concept to develop and promote state socio-economic programmes that would make the "good life" possible for all citizens.

Fourth, Polanyi concluded from his study of Aristotle that the Philosopher had foreseen the development of nineteenth-century industrial capitalism "two thousand years before its advent."[11] Moreover, Polanyi argues that Aristotle warned of the dangers of market trade to the self-sufficiency of a household or state in the same way as that problem arose in the eighteenth and nineteenth centuries in the English countryside.

Fifth, Polanyi adopted Aristotle's distinction between production for use and production for a market, and Aristotle's conclusion that gain was a motive peculiar to production for a market.[12]

Sixth, Polanyi saw in Aristotle an early proponent of "the substantive meaning of economic," in contradistinction to the Greek statesman Solon who articulates a principle of gain.[13]

Seventh, Polanyi applied Aristotle's view that exchange in ancient Greece is a "status transaction," and the research of anthropologists on status transactions in non-market societies, to argue that status continues to play a role in exchange transactions today.

All in all, Polanyi appreciates Aristotle's critique of political economy more than even Marx, who, we remember, praises Aristotle as "the great thinker who was the first to analyze the form of value,"[14] for Polanyi puts aside the modern claim that market economy must be the core of society but which Marx, because of his "too close adherence to Ricardo and the traditions of liberal economics," accepts.[15] Marx did not recognize the many fertile concepts in Aristotle by which Polanyi understands contemporary society.

Oikonomia and self-sufficiency

Polanyi credits Aristotle and the Greeks with the concept of *oikonomia*. He defines *oikonomia* as "production for one's own use," and distinguishes it from "production for gain" or "for the market," and from "money-making."[16] He elaborates: "The economy – as the root of the word shows, a matter of the domestic household or *oikos* – concerns directly the relationship of the persons who make up the natural institution of the household."[17] For the Greeks, the *oikos* is the foundation of the economy, for the *oikos* is the elemental organization of the citizens of the *polis* and of their economic activity. That is why – as Aristotle says in the *Politics* – *oikonomia* is a matter of concern for the *polis* and statesmen, for the task of *oikonomia* is to establish self-sufficiency of the *polis* and of the households that constitute it.[18] Such self-sufficiency, Polanyi says, is natural, for

> Man, like any other animal, was presented by [Aristotle] as naturally self-sufficient. The human economy did not, therefore, stem from the boundlessness of man's wants and needs, or, as it is phrased today, from the fact of scarcity . . . The rejection of the scarcity postulate . . . is based on the conditions of animal life, and is thence extended to those of human life. Do not animals from their birth find their sustenance waiting for them in their environment? And do not men, too, find sustenance in mother's milk and eventually in their environment, be they hunters, herdsmen, or tillers of the soil?[19]

Polanyi's discussion here paraphrases Aristotle's *Politics*, Book i, Chapter 8.[20] Nature provides sustenance to animals from birth, and likewise provides sustenance to human households. The *oikos* organizes the family's relationship to nature: it harvests from nature what it can, it produces what other necessities it is able to, and obtains through exchange with other households whatever else it needs. Accordingly, Aristotle says there are degrees of self-sufficiency: a household is more self-sufficient than an individual, and a city-state more so than a household.[21] Even a poor farmer's family with a cottage, a plot of land and a work animal or two has a degree of self-sufficiency without which his life would be much more difficult. The complete community of several villages that have reached the limit of self-sufficiency is a *polis*.[22]

The concept of self-sufficiency is based on the fact that the necessary needs of a human being are by nature finite and determined, for otherwise self-sufficiency would not be possible. To have such self-sufficiency, says Aristotle, *oikonomia* "must either possess or acquire a storehouse of the goods necessary for life and useful for the community of city-state and household,"[23] through harvests, production or exchange. The goal is to establish "the self-sufficiency (*autarkia*) of that sort of property acquisition for a good life (*agathē zōē*)."[24] That self-sufficiency is not unlimited (*apeiros*). Aristotle contrasted his viewpoint with that of Solon, who said, "No boundary to wealth is established for human beings," a statement that sums up the principle of gain without limit. In response to Aristotle, Polanyi engages in Socratic questioning of the Philosopher's critique of political economy:

> [W]hy did he have to probe into the economy at all? . . . To what purpose did he develop a theorem comprising the origins of family and state, solely designed to demonstrate that human wants and needs are not boundless and that useful things are not, intrinsically, scarce? . . . The explanation is obvious. Two policy problems – trade and price – were pressing for an answer. Unless the question of commercial trade and the setting of prices could be linked to the requirements of communal existence and its self-sufficiency, there was no rational way of judging of either, be it in theory or in practice. If such a link did offer, then the answer was simple: first, *trade that served to restore self-sufficiency was in accordance with nature; trade that did not, was contrary to nature.* Second, *prices should be such as to strengthen the bond of community; otherwise, exchange will not continue to take place and the community will cease to exist.* The mediating concept was in either case the self-sufficiency of the community. The economy, then, consisted in the necessaries of life – grain, oil, wine, and the like – on which the community subsisted. The conclusion was stringent and no other was possible. So either the economy was about the material, substantive, things that sustained human beings, or else there was no empirically-given rational link between matters such as trade and prices on the one hand, and the postulate of a self-sufficient community, on the other. The logical necessity for Aristotle's insistence on the substantive meaning of economic is therefore evident. Hence also that astonishing attack on the Solonic poem in an overture to a treatise on economics.[25]

We will discuss below how this passage reveals Polanyi's indebtedness to Aristotle for his substantive theory of political economy. But first we cover a different problem which he explored first in *The Great Transformation*: the relation of market exchange and trade to the self-sufficiency of the *oikos* and the *polis*. In the *Politics,* Aristotle says that trade and market exchange is necessary for the self-sufficiency of households and of the *polis,* for "people have to be able to buy and sell in order to satisfy each other's necessary needs."[26] Within the *polis,* such exchange among households is normal and "not contrary to nature," for its purpose is "the completion of natural self-sufficiency."[27] But when people expand such trade and import from distant foreign sources, the self-sufficiency of the *polis* is undermined.[28] Therefore, neither the household nor the city-state should become dependent upon trade. By that Polanyi means that the household must not produce for the market, must not become dependent on income from such market sales, for then it would no longer be self-sufficient. Moreover, because of the distances involved, money was devised to settle transactions, and that gave rise to commerce, which lead to production of goods for the market. That sort of trade was contrary to nature,[29] for it undermined self-sufficiency, and, because it was driven by the principle of gain, diverted attention away from the goal of self-sufficiency, namely, to experience the good life. Polanyi sees in Aristotle's text the understanding that dependence upon distant market trade, whether real in the case of necessities, or merely psychological in the case of other goods, *imposes the perception of scarcity upon a community* where there was not scarcity by nature. Thus Polanyi finds in Aristotle's critique of political economy a criticism of an early form of the scarcity postulate of contemporary economic theory, for he says that Aristotle sought "to demonstrate that human wants and needs are not boundless and that useful things are not, intrinsically, scarce."

Moreover, for Polanyi a social problem of the nineteenth and twentieth centuries is that households are no longer self-sufficient, but are desperately dependent upon sources of external income. Such dependence undermines the experience of the "good life" and of freedom.[30] Writing about the late eighteenth and early nineteenth centuries, Polanyi says:

> The war on cottages, the absorption of cottage gardens and grounds, the confiscation of rights in the common deprived cottage industry of its two mainstays: family earnings and agricultural background. As long as domestic industry was supplemented by the facilities and amenities of a garden plot, a scrap of land, or grazing rights, the dependence of the laborer on money earnings was not absolute; the potato plot or "stubbing geese," a cow or even an ass in the common made all the difference; and family earnings acted as a kind of unemployment insurance. The rationalization of agriculture inevitably uprooted the laborer and undermined his social security.[31]

For Polanyi, the point of Roosevelt's "New Deal" was to return some such "social security" to the labourer. The point is that to the degree that a household in the ancient world was self-sufficient, in case of a breakdown of society its members could survive for some time, but today that degree of self-sufficiency has been eliminated. The whole process by which capital tore up the social structure and culture of the British countryside, Polanyi, with insight, interprets from Aristotle:

> In denouncing the principle of production for gain as boundless and limitless, "as not natural to man," Aristotle was, in effect, aiming at the crucial point, namely, the divorcedness of a separate economic motive from the social relations in which these limitations inhered.[32]

In other words, in denouncing the principle of gain, Aristotle was criticizing the attempt to "divorce," or as Polanyi also says, *disembed*, economic activity from the social relations from which it originally developed, the preservation of which social relations is the healthy aim of economic activity. Those social relations will naturally place limits upon economic activity that saps the life blood of the community. They place such restrictions, such regulations, in a counter-movement to protect those human social relations, to protect the capacity of households and the *polis* to experience "the good life."[33] In the passage, Polanyi seems to attribute to Aristotle some awareness of the "double movement," as he called it, through which society seeks to contain those acting on the principle of gain.

"Living well" (*eû zên*) as a normative principle

A central concept that Polanyi drew from Aristotle's work is the concept of the "good life" or "living well" (*eû zên*). Polanyi says that Aristotle "reached the conclusion, that the broader concept of the *good life* is the key to the solution" of the problem of political economy.[34] In other words, the dos and don'ts of political economy are developed in references to the actions that make the good life easier, or more difficult, to experience. Polanyi says "the good life (*eû zên*)" is "the ways in which men seek a life over and above the elementary requirements of animal life (*zên*)."[35] That accords with Aristotle's account, for he says that there cannot be a city-state of animals since animals cannot experience the good life.[36] "The elixir of the good life," explains Polanyi, is "the elation of day-long theater, the mass jury service, the holding in turn of offices, canvassing, electioneering, great festivals, even the thrill of battle and naval combat,"[37] in a phrase, a life of culture and participation in the affairs of one's nation, all of which are out of reach from the vast majority of humanity today, even in the advanced sector. Polanyi notes that "under the sway of a *utilitarian value scale* the craving for *money is boundless*. Yet apart from the necessaries, the objects money can buy do not form part of the *good life*."[38] In contrast, *eû zên* defined Athenian identity.[39] As we will see in Part II, in order that all fully enjoy *eû zên*, the better-off assist the less-advantaged through the reciprocity, redistribution and civic friendship that sustain community.[40]

In the last chapter of *The Great Transformation* and in a discussion of Galbraith's *Affluent Society*, Polanyi enlarged Aristotle's concept to articulate "the good life in an industrial society." He proposed several principles of "freedom" to protect the individual from 1) "the technology of *efficiency*," 2) "the *totalitarian or conformist tendency* inherent in a technology of mass production and mass communications," and 3) the power of money.[41] He elaborates that "*The dethroning of efficiency as a unique diremptive principle is inevitable in free society*. Only in competition with other aims, values and ideals can efficiency be accepted."[42] In the last chapter of *The Great Transformation*, Polanyi develops these ideas in more detail. He says that "the right to nonconformity must be institutionally protected. The individual must be free to follow his conscience without fear of the powers that happen to be entrusted with administrative tasks in some of the fields of social life." He continues, "The true answer to the threat of bureaucracy as a source of abuse of power is to create spheres of arbitrary freedom protected by unbreakable rules."[43]

For Polanyi, the good life is a "*normative principle* in regard to the society of which the economy forms a part";[44] that is we can rate or judge societies by whether and how well they support the good life for their citizens. An attempt to do that is developed in Parts III and IV of this book.

Historic impact of wealth acquisition that is not in accordance with nature

For both Aristotle and Polanyi, the antithesis between mere living (animal life) and living well (human life) corresponds to two different kinds of wealth acquisition: *oikonomia*, which is "wealth in accordance with nature" (*ho ploûtos ho kata phusin*), on the one hand, and the craft of wealth accumulation or "money-making" (*chrēmatistikē*), as Marx rendered Aristotle's Greek, on the other.[45] The craft of wealth accumulation seeks, as Solon said, to increase wealth without limit, while *oikonomia* is concerned only with acquiring the goods necessary for the self-sufficiency of household and *polis*. Those who pursue the craft of wealth accumulation misunderstand the function and purpose of economic activity, says Aristotle. They persevere in increasing their wealth without limit. "Anxiety for living, rather than living well (*eû zên*), is a cause of this disposition," he says.[46] Since the desire for life is unlimited, they desire also that the things productive of it be unlimited. Such people crave the means for life, not the end of living well. Polanyi comments:

> In Aristotle's logic, of course, means are always limited by ends – tools, serving a purpose, are limited by their purpose. Hence he concludes that the introduction of money and monetary gain must unsettle the concept of the good life, and reduce it to utilitarian items. *Money is an end in itself, the craving for it is therefore limitless.* Once accepted as the means of acquiring more and more enjoyable things the idea of the good life is perverted.[47]

Here Polanyi argues that since money is a tool, it is supposed to be limited by its purpose, namely – for Polanyi and Aristotle – to support the good life. But when people make money and monetary gain the purpose of their activity, money ceases to function as a means to the good life, and instead become a thing-in-itself towards which all else is oriented. The purpose of money becomes to acquire whatever "enjoyable things" the possessor desires, but the point of the good life, of living well, is not to acquire objects but to participate in civic discourse and deliberation with other citizens. Summarizing the point in contemporary jargon, Polanyi says:

> [I]f scarcity springs "from the demand side," as we would say, Aristotle attributes it to a misconceived notion of the good life as a desire for a greater abundance of physical goods and enjoyments.[48]

Here Polanyi is saying that the modern notion of scarcity has a psychological origin in a "misconceived notion of the good life," a "false notion of the good life as a utilitarian cumulation of physical pleasures"[49] (just as so many today are obsessed with luxury goods). That gives rise to an unsatisfiable craving for money which, like all such cravings, such as for drugs, makes its victims feel that desirable goods are scarce. Those who practise the craft of wealth acquisition without limit are concerned with mere living, not with living well. So, the distinction between *oikonomia* and wealth accumulation corresponds to two conditions of mind, two subjectivizations of the purpose of life. Yet this psychological divergence has historic implications when the minority that adheres to the "misconceived notion of the good life" becomes increasingly powerful. They emerge as a new class obsessed with, enslaved to, the principle of gain, and through their obsession transform feudal society into something very different. About that, Polanyi writes in *The Great Transformation*:

> [Aristotle's] famous distinction of householding proper [*oikonomia*] and money-making, in the introductory chapter of his *Politics*,[50] was probably the most prophetic pointer ever made in the realm of the social sciences . . . Aristotle insists on production for use as against production for gain as the essence of householding proper; yet accessory production for the market need not, he argues, destroy the self-sufficiency of the household as long as the cash crop would also otherwise be raised on the farm for sustenance, as cattle or grain; the sale of the surpluses need not destroy the basis of householding . . . Only a genius of common sense could have maintained, as he did, that gain was a motive peculiar to production for the market . . . yet, nevertheless, as long as markets and money were mere accessories to an otherwise self-sufficient household, the principle of production for use could operate . . . *the distinction between the principle of use and that of gain was the key to the utterly different civilization the outlines of which Aristotle accurately forecast two thousand years before its advent* out of the bare rudiments of market economy available to him."[51]

The passage says that Aristotle predicted the advent of the industrial age of the nineteenth century. We will analyse the passage at length below, for Polanyi makes some rather strong claims about Aristotle's *Politics* therein. But this is not the only work in which Polanyi attributes such historic foresight to Aristotle. Stating his claim again in the essay, "Aristotle discovers the economy," Polanyi writes that "Aristotle divined the full-fledged specimen [of industrial capitalism] from the embryo" that he observed in the fourth century BC.[52]

In the text above, Polanyi refers to Aristotle's key concept of "*oikonomia*," the term that Polanyi translates as "householding." *Oikonomia* refers to the production of goods for the use of both *oikos* (household) and *polis*. Polanyi claims that Aristotle says that the craft of wealth acquisition (*chrēmatistikē*) involved the production of goods only for sale in the market. That is an important claim, for in producing goods only for the market, commerce introduces a process that can destroy the self-sufficiency of the household and of the *polis*: If the household begins to produce for the market, it becomes dependent on those market sales for its livelihood. That destroys the self-sufficiency of the household, which for Aristotle is the key to living well.[53] Such is the predicament of the modern household, and that predicament came into being in the eighteenth century as commerce drew independent householders into its network of cottage industry for production for the market, and later forced them off their land and into the cities to be dependent on the sale of their labour.[54] That phenomenon, the production of goods by commerce for the market, was the "embryo" in ancient Athens from which "Aristotle divined the full-fledged specimen" of modern capitalism.

But we must first determine whether Aristotle actually says that commerce produces goods exclusively for the market. Only then can we claim that Aristotle divined the "specimen from the embryo." For Aristotle's commercial trader may have been only a mere merchandiser, who buys cheap and sells dear.[55] No, Aristotle says in the *Politics*,

(1) Commerce is productive of goods, not in all respects, but through the exchange of goods (*hē de kapēlikē poiētikē chrēmatōn ou pantōs, alla dia chrēmatōn metabolēs*)[56]

By exception we highlight a passage from Aristotle in this chapter on Polanyi, because getting that passage right is key to interpreting Polanyi's understanding and use of Aristotle. The passage says that commerce produces goods only for exchange, for the market, not for use. As Polanyi says in the passage above, Aristotle "maintained . . . that gain was a motive peculiar to production for the market." To us living in the twenty-first century, that seems rather obvious. Apple makes iPhones to sell them, not to use them itself. Polanyi cites the example of the English cottage wool industry in the eighteenth century "where production was organized by the clothier," that is by the merchant.[57] But that, Polanyi argues, was rare in fourth-century Athens. The customary practice in Greece was production for use, and if there was any excess product, beyond what a household would use, one would sell it to one's neighbours or at the market. Aristotle warns, however, that market exchange is a double-edged sword: Exchange of one's excess for necessities that one needs and can receive from fellow citizens plays a role in sustaining self-sufficiency for all citizens of the *polis* and does not involve the type of wealth acquisition that is contrary to nature.[58] So, Polanyi says above, production is for use, even when there is an excess product, for "accessory production for the market need not, [Aristotle] argues, destroy the self-sufficiency of the household as long as the cash crop would also otherwise be raised on the farm for sustenance, as cattle or grain; the sale of the surpluses need not destroy the basis of householding."

But, on the other hand, when people import what they need from distant foreign sources, or sell their product in distant markets, they become dependent on those foreign supplies and markets, and self-sufficiency is undermined.[59] Moreover, in that same way, money making is introduced into acquisition of necessary foodstuffs, further undermining self-sufficiency.

All in all, the household is made dependent and must throw itself upon the mercy of commerce. Thus Aristotle saw "the key to the utterly different civilization": He "divined the full-fledged specimen from the embryo," and, as Polanyi argues, envisioned a civilization in which livelihood was dependent upon the market. But how is this distinction between the principle of use and that of gain "the key to the utterly different civilization the outlines of which Aristotle accurately forecast two thousand years before its advent"? Because the principle of gain drives people to use fellow citizens as instruments to their objective to make money, rather than cooperate with those others as sharers in the same community.[60] That reminds us of Kant's rule – which he enunciated in criticism of capitalist culture – that "all rational beings stand under the law that each of them should treat himself and all others never merely as means but always at the same time as an end in himself."[61]

Polanyi's interpretation of passage (1) in *The Great Transformation* contradicts the translations of his contemporaries Ernest Barker and Benjamin Jowett, but is confirmed by Reeve's recent translation, which has roughly the same meaning as above.[62] Jowett, and Barker and Stalley render the lines with a very different sense so that they miss the point of the phrase "productive of goods" (*poiētikē chrēmatōn*): The disagreement attests to Polanyi's mastery of Greek, which, combined with his knowledge of economy, yielded the proper interpretation of passage (1).[63]

In his essay on Aristotle, Polanyi went so far as to say:

> It may seem paradoxical to expect that *the last word* on the nature of economic life should have been spoken by a thinker who hardly saw its beginnings. Yet Aristotle, living, as he did, on the borderline of economic ages, was in a favored position to grasp the merits of the subject.[64]

Whether this is true is separate from the significance of that conclusion for Polanyi's own work, for Polanyi's *Great Transformation* is occupied with the very development of the "full-fledged specimen" of industrial capitalism, and how societies engage in counter-movements to protect themselves from those acting in accordance with the principle of gain. Polanyi came to the conclusion that Aristotle had foreseen the very problem for which he struggled in his book to advance a solution. That problem is how to protect the people of a country from the destructive effects of an unregulated market economy upon their lives and livelihoods. Such a concern was also natural to Aristotle, because:

> Aristotle's approach to human affairs was sociological . . . Community, self-sufficiency, and justice were the focal concepts. The group as a going concern forms a community (*koinonia*) the members of which are linked by the bond of good will (*philia*). Whether *oikos* or *polis*, there is a kind of *philia*, specific to that *koinonia*, apart from which the group could not remain [together]. *Philia* expresses itself in a behavior of reciprocity (*antipeponthos*), that is, readiness to take on burdens in turn and share mutually.[65]

In Part II, we will discuss how Aristotle analyses and treats social problems that arise from commerce.

Polanyi's two interpretations of "economic"

Polanyi argues that the "substantive" meaning of economic is the proper grounding for a conceptual framework with which to evaluate market economy.[66] The substantive meaning refers to the process of human social reproduction, which Polanyi describes as "man's interchange with his natural and social environment, insofar as this results in supplying him with the means of material want-satisfaction."[67] Polanyi's insistence that the substantive be the grounding for evaluating the market system is a departure from the thought of Max Weber who also distinguished the "substantive" from the "formal" in economics, but regarded them to coincide in practice.[68] Polanyi rejects Weber's approach and argues that no coincidence is possible between "formal economics" and the separately existing process of human social reproduction defined above.[69] Polanyi contrasted the substantive understanding of economy with "catallactics," a theory of the way the free market system reaches exchange ratios and prices that was used by Ludwig von Mises.[70] The term catallaxy was drawn by Friedrich Hayek from Greek to describe "the order brought about by the mutual adjustment of many individual economies in a market."[71] Hayek was dissatisfied with the usage of the word "economy" because its Greek root, which translates as "household management," implies that economic agents in a market economy possess shared goals, a conception that he rejected.

The disagreement between Weber and Polanyi is fundamental for the study of political economy, and we take time to review it here, for the kernel of Polanyi's view is that there exist two parallel, co-existent processes of economy: the process of reproduction of humanity through agriculture, manufacturing and auxiliary activities, and on the other hand, the circulation of financial paper that is alleged to represent the value of the former. Please bear with our review of Weber's somewhat abstract formulations in *Wirtschaft und Gesellschaft*.

Weber summarized his distinction between formal and substantive as follows: He said that *formal* rationality (*formale Rationalität*) of an economy signifies the extent to which quantitative calculation or accounting is both possible in an economy and actually carried out. By contrast, substantive rationality (*materiale Rationalität*) signifies the degree in which the providing and caring (*Versorgung*) of given groups of people with goods through economically oriented social action is shaped by some evaluative assumption, for example the achieving of equality.[72] Weber explains that an economy will be called *formally* rational according to the degree in which the providing and caring, which is essential to every rational economy, can be expressed in numerical, calculable terms, and is so expressed. The monetary form represents the highest degree of *formal* calculability.[73] In contrast, in any "substantive rationality" of economy, some moral criterion guides decision making. That is, those involved posit ethical, political, utilitarian, hedonistic, feudal, egalitarian or whatever demands, and measure the results of the economy against such values.[74] In formal rationality, on the other hand, decisions are carried out (not made) by individuals in accordance with the prescribed rationalized rules and procedures of an organization of which they are a part and which seeks to maximize some criterion, for example, utility, or profit, or some other such metric.[75] As C. W. Mills says, human beings in corporate or bureaucratic organizations "often carry out series of apparently rational actions without any ideas of the ends they serve . . . The soldier, for example, 'carries out an entire series of functionally rational actions accurately without having any idea as to the ultimate end of this action' or the function of each act within the whole . . . It is not too much to say that in the extreme development, the chance to reason of most men is destroyed, as rationality increases and its locus, its control, is moved from the individual to the big-scale organization."[76]

In spite of his elaborate distinction between formal and substantive, Weber concludes that "formal and substantive rationality coincide to a relatively high degree,"[77] which is odd, for how can the rate of profit be maximized under moral criteria? Polanyi criticized Weber for "fusing the two meanings of 'economic' [substantive and formal] for the sake of common usage":

> Weber consciously included *both* the substantive and the formal meaning in the definition of "economic" (in conformity with common usage). He asserted that "economic" meant provision for the means of material want-satisfaction, but also insisted that the intrinsically *"economic" behavior* was of "pure rationality," the most typical form of which we encounter on the stock exchange. Owing to this ambiguity, Weber's terms proved a very useful instrument of inquiry into capitalist economy, in which the same conjunction of meanings prevails. However, outside of capitalism, the inclusion of pure rationality into the definition of "economic behavior" made that term unsuitable for general economic history . . . Weber's attempt at a synthesis of societal and economistic approach is open to criticism. His inability to decide in favor of the substantive meaning of "economic" vitiated his endeavors to clarify the problems of general economic history.[78]

Weber's terms coincide with capitalist economy because that form of economy is dominated by rationalized organizations that impose standards of decision making upon the individual. But that sort of "rational" social organization does not exist outside capitalism. As a result, Weber's analysis is historically and culturally limited. Moreover, I am not pleased with Polanyi's concession to Weber that his "terms proved a very useful instrument of inquiry into capitalist economy," for crises in modern capitalism coincide with a widening divergence between "numerical calculable" monetary values in an economy, and the providing and caring of human beings with goods.

Polanyi intervened into the Weberian discourse over the nature of civil society with his essay, "The economy as instituted process." There he announces his "substantivist" school of political economy, and develops the distinction between formal and substantive in a way that pertains to the physical economy. He says "the term economic (*oikonomia*) is a compound of two meanings that have independent roots." The two roots to which Polanyi refers are *oiko-* from *oikos* ("house, household, substance") and *-nom-* from *nomos* ("custom, law"). Polanyi argues that "economic" (*oikonomikē*) is homonymous: He names the study of what Aristotle calls property acquisition for the household and city-state "the substantive meaning of economic," and says that Aristotle's adhered "to the substantive meaning of economic,"[79] which Polanyi says

> derives from man's dependence for his living upon nature and his fellows. It refers to the interchange with his natural and social environment, insofar as this results in supplying him with the means of material want-satisfaction.[80]

This is very different from Weber's definition of "substantive rationality" insofar as it is based on *action* upon nature together with other human beings, rather than subjective "criteria of ultimate ends."[81] Polanyi's formulation abandons such criteria, whether they be ethical, political, utilitarian, hedonistic, feudal, egalitarian or whatever. He contrasts the substantive meaning with:

> The formal meaning of economic [which] derives from the logical character of the means–ends relationship, as apparent in such words as "economical" or "economizing." It refers to a definite situation of choice, namely, that between different uses of means induced by an insufficiency of those means. If we call the rules governing choice of means the logic of rational action [i.e. Weber's "formal rationality of economic action" – RG], then we may denote this variant of logic, with an improvised term, as formal economics.[82]

Polanyi explains:

> The last two centuries produced in Western Europe and North American an organization of man's livelihood to which the rules of choice happened to be singularly applicable. This form of the economy consisted in a system of price-making markets. Since acts of exchange, as practiced under such a system, involve the participants in choices induced by an insufficiency of means, the system could be reduced to a pattern that lent itself to the application of methods based on the formal meaning of economic.[83]

He concludes:

> The relation between formal economics and the human economy is, in effect, contingent. Outside of a system of price-making markets economic analysis loses most of its relevance as a method of inquiry into the working of the economy. A centrally planned economy, relying on non-market prices is a well-known instance.[84]

Thus,

> The two root meanings of economic, the substantive and the formal, have
> nothing in common. The latter derives from logic, the former from fact.[85]

Aristotle did not speak about the formal meaning of economic: Economic
was not used in that sense in the fourth century. For Aristotle, the antithesis
of the type of property acquisition that is by nature (the substantive meaning)
was wealth acquisition, money–making, via commercial trading, the type of
property acquisition that is *contrary* to nature. But by Polanyi's time, modern
economics, with its theories of scarcity, rational behavior and risk, had come
into being. So, Polanyi's point is that there are two fields of economics, one
that deals with the production and consumption of real goods and services
for the reproduction of humanity, and the other that concerns itself with the
imagined behaviour of an individual in a market. Polanyi's substantive meaning signifies the same type of activity as Aristotle's concept of property acquisition in accordance with nature. Polanyi advances his substantive theory as an
alternative to modern formal, neo–classical economy. His theory is truly an
Aristotelian theory of political economy. Polanyi's essay inaugurated a new
school of political economy, which was advanced by economic historians and
anthropologists.[86]

Status versus contractus

In his essays, Polanyi sketches out a way that we can understand that status continues to determine the terms of exchange in the modern world today. In the
essay "Aristotle discovers the economy," Polanyi acknowledges that Aristotle is
the first to represent the role of status in exchange transactions. Polanyi writes:

> Prices are justly set if they conform to the standing of the participants
> in the community, thereby strengthening the good will on which com-
> munity rests . . . The rate of exchange must be such as to maintain the
> community.[87] Again, not the interests of the individuals, but those of the
> community were the governing principle. The skills of persons of different
> status had to be exchanged at a rate proportionate to the status of each.[88]

Polanyi here refers to Aristotle's formulation of exchange in ancient Athens:
Aristotle represents how relative social status or power affects an exchange
with a proportion. He expresses the problem in algebraic symbols, which he
places into proportion with each other. "Let a farmer be α, nourishment γ, a
shoemaker β, his *ergon* that is equalized δ."[89] He proposes for consideration the
following proportion:

(2) As farmer is to shoemaker, so the *ergon* of the shoemaker is to that of the
farmer.

Or restating (2) with the symbols he assigns:

(A)
$$\frac{\alpha}{\beta} = \frac{\delta}{\gamma}$$

To clearly show the meaning of (A), consider this:

(A$_1$)
$$\delta = \frac{\alpha}{\beta}\gamma,$$

which means that the exchange of the *erga* of two parties is determined by their relative social status $\frac{\alpha}{\beta}$. In his comment on Aristotle's treatment of status, Polanyi again shows himself to be a skillful reader of Greek, for he renders *ergon* as "skill," rather than simply product or work, for Polanyi recognizes that *ergon* is homonymous and understands that Aristotle holds that the product (*ergon*) stands for the individual who supplies it, and represents his function (*ergon*) in the community, which is therefore prior to the product and the source of its being.[90] Polanyi and many others have recognized that status transactions were the norm in archaic and primitive economies, but while others have maintained that status transactions gave way to purely contractual ones, Polanyi maintains that status continues to play a role in contemporary society. In an essay written in the 1950s but only recently published, Polanyi sketches out his idea:

> [M]odern social classes *are* classes formed through incomes determined in specific markets, the modern social struggle is a struggle between economic classes – that is, groups the status of which is defined in market terms and the conflicts of which are conflicts about those terms.[91]

Chapter 8, p.125, presents an example from the work of Wolff.

Reciprocity and redistribution

Polanyi's views on reciprocity and redistribution differ from Aristotle's, developed as they were, through study of Malinowski, Mead, Thurnwald and others.[92] Polanyi says that redistribution involves the return of all, or a substantial amount, of the social product to a centre, from which it is distributed, while reciprocity is the return received from a distant source for a deed performed for proximate others.[93] About Aristotle's views, Polanyi says:

> Aristotle taught that to every kind of community (*koinonia*) there corresponded a kind of good will (*philia*) amongst its members, which expressed itself in reciprocity (*to antipeponthos*) . . . In our terms this implies a tendency in the larger communities to develop a multiple symmetry in regard to which reciprocative behavior may develop in the subordinate

communities. The closer the members of the encompassing community feel drawn to one another, the more general will be the tendency among them to develop reciprocative attitudes in regard to specific relationships limited in space, time, or otherwise . . . Reciprocity as a form of integration gains greatly in power through its capacity of employing both redistribution and exchange as subordinate methods.[94]

To illustrate the passage, let a *polis*, such as Athens, be composed of tribes, and the tribes of clans. Reciprocating behaviour may develop involving clans of different tribes. Importantly, Polanyi subordinates redistribution and exchange to reciprocity: In other words, redistribution and exchange are ways to exhibit "reciprocative behavior." About reciprocity and redistribution specifically in Attica, Polanyi says:

> Not exchange, but reciprocity and redistribution were the forms of integration that originally dominated the economic life of Attica. True, the *reciprocity* elements were greatly weakened with the loosening of the clan tie in the eighth/seventh century (with its blood feud, family rights in landed estate, inalienable property). Gift trade and the other, highly developed, gift and countergift systems common in the times of the epics were now fading out. But the *redistributive* forms of tribal life did not disappear in the same manner as reciprocating ones. The *polis* took over much of the redistributive inheritance of the tribe. The distribution of land (*kleroi*),[95] of booty, of a lucky strike in the Laurion mines[96] − similarly, of the gold mined on the isle of Syphnos; the claim to maintenance or to corn distribution in an emergency[97]; the claim to participation in public displays or to payment for the performance of citizens' duties[98] − all this is a very real tribute to the strength of the *redistributive factor in classical communities*. The basic economic organization of the *polis* was redistribution of the proceeds of common activity, share in booty and tribute, share in conquered land and in colonial ventures, in the advantages to be gained from third-party trade.[99]

In other words, according to Polanyi's account, an Athenian could sustain his household to a large degree as the recipient of a variety of distributions, whether that of land, or of payments for serving in offices or for involvement in festivals, or of episodic distributions of booty, of precious metals, or emergency distributions of corn. The Athenian was not left to his own resources to care for his household. That is the distinguishing mark of redistribution, and it highlights the way that redistribution supports *eû zên*, namely, the citizen is not on his own to support his household, as s/he is today, but can rely on support from the city-state. That enables the citizen to involve himself in the affairs of the *polis,* in political deliberation, in cultural exhibitions and festivals, and in its defense. As Polanyi says, "community creates the good life."

But this interesting passage says that reciprocity per se was "greatly weakened" long before the fourth century in which Aristotle wrote. Redistribution, formerly a responsibility of the tribes that composed ancient Athens, became the responsibility of the *polis*, says Polanyi, who refers to this being practised at least down to the defeat in the Peloponnesian Wars. Polanyi's account is confirmed by Aristotle's *The Constitution of Athens*, where the Philosopher describes the highpoint in Athenian policies of redistribution during the Penteconteitia, the interval of 45 years between the defeat of Persia and the onset of the Peloponnesian Wars.[100]

> [Aristides[101],] seeing the state growing in confidence and much wealth accumulated, advised the people to lay hold of the leadership of the [Delian] league,[102] and to quit the country districts and settle in the city. He pointed out to them that all would be able to gain a living there, some by service in the army, others in the garrisons, others by taking a part in public affairs . . . This advice was taken . . . They also secured an ample maintenance for the mass of the population in the way which Aristides had pointed out to them. Out of the proceeds of the tributes and the taxes and the contributions of the allies more than twenty thousand persons were maintained . . . Such was the way in which the people earned their livelihood.[103]

By 20,000 persons Aristotle means 20,000 heads of households, for the number of those directly employed by the state in wartime is over 9,750. In 431 BC at the height of Athenian population before the Peloponnesian Wars, there were in Athens 25,000 men of hoplite rank or above, and 18,000 labourers,[104] so if 20,000 "were maintained," as Aristotle says, that would constitute roughly half the households of Athenian citizens. We can surmise that the wealthy would not be on the receiving end of these distributions, both because they did not need them and did not care to hold most of the paying positions, and because the poor through their heroic role in the Second Persian War merited the distributions.[105] "Such was the way in which the people earned their livelihood," Aristotle emphasizes in concluding.[106] The point here is that *redistribution was a central feature of Athenian social life* and one that enabled the people to involve themselves closely in the cultural and political affairs of Athens, which they would not have been able to do had they to work a farm or craft. Thus Pericles, in his famous funeral speech, could claim with some justification that poverty in classical Athens was no barrier to political participation.[107] Aristotle's account provides strong support for Polanyi's. The point here, however, is not to make an historical argument for how distribution occurred in ancient Athens, but rather to understand what Polanyi means when he proposes εὖ ζῆν as a normative principle.

Finally, it is appropriate here to rebut some of the criticisms of Polanyi advanced by contemporary writers. Booth has rejected as "not useful" Polanyi's claims that ancient economies were typified by "the absence of a concept of scarcity," "the absence of an idea of surplus as the goal and consequence of economic activity," and the absence of "economizing, or rational action based on scarcity."[108] First of all, though – as discussed above and as Polanyi himself points out – merchandising trade was introducing a perception of scarcity in ancient Athens, previously a concept of scarcity did not exist as people did not experience scarcity in a culture where it was the nature of the ancient community to take care of its people in any time of difficulty through distributions of various sorts, as discussed above. In contrast to modernity, where the concept of scarcity grows from my lack of job security or adequate income since I am totally dependent on my own resources for my livelihood, in the ancient world my livelihood is provided to a large degree by my *polis*. Therefore, "rational action based on scarcity" (a Weberian construct) was not necessary, since scarcity in the modern sense of total dependence on oneself was rarely experienced. Second, the avowed aim of economic activity in ancient Greece was to support the good life for the households of its citizens; it was not to produce a surplus for its own sake. Marx would laugh at Booth's claim that for a household to store up some surplus goods to enable them to enjoy some leisure is tantamount to the production of surplus value for its own sake in modern industry. Any modern household tries to accumulate a "nest egg," for a vacation or some independence. The fact that Aristotle devotes some time to criticizing the behaviour and psychology of those who practise *chrēmastikē* for the purpose of gain does not mean that capital accumulation was the purpose of the ancient economy.

Conclusion

In *The Great Transformation*, Polanyi says, "In retrospect our age will be credited with having seen the end of the self-regulating market."[109] The return to policies supporting a self-regulating free market in the last quarter of the twentieth century has shown this hope not to be true. As Kari Polanyi Levitt has recently said, "In the western heartlands of capitalism a malaise of stagflation and declining returns on domestic investment triggered a neoliberal regime change in the 1970s."[110] With all his insights and the power of his analysis of contemporary capitalism, so relevant to today's world, his opposition to Classical Political Economy obscured for Polanyi the relevance of the falling rate of profit, which explains why capitalists were driven to establish a free-market after the stagnation of the post-World War II "New Deal" economy in its series of recessions in 1958, then in the 1960s and 1970s.

This discussion of the work of Karl Polanyi and his relationship to Aristotle has also provided grounds for holding that Aristotle advances a theory of political economy. Polanyi himself develops a theory of political economy based on his study both of Aristotle's theory and of modern anthropology. He argues that Aristotle foresaw the development of nineteenth-century industrial capitalism. Moreover, Polanyi's own critique of market society was Aristotelian, for he wrote that:

> The true criticism of market society is not that it was based on economics – in a sense, every and any society must be based on it – but that its economy was based on self-interest. Such an organization of economic life is entirely unnatural, in the strictly empirical sense of exceptional.[111]

In that passage, Polanyi echoes Aristotle's argument that the pursuit of unconstrained wealth acquisition is contrary to nature and destructive to community life. Polanyi's Aristotelian theory and his interpretation of nineteenth- and twentieth-century economic history provide insights to help us understand contemporary political economy.

Notes

1 Polanyi (1944), 124 draws the conclusion of an argument that runs from p. 68 to p. 129.
2 Cf. Polanyi (1944), 126.
3 Cf. Polanyi (1944).
4 Cf. Polanyi (1957b).
5 There are many publications illustrating Polanyi's contemporary influence. For example, cf. Orum and Dale (2009), Chap. 5; Blyth (2002); Hann and Hart (2011); Rieger and Liebfried (2003); Munck (2006); Granovetter and Swedberg (2011); even among his detractors, for example McCloskey (2016), Chaps. 57–58.
6 Cf. Polanyi (1959), 2.
7 Cf. Polanyi (1944), 47–55.
8 Cf. Polanyi (1944), 53–55; Polanyi (1957a). Polanyi (1944), 47 acknowledges the influence of also Malinowski and Thurnwald on reciprocity and redistribution.
9 Cf. Polanyi (1957a), 79.
10 Cf. Polanyi (1944), 254–258; Polanyi (1959).
11 Cf. Polanyi (1944), 54.
12 Cf. Polanyi (1957a).
13 Cf. Polanyi (1957a), 99, on Solon, 97, 100 and cf. Aris. *Pol.* i.8.1256b32.
14 Marx (1962), 100.
15 Cf. Polanyi (1944), 126.
16 Cf. Polanyi (1944), 53–55.
17 Cf. Polanyi (1957a), 98–99.
18 Cf. *Pol.* i.8.1256b28–39.
19 Cf. Polanyi (1957a), 79, 98.
20 Cf. *Pol.* i.8.1256b7–22.
21 Cf. *Pol.* ii.2.1261b11–13.
22 Cf. *Pol.* i.2.1252b27–29.
23 Cf. *Pol.* i.8.1256b29–30.
24 Cf. *Pol.* i.8.1256b31–32.
25 Cf. Polanyi (1957a), 99–100, italics added. Polanyi's comment suggests that much of the *Politics* responds to contemporary development in Greek trading and market activities, a question I have to put aside for now.
26 Cf. *Pol.* vi.8.1321b14–16.
27 Cf. *Pol.* i.9.1257a29–30.
28 Cf. *Pol.* i.9.1257a31–33.
29 Cf. *Pol.* i.9.1257a31–b22.
30 Cf. Polanyi (1944), 249–258.
31 Cf. Polanyi (1944), 92.
32 Cf. Polanyi (1944), 54.
33 Cf. his discussions of the "double movement" in Polanyi (1944).
34 Cf. Polanyi (1959), 5, emphasis in original.
35 Cf. Polanyi (1959), 3; Greek is from Polanyi's text.

36 Cf. *Pol.* i.2.1252b28–29; iii.9. 1280a31–32, b39.
37 Cf. Polanyi (1957a), 98.
38 Cf. Polanyi (1959), 4, emphasis in original.
39 Cf. Pericles' funeral speech in Thucydides (1954).
40 Cf. *EE* 1242b15–16, 1244a24, 27–30.
41 Cf. Polanyi (1944), 254–58, Polanyi (1959), 6, emphasis in original.
42 Cf. Polanyi (1959), 7, emphasis in original.
43 Cf. Polanyi (1944), 255.
44 Cf. Polanyi (1959), 2.
45 Cf. *Pol.* i.9.1257b19–20. Liddell and Scott (1897) also render *chrēmatistikē* as "the craft of making-money." Natali (1990) shows that Aristotle distinguishes two types of *chrēmatistikē*, "bonne" and "mauvaise," of which the first serves *oikonomia*, and the other with which we are here concerned is the "craft of money-making," which Natali designates "*chrematistique*".
46 Cf. *Pol.* i.9.1257b38–58a2.
47 Cf. Polanyi (1959), 6, emphasis in original.
48 Polanyi (1957a), 98.
49 Polanyi (1957a), 99.
50 Polanyi means Book I.
51 Polanyi (1944), 53–54, italics added; cf. Aris., *Pol.* i.9.
52 Polanyi (1957a), 81.
53 Cf. *Pol.* i.2.1352b27ff; ii.2.1261b14; iii.9.1280b31–34.
54 Cf. Polanyi (1944), 74.
55 "Buy cheap and sell dear," is attributed to Baron Rothschild.
56 Cf. *Pol.* i.9.1257b20–22.
57 Cf. Polanyi (1944), 74.
58 Cf. *Pol.* i.9.1257a21–30; vi.8.1321b12–18.
59 Cf. *Pol.* i.9.1257a31–34.
60 Cf. *EN* ix.1.1163b32–35.
61 Kant (1993), 39, Menzer, 433.
62 Cf. Aristotle (1998), 17: "Commerce has to do with the production of goods, not in the full sense, but *through their exchange.*"
63 Stalley's revision of Barker's translation reads: "retail trade serves to make money, and that only by the exchange of commodities" (cf. Aristotle, 1995, 27). In their rendering, Barker and Stalley translate χρήματα two different ways, first as "money," then as "commodities." That is clearly problematic. The word can indeed mean either "goods" or "money" within a single context, but can hardly mean both in the same sentence. That error in translation comes from the translator's failure to understand that Aristotle is referring to production of goods solely for a market, for the production of such goods results in gain only if they are exchanged. Jowett's translation is ambiguous; he writes: "Retail trade is the art of producing wealth, not in every way, but by exchange" (cf. Aristotle, 1984, v.2, 1995). Jowett omits any translation at all of the second χρημάτων in the passage since a translation consistent with his rendering of the first phrase would be "by exchange of wealth" and that would not make sense. Both occurrences of χρημάτων must be translated as "of goods."
64 Polanyi (1957a), 95, emphasis added.
65 Polanyi (1957a), 96.
66 Cf. Polanyi (1957b), 270.
67 Cf. Polanyi (1957b), 243.
68 Cf. Weber (1978), Vol. I, part 1, Chap. 2, section 7, and p. 109.
69 Cf. Polanyi (1957b), 243.

70 Cf. von Mises, *Human Action,* Mises Institute. In his edition of Polanyi's essays, G. Dalton excised all but one instance of "catallactic" from Polanyi (1957b), and thereby removed Polanyi's reference to von Mises and Hayek and replaced clarity with confusion; cf. Polanyi (1968), 158n5.
71 Cf. Hayek, F.A. *Law, Legislation, and Liberty,*Vol. 2 (1976), 108–109.
72 For German text, cf.Weber (1922),Vol. I, part 1, Chap. 2, section 9, p. 44; for translation, cf.Weber (1978), 85.
73 Cf.Weber (1922), 45;Weber (1978), 85.
74 Cf.Weber (1922), 45;Weber (1978), 85–86.
75 Cf. Mills (1959).
76 Mills (1959), 168, 170. Example of soldier drawn from Mannheim (1940), 54.
77 Weber (1978), 109.
78 Polanyi (1968b), 136, emphasis in original.
79 Polanyi (1957a), 82.
80 Polanyi (1957b), 243.
81 Weber (1978), 85–86.
82 Polanyi (1957b), 243.
83 Polanyi (1957b), 244.
84 Polanyi (1957b), 247.
85 Polanyi (1957b), 243.
86 On the substantivist school, cf. Hann and Hart (2011), 55–71.
87 Cf. *EN* 1133b16, 1133b8.
88 Polanyi (1957a), 97, 107.
89 *EN* v.5.1133b4–5.
90 Cf. Part II for further discussion.
91 Cf. Polanyi (2014b), 153.
92 Cf. Polanyi (1944), 47; Polanyi (1957a). 86–93.
93 Cf. Polanyi (1944), 47–53.
94 Polanyi (1957b), 152–153.
95 Aristotle speaks of distribution of *klēroi* in Attica to citizens in *Pol.* ii.6.1265b3–4; often allotments were in recently conquered foreign territory, for example Lesbos, where the new Athenian owners would continue to live in Athens, but retain the former owners as tenant farmers; cf. Liddell and Scott (1897), 814 comment on *klērouxia*;Thuc. iii.50; cf. Herod. vi.100 on the case of Chalcis; Plutarch, "Life of Pericles."
96 Howatson (1989), 366 tells us:"The silver mines of Laurium . . . were the source of great wealth to fifth-century Athens." Cf. also Thuc. ii.55, vi, 91.
97 Cf. Paley (1921).
98 Pritchard (2015), 52ff says that "In the 450s the Athenians voted to introduce *misthos* ("pay") for jurors. In the 440s or the 430s they began to pay councilors and magistrates. By the 390s the *dēmos* were drawing pay to attend assembly meetings." On pay for assembly attendance, cf. Aristop. *Eccl.,* l. 378–379. On payment for jurors cf. Pl. *Gorg.* 515e, Aris. *Pol.* 1294a37. Pay was raised from 2 to 3 obols by Cleon early in the Peloponnesian war.
99 Polanyi (2014b), 157–158.
100 On the Pentecenteitia, cf.Thuc. i. 89–117.
101 Known as "the Just," he was an Athenian statesman, one of the generals at the battle of Marathon in 490, held a command at Salamis, and led the Athenian forces at Platea. He apportioned the tribute among the members of the Delian League. Cf. Howatson 1989.

102 The League was the alliance formed to prosecute the war against Persia. It included almost all the Greek islands. Cf. Howatson, 1989.

103 *Ath. Res.* 24–25. Translation from Aristotle (1984b), 24–25.

104 Cf. Cary (1933), 224–225.

105 Cf. *Pol.* ii.12.1274a13

106 We might object that the Athenians lived off of tribute paid by the allies whom they had freed from Persian domination, but Pritchard (2015) shows that the Athenians supported their democracy and grand festivals from internal funds, and only used the tribute for alliance and military expenditures.

107 Cf. Thuc. ii.37.

108 Cf. Booth (1993), 80, cf. 78.

109 Polanyi (1944), 142.

110 Levitt (2014), xiv.

111 Cf. Polanyi (1944), 249.

3   John Rawls

I argue that John Rawls in his theory of justice as fairness presents a Kantian version of an Aristotelian social welfare policy. Rawls employs Aristotle's critique of political economy in his theory of the distribution of human natural assets, in his difference principle, and in his theory of reciprocity, all of which I discuss below. Moreover, he constructs an Aristotelian principle of human motivation to support his theory, which he calls "the Aristotelian Principle." I also consider some areas in which Rawls clearly disagrees with Aristotle in regards to the nature of the state, the nature of human beings, and the nature of justice.

Rawls himself says that his theory is Kantian. But to say that his theory is Aristotelian is perhaps a surprise to many. I do not say that Rawls himself is Aristotelian, but only that he reforms Aristotle's proposals from a Kantian standpoint for the sake of making them more palatable to contemporary culture. The difference principle, which is very much the heart of Rawls' theory, is a principal locus of the Aristotelian influence.

Community

To begin, I review two of Rawls' fundamental political principles and contrast them with Aristotle's views in order to set the context in which Rawls brings Aristotelian social welfare policy into his political theory. First, in *Justice as Fairness: A Restatement*, Rawls says rather surprisingly

> I believe that *a democratic society is not and cannot be a community*, where by a community I mean a body of persons united in affirming the same comprehensive, or partially comprehensive, doctrine. *The fact of reasonable pluralism which characterizes a society with free institutions makes this impossible.* This is the fact of profound and irreconcilable differences in citizens' reasonable comprehensive religious and philosophical conceptions of the world, and in their views of the moral and aesthetic value to be sought in human life.[1]

Rawls' statement is consistent with his belief, following Kant, that human beings in contemporary civil society act heteronomously,[2] that is they are driven by passions and desires rather than directed by reason. Rawls contrasts a modern democratic society with "conditions in other historical ages when people are said to have been united," as in classical Athens, but adds the cynical caveat "though perhaps they never have been" united. [3]

In contrast to Rawls, Aristotle says in the very first line of the *Politics* that "every city-state is a community (*koinōnia*) of some sort."[4] He bases that community on "oneness of mind" (*homonoia*) and civic friendship. He explains that as follows:

> It is peculiar to human beings alone, in comparison to the other animals, to have perception of what is good and bad, just and unjust, and the rest. And it is the community in these things that makes a household and a city-state.[5]

For Aristotle, a community is constituted out of agreement concerning "what is good and bad, just and unjust," and so on among the human beings who form that community. Those topics fall under what Rawls names "views of the moral . . . value to be sought in human life." Rawls' view, again following Kant, is that contemporary citizens of Western democracies, such as the United States, cannot agree in their "views of the moral and aesthetic value to be sought in human life," that is the "perception of what is good and bad, just and unjust," and so on and therefore that such a "democratic society" cannot be a community.[6] Rawls' point is that contemporary policies of redistribution, for example, cannot be based on the proposition that all members of a community merit this or that, as Aristotle argued, since there is no such community of the "perception of what is good and bad, just and unjust," and so on, and therefore no agreement on what people merit. Perhaps Rawls considers that in contemporary capitalist society the possibility of the civic friendship and *homonoia* that united Athens, is greatly diminished. Therefore, it is necessary to formulate alternative, contemporary justifications for redistribution and other such policies characteristic of communities. What separates Rawls and Aristotle in that discussion is that Rawls holds the Kantian view that we cannot agree on our views of the moral value in life, while Aristotle holds that we can.

Man as a political animal

Second, Rawls rejects Aristotle's account of the human as "a political animal."[7] He says:

> [J]ustice as fairness . . . rejects civic humanism. To explain: in the strong sense, civic humanism is (by definition) a form of Aristotelianism: it holds that we are social, even political, beings whose essential nature is most fully achieved in a democratic society in which there is widespread and active participation in political life. This participation is encouraged not merely as possibly necessary for the protection of basic liberties but because it is the privileged locus of our (complete) good.[8]

Rawls says that he follows Kant in rejecting civic humanism.[9] Since many people today do not consider "widespread and active participation in political life" as part of their "(complete) good," Rawls reasons, civic humanism is "incompatible with justice as fairness as a political conception of justice."[10] Rawls elaborates his explanation for why he must reject civic humanism:

> Justice as fairness . . . regards the equal political liberties (the liberties of the ancients) as having in general less intrinsic value than, say, freedom of thought and liberty of conscience (the liberties of the moderns). By this is meant . . . that in a modern democratic society taking a continuing and active part in public life generally has . . . a lesser place in the conceptions of the (complete) good of most citizens. In a modern democratic society politics is not the focus of life as it was for native-born male citizens in the Athenian city-state.[11]

In these two passages, Rawls puts aside Aristotle's description of the human being as "a political animal," for if involvement in the affairs of one's state "is not the focus of life" then the human is not a political animal. But this is also a rejection of the Greek conception of *eû zên* or "living well," for a city-state "exists for the sake of living well (*eû zên*),"[12] and is "a community for households and families to live well (*eû zên*) together,"[13] so someone who does not participate in the affairs of his or her state abandons it and so abandons "living well" or "the good life."[14] Thus Rawls rejects *eû zên*, for the Greeks considered *eû zên* to be constituted of participation in their social and political life as the "locus of [their] (complete) good."

But the narrow conception of civic involvement that Rawls embraces fits his undertaking to develop a social welfare policy that though in some respects is similar to that of the ancients, yet at the same time is acceptable to less politically involved moderns, for one cannot today expect to justify that support be provided for the less advantaged so that they can participate in political life, as Aristotle argued and as Pericles so provided such support, since widespread such participation is not viewed as in the interests of all. Therefore, we must arrive at some other justification for assisting the poor, if we are to do so. It is almost as if Rawls envisions that the New Deal policies of Roosevelt would be jettisoned, as many of them were in the 1970s and 1980s, and that some less generous policy would come to the fore to which we need respond in new ways.[15]

Rawls' disagreements with Aristotle's views that the human is a political animal and that a polity need be a community of the "perception of what is good and bad, just and unjust," and so on confirm that Rawls and Aristotle express fundamentally different politico-theoretical views. There would seem to be dubious grounds for holding that Rawls is influenced by Aristotle.

Rawls' Aristotelian Principle and his theory of the distribution of natural assets

In Part III of *A Theory of Justice*, however, Rawls presents his "Aristotelian Principle," which he defines as follows:

[O]ther things equal, human beings enjoy the exercise of their realized capacities (their innate or trained abilities), and this enjoyment increases the more the capacity is realized, or the greater its complexity.[16]

Rawls says the principle "characterizes human nature as we know it."[17] He explains:

The Aristotelian Principle is a principle of motivation. It accounts for many of our major desires, and explains why we prefer to do some things and not others by constantly exerting an influence over the flow of our activity. Moreover, it expresses a psychological law governing changes in the pattern of our desires . . . it states a deep psychological fact which, in conjunction with other general facts and the conception of a rational plan, accounts for our considered judgments of value.[18]

Rawls justifies his naming the principle Aristotelian by citing *Nicomachean Ethics* Book vii, Chapters 11–14, and Book x, Chapters 1–5 as texts from which he derives it. Those texts present Aristotle's view of pleasure. Rawls explains in a note:

Aristotle certainly affirms two points that the principle conveys: (1) that enjoyment and pleasure are not always by any means the result of returning to a healthy or normal state, or of making up deficiencies [as when we eat or drink – RG]; rather many kinds of pleasure and enjoyment arise when we exercise our faculties; and (2) that the exercise of our natural powers is a leading human good. Further, (3) the idea that the more enjoyable activities and the more desirable and enduring pleasures spring from the exercise of greater abilities involving more complex discriminations is not only compatible with Aristotle's conception of the natural order, but something like it usually fits the judgments of value he makes, even when [he] does not express his reasons.[19]

Here Rawls endorses Aristotle's notion that pleasure need not be corporeal or emotional, and attributes to him the view that "the exercise of our natural powers is a leading human good." Furthermore, he expresses agreement with Aristotle's view that some pleasures are "more desirable and enduring" than others, and argues that such pleasures originate from "the exercise of greater abilities involving more complex discriminations." This amounts to a brief sketch of a non-liberal theory of aesthetics, from which one could argue that, for example, certain music is "more desirable" than other.[20] Moreover, Rawls says that the principle coheres with "Aristotle's conception of the natural order" and the way that Aristotle makes "judgments of value." But "Aristotle's conception of the natural order" revolves around his notion of teleology, which expressed through the Aristotelian Principle would state that "the exercise of our natural powers" is a purpose (*telos*) of our existence. Rawls strikingly seems to be highlighting portions of Aristotle's thought with which he seems to agree. But we should ask whether Rawls' account of Aristotle is accurate. Could he simply have cited Aristotle to bolster the credibility of *A Theory of Justice*? No: towards the end of the passages cited by Rawls, Aristotle expresses something like Rawls' Aristotelian Principle:

> One might think that all men desire pleasure because they all aim at life; life is an activity, and each man is active about those things and with those faculties that he loves most; e.g. the musician is active with his hearing in reference to tunes, the student with his mind in reference to theoretical questions, and so on in each case; now pleasure completes the activities, and therefore life, which they desire.[21]

Thus Aristotle agrees that "human beings enjoy the exercise of their realized capacities." At the end of the passages cited by Rawls, Aristotle concludes that the best pleasures correspond to the best activities:

> [O]f those that are thought to be good what kind of pleasure or what pleasure should be said to be that proper to man? Is it not plain from the corresponding activities? The pleasures follow these. Whether, then, the perfect and supremely happy man has one or more activities, the pleasures that perfect these will be said in the strict sense to be pleasures proper to man, and the rest will be so in a secondary and fractional way, as are the activities.[22]

Although Rawls does not say that there is a pleasure "proper to man" – a quite non-liberal view – he does come close to saying so, when he writes, "this enjoyment increases the more the capacity is realized, or the greater its complexity," [23] so that the pleasure experienced in realizing complex capacities is "proper to man."

Now, what role does the Aristotelian Principle play in Rawls' theory of justice? What does it have to do with justice? First, the Aristotelian Principle, with its focus on motivation and on realizing "natural capacities" and "innate or trained abilities," places emphasis on Rawls' theory of the distribution of human natural assets, and that theory is embedded in his theory of primary goods. Rawls says that there are "natural" as well as "social" primary goods:

> the chief primary goods at the disposition of society are rights, liberties, and opportunities, and income and wealth . . . These are the social primary goods. Other primary goods such as health and vigor, intelligence and imagination, are natural goods; although their possession is influenced by the basic structure, they are not so directly under its control.[24]

The point of the last clause is that natural assets, such as intelligence, or imagination, which make all the difference in someone's ability to succeed, are not under the control of "the basic structure of society," that is society cannot distribute them: some people have greater natural assets than others, and there is nothing that anyone can do about it. Rawls proposes to give those people more challenging tasks that, once completed, benefit all.[25]

Second, Rawls would have it that the more advantaged members of society, who he says are "more gifted," that is have "natural" primary goods that others lack, are guided by the Aristotelian Principle in making decisions that affect others, that is, in making "judgments of value," for the Aristotelian Principle "accounts for many of our major desires," and is "constantly exerting an influence over the flow of our activity." Moreover, as the more advantaged has "greater abilities," according to the Aristotelian Principle they will be motivated to use them in particularly creative ways. If those who are more gifted are motivated in accordance with the Aristotelian Principle, as Rawls proposes, he hopes that they will turn away from desire for material goods and towards the enjoyment of the realization of their natural capacities. Rawls intends that potentiality to support the principle of generosity that underlies the difference principle.[26] Rawls argues:

> Thus the more advantaged, when they view the matter from a general perspective, recognize that the well-being of each depends on a scheme of social cooperation without which no one could have a satisfactory life; they recognize also that they can expect the willing cooperation of all only if the terms of the scheme are reasonable. So they regard themselves as already compensated, as it were, by the advantages to which no one (including themselves) had a prior claim.[27]

Rawls argues that it is in the interest of the more advantaged that the less advantaged "have a satisfactory life." This sounds like Aristotle's argument from the *Politics* that the leaders of the *polis* must make sure that the poor have the means to participate in the political affairs of the city, to establish a homestead and to join in the common meals.[28] But that argument is based on the recognition that the *polis* is a community held together by civic friendship or *philia*, concepts rejected by Rawls. Rawls rejects any such basis for justice as fairness, since he dismisses Aristotle's essential premise concerning a harmony of interests in the community. Rawls, however, believes in the existence of a community of interest so that each can "have a satisfactory life." But such a community of interest is precisely what is lacking in democratic societies, as he describes them. For why should people who have very different beliefs, priorities and values help others who don't share them? No reason is given.[29]

As noted above, it is a fundamental premise of Rawls' theory of justice that human natural assets are distributed unequally, that is that people differ in nature, and are not the same. This is a pre-Enlightenment concept. It is *not* Kantian. Rawls uses that premise to motivate the difference principle:

The difference principle represents, in effect, an agreement to regard the distribution of natural talents as in some respects a common asset and to share in the greater social and economic benefits made possible by the complementarities of this distribution. Those who have been favored by nature, whoever they are, may gain from their good fortune only on terms that improve the situation of those who have lost out. The naturally advantaged are not to gain merely because they are more gifted, but only to cover the costs of training and education and for using their endowments in ways that help the less fortunate as well. No one deserves his greater natural capacity nor merits a more favorable starting place in society. But, of course, this is no reason to ignore, much less to eliminate these distinctions. Instead, the basic structure can be arranged so that these contingencies work for the good of the least fortunate.[30]

Rawls argues that since human talents are unevenly distributed, they must be viewed as the common asset of all, rather than something that makes their possessor "superior." Rather, possession of greater abilities obligates us to use our endowments "in ways that help the less fortunate."

Given that Rawls' theory of the distribution of natural assets conflicts with Enlightenment thought, we must consider what its source could possibly be. Simply stated, the view that natural assets differ from person to person, and yet are at the same time a common asset of humanity, originates with Plato and Aristotle. In the *Republic* Socrates advances the view that "each of us was born not quite like one another, but differing in nature (*phusis*), one suited to the doing of one task, another to another."[31] So, natural assets are distributed unequally. Socrates argues that each of us needs to associate with others who have different talents than us, and form cities, "because none of us is self-sufficient, but we all need many things."[32] Thus we call upon others who have different natural assets in order to fulfill our needs. This is more than the modern concept of the division of labour, for that concept does not acknowledge that people "differ in nature" and because of that, must come together into a community. Their different needs "will make the city,"[33] Socrates explains, "because people need many things, and because one person associates with a second because of one need, and with a third because of a different need, many people gather together in a single homeland to live together as sharers and helpers."[34] In sum, the city is based on all sharing in the natural assets of each other. In the *Republic*, each member of that community is free to call upon any other to meet his or her needs, for collectively their talents are a common asset.

Following what Socrates says in the *Republic*, Aristotle argues in the *Politics* that a fundamental characteristic of city-states is that they are necessarily composed of "people who differ in kind (*eídos*)."[35] Moreover, Aristotle holds that it is a special function of "superior" members of a community to benefit weaker ones, and that relationship characterizes for Aristotle a special sort of civic friendship, whose aim is to maintain the existence of the lesser party.[36] Thus Plato and Aristotle propose that natural assets differ from person to person, and that the totality of human natural assets are a common asset insofar as each draws on the natural assets of the other. That view influenced social and political organization until the Enlightenment. Therefore, it is reasonable to conclude that in his theory of the distribution of natural assets, Rawls again shows that he is influenced by Greek economic thought. He acknowledges that natural assets differ and that we should consider them common. Nonetheless, however, he rejects the basis of that commonality in the civic friendship of a community. By contrast, Aristotle's view is predicated on "oneness of mind" (*homonoia*) and friendship (*philia*) among members of a community.[37] Aristotle goes so far as to say that where there is *philia*, there is no need for justice. But Rawls has no notion of the affection that binds a community together.

Having seen how Rawls' Aristotelian Principle is linked to his theory of the distribution of natural assets, we now turn to discuss the difference principle, which is dependent on both of those other theories.

The difference principle

Rawls' difference principle is a contemporary scheme of distributive justice, which he hopes will compensate for the uneven distribution of natural asserts in a society.[38] In *A Theory of Justice*, Rawls proposes the difference principle as a distribution scheme, based on comparison of the expectations of two persons, one more advantaged, the other less advantaged.[39] Rawls' scheme is strikingly similar to Aristotle's model of exchange between two persons of different worth (*axia*) which one can see by substituting wealth for "expectations" or "worth" in either model, which is fair, since Rawls speaks of expectations in terms of income and goods, and Aristotle says that worth is measured in an oligarchy by wealth.[40]

In motivating the difference principle, Rawls asks what can justify the initial inequalities that exist in life prospects among the people who make up a society.[41] He answers that "According to the difference principle, [inequality] is justifiable only if the difference in expectation [of the more advantaged] is to the advantage of the representative man who is worse off, in this case, the representative unskilled worker."[42] But how could inequality be to the advantage of the one who is worse off? Rawls means that the more advantaged should only acquire more wealth, if, at the same time, the position of the less advantaged is also benefited as much as it can be under the circumstances.[43] In other words, we can justify inequality only if the growth in the income of the more advantaged results in the highest income possible for the less advantaged under a variety of possible scenarios for the growth of the income of both.[44] Rawls believes that inequality is necessary, for without it, he argues, the more advantaged would not be motivated to take initiative to employ the less advantaged in productive cooperation, and as a result, society would not be properly organized.[45] Those more advantaged are born with, or acquire (through privilege) talents that the less advantaged lack, says Rawls, and those talents are useful to society as a whole in organizing productive cooperation.[46] In *Theory*, Rawls advances the example that the more advantaged are the entrepreneurial class, and the less advantaged the class of unskilled workers.[47] In *Justice as Fairness: A Restatement*, Rawls says that the difference principle pertains to social cooperation in producing goods and services, that is the usual employer/employee arrangement that characterizes the capitalist age, in which employee exchanges labour for wages proposed by employer.[48] In Rawls' model of the difference principle, the higher expectations allowed to entrepreneurs encourage them to do things that raise the prospects of the labouring class.[49] All in all, Rawls views contemporary capitalist relations as "fair" or at least potentially fair. That is, today's exchange of labour for wage income is a fair exchange. Admittedly, Rawls wrote the first edition of *A Theory of Justice* when conditions were better for working people in America than they are today. But the rapid growth of inequality that has occurred since suggests that his theory embodies fundamental error, error in understanding the nature of society, in understanding human nature and in understanding justice, as we will see below. We have seen that when the more advantaged with so-called "greater abilities" are given the freedom, they will try to grab everything for themselves. They "regard persons as means" and are "prepared to impose on those already less favored still lower prospects of life for the sake of [their own] high expectations."[50] Moreover, it seems clear that in Rawls' view contemporary capitalist relations of employer to employee are prior to other forms of social organization, such as within a community or a household, contrary, needless to say, to Aristotle and Polanyi. Nonetheless, Rawls follows Aristotle in recognizing inequality within a society, and incorporating it into his theory, for Aristotle was the first to do so, as far as we know. Though Rawls intended his theory as reform, in the final analysis it is another apology for capitalism.

Rawls' famous figure representing the difference principle in *A Theory of Justice* (reproduced as Figure 3.1 here) plots the benefits of productive cooperation to representative individuals of the more and the less advantaged groups, represented by x_1 and x_2.[51] The straight line rising to the right through Figure 3.1 (the 45° slope) represents growth in which both parties would benefit equally (i.e. in the figure, $x_1 = x_2$) from a distribution/transaction or productive cooperation,[52] a condition that never holds since there is inequality. Rawls argues that any curve representing distributions or transactions involving two such unequal parties, labelled OP in Figure 3.1, is always below the 45° line, since x_1 is always better off.[53] Within that constraint, the difference principle judges the most effective scheme to be the one which gives the greatest return to the less advantaged regardless of the return to the more advantaged.[54] The difference principle maximizes the value of x_2: It picks out the highest point on any curve OP representing the relation between the incomes of x_1 and x_2 (cf. Figure 3.1).[55] In the Figure, the difference principle picks out the point where OP is tangent to the horizontal (whose x_1 value is labeled *a*), as the most effective relative distribution since "it gives a greater return to the less advantaged for any given return to the more advantaged,"[56] for all other points on curve OP gives a lower return to x_2. Following Rawls' later practice,

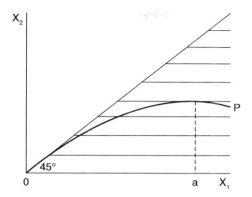

Figure 3.1 Rawls' figure illustrating the difference principle. Figure reprinted by permission of the publisher from Figure 6, page 66 *of A THEORY OF JUSTICE: REVISED EDITION* by John Rawls, Cambridge, Mass.: The Belknap Press of Harvard University Press, Copyright © 1971, 1999 by the President and Fellows of Harvard College.

I name that tangent point D.[57] The upper left portion of Figure 3.1 is blank, explains Rawls, since in that region the less advantaged party x_2 would benefit materially *more* than the more advantaged x_1, which prospect Rawls rules out.[58]

As we noticed in Chapter 2, and will see in subsequent chapters, Aristotle, like Rawls, analyses the inequality that exists in society.[59] To do this, unlike Rawls, he formulates a theory of value and includes relative worth or social status $\frac{\alpha}{\beta}$ (e.g. relative income) as a term. With that instrument, he analyses all exchanges. One can plot values of Aristotle's terms, α, β, on Rawls' Figure 3.1 (where α is the more advantaged, and β is the less advantaged), as follows: $\alpha = x_1$, $\beta = x_2$, and they will determine points in the lower right of the figure, as in the cases that Rawls studies. Moreover, like Rawls, Aristotle is interested in improving the condition of the less advantaged, but – unlike Rawls – not only for their sake, but also for the sake of the community of the *polis* of which they are a part, for, insofar as they are less advantaged, they can contribute only so much to the community, whereas, if they were better off, they might contribute more. Also like Rawls, Aristotle is interested in raising the absolute wealth of the less advantaged. But unlike Rawls he proposes, in the *Eudemian Ethics*, that in individual transactions between more advantaged and less advantaged parties, the more advantaged ought to materially benefit the less advantaged, so that the less advantaged will benefit more materially from such transactions than the more advantaged.[60] For example, we relate Aristotle's terms to Rawls' as follows: $\alpha = x_1$, $\beta = x_2$, and the initial position is the tangent point which we have named D on OP in Figure 3.1. Suppose the more advantaged party sells the less advantaged party a house at a price less than its value,[61] so that each has a new position: $x_1' = x_1 + dx_1$ and $x_2' = x_2 + dx_2$, where $dx_1 < 0$ and $dx_2 > 0$. Such a transaction moves point D off OP to D' towards the upper

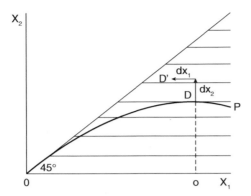

Figure 3.2 Modification of Figure 3.1 to represent transaction benefiting lesser party (proposed by Aristotle). Differentials dx_1 and dx_2 represent changes in incomes of the two parties resulting in movement of D to D' (see text).

left (cf. Figure 3.2). After repeated such transactions, D will cross the $x_1 = x_2$ line as the more advantaged materially assist the less advantaged. But a transaction in which the more advantaged benefits the less advantaged would not be proportional, as Aristotle puts it, or "Pareto efficient," as Rawls would say, for it makes one person better off (the less advantaged) while making another one worse off (the more advantaged).[62] We discuss in Chapter 9 how proportionality is restored in Aristotle's example by the community rewarding the more advantaged in a non-material way. Part of that discussion, however, shows that insofar as the less advantaged is better off and is able to contribute more to the community, the more advantaged benefits as a result.

Rawls on reciprocity

Rawls' difference principle and Aristotle's theory of exchange have similarities. It is reasonable to conclude that Aristotle's theory influenced Rawls' formulation of the difference principle.[63] Rawls' detailed discussion of Aristotle's theory of worth also suggests that.[64] Moreover, as Aristotle claims his theory of exchange upholds reciprocity, Rawls argues that "the difference principle expresses a conception of reciprocity. It is a principle of mutual benefit."[65] Rawls imagines that the arrangement where the better endowed are motivated to organize productive cooperation so that the less endowed are somewhat benefited, is one of reciprocity such as he describes among members of a family:

> Members of a family commonly do not wish to gain unless they can do so in ways that further the interests of the rest. Now wanting to act on the difference principle has precisely this consequence. Those better circumstanced are willing to have their greater advantages only under a scheme in which this works out for the benefit of the less fortunate.[66]

Now, obviously, there is something awry here, for by comparing society to a family, Rawls assumes that there is a community of interests in society, as in a family, precisely what he rejects in the passages we discussed at the beginning of this chapter. But Rawls here is simply attempting to construct a model of reciprocity not based on community, but based on his hope that the more advantaged will conceive it in their interest to benefit the less advantaged, and that the less advantaged will not resent the greater wealth and power of the more advantaged. It is a weaker form of reciprocity than that proposed by Aristotle, yet Rawls, in justifying his theory as reciprocative, and in arguing that reciprocity is good for society, nonetheless follows Aristotle's thought.

One of the most controversial features of Rawls' theory is that the difference principle is chosen "behind a veil of ignorance." I resituate Rawls' veil as follows: In a revision of the myth of Er in Plato's *Republic* a group of souls (Rawls' "noumenal selves"[67]) is having tea before they go before Lachesis, the daughter of Necessity, to choose their *daimon* or guardian spirit for their future lives.[68] Before they make their choices, they are allowed to set down basic principles of justice in the world they will inhabit. Because they do not know what sort of life they will be able to choose when they come before Lachesis, they want to make sure that their needs are satisfied no matter where they end up in the social hierarchy, that is whether they are a party x_1 or a party x_2 in Rawls' model (or a party α or a party β in Aristotle's). So, they agree on the difference principle. Rawls' fundamental view is that each of us has our talents and position in the social hierarchy by accident.[69] We were born with those talents or into that social position, or we acquired them through privilege. Therefore, we must reason about what are the best principles of justice, not from the standpoint of our actual social position, but as though we could have ended up anywhere in the hierarchy. Thus we agree on the difference principle, basically, to save our skins no matter where we end up. Unfortunately, however, in formulating a basis of interpersonal comparison, Rawls places outside of consideration the very natural assets or natural primary goods that in many ways distinguish the more advantaged from everyone else. He blandly states that "These comparisons are made in terms of expectations of primary social goods."[70] Subsequently, Rawls drops discussion of natural primary goods entirely, so that in *Justice as Fairness: A Restatement*, he makes no mention of them.[71] They seem set aside from the primary goods approach altogether. In this way, surprisingly so, Rawls neglects difference.

Rawls and Aristotle on Aristotle's theory of justice

The difference principle is both Aristotelian and Kantian. The Kantian adopts it under the doctrine that each human is an end in him- or herself.[72] Rawls explains:

> [T]he difference principle interprets the distinction between treating men as a means only and treating them also as ends in themselves. To regard persons as ends in themselves in the basic design of society is

to agree to forgo those gains which do not contribute to everyone's expectations. By contrast, to regard persons as means is to be prepared to impose on those already less favored still lower prospects of life for the sake of the higher expectations of others.[73]

The Aristotelian, on the other hand, perceives the difference principle to be a step in the right direction, for Aristotle views each member of a community as necessary to the life of all the others, but would have us not only "forgo those gains which do not contribute to everyone's expectations" but rather be generous and constructive towards our partners in exchange to strengthen civic friendship and to enable them to experience *eû zên*.[74]

Rawls recognizes that imbalances, inequalities, will come to be, and hopes with the difference principle to prevent them from becoming overwhelming for the less advantaged. Aristotle likewise is concerned that inequality will lead to exploitation, social injustice and civil strife.[75] Unlike Rawls, however, and as we will see in Chapter 9, Aristotle does not accept the view that the more advantaged must always benefit more from a distribution or transaction than the less advantaged party.

The difference between Rawls' and Aristotle's theories is brought out in Rawls' account of Aristotle's definition of justice, for he says

> The more specific sense that Aristotle gives to justice . . . is that of refraining from *pleonexia*, that is, from gaining some advantage for oneself by seizing what belongs to another, his property, his reward, his office, and the like, or by denying a person that which is due to him.[76]

With that, Rawls presents rather Aristotle's definition of *injustice*, which is to commit *pleonexia*.[77] Aristotle himself does not define justice in terms of wrongdoing, but rather with respect to beneficence, for he says

> Justice is the only virtue that is another person's good, for it is related to another; for it does what benefits another.[78]

Under Aristotle's notion of justice, I am not just if I simply follow Rawls' account of justice in the passage, that is adhere to my contractual commitments, do not violate the rights of others and so on. I am just only if I positively benefit others. In the *Eudemian Ethics*, Aristotle provides an example of his sense of justice by formulating a procedure for establishing terms of exchange between unequal parties, so that the party superior in wealth or power grants generous terms to his less prosperous partner in proportion to their relative social status.[79] For the more advantaged to exploit the less advantaged, as seems allowed in justice as fairness, Aristotle says "the better supposes that it is fitting for him to have more (*pleon echein*)," that is commit *pleonexia*.[80]

Our investigation of Rawls' theory of justice shows that Aristotle's critique of political economy influenced Rawls' development of his own economic theories. We leave to Part III discussion of Rawlsian attempts to measure social welfare.

Notes

1 Rawls (2001), 3. Italics added. I agree with Rawls that there is only limited community in the United States. As Marx explains, American capitalism "did not develop on the foundation of a feudal system, but developed rather from itself . . . not as the result of a centuries-old movement, but rather as the starting-point of a new movement" (1972, 884). As a result, the mediaeval traditions of community and of feudal ties among individuals and classes that exists in Europe do not exist in America.

2 Rawls (1999), 222. Rawls seems to follow Protagoras.

3 Rawls (2001), 4. I am not going to debate here Rawls' suggestion that ancient Athens was not "a society with free institutions."

4 Aris. *Pol.* 1252a1.

5 Aris. *Pol.* 1253a16–18.

6 Cf. Rawls (1999), 221–227. The view that "a democratic society is not and cannot be a community," however, conflicts with other views expressed in *A Theory of Justice*, for there Rawls says: "the value of education should not be assessed solely in terms of economic efficiency and social welfare. Equally if not more important is the role of education in enabling a person to enjoy the culture of his society and to take part in its affairs, and in this way to provide for each individual a secure sense of his own worth." On another issue, it is certainly odd that Rawls seems to say that ancient Athens, the first democracy, was not "a democratic society."

7 Cf. *Pol.* i.2.1253a2–3.

8 Rawls (2001), 142.

9 Rawls (2001), 142n8.

10 Rawls (2001), 143. Rawls' theory justifies the US government conducting foreign military policy on which citizens do not deliberate or of which they are ignorant.

11 Rawls (2001), 143. One wonders if the tens and tens of thousands of Illinois citizens who stood for hours and hours listening to the Lincoln–Douglas debates would agree with Rawls here. I also find it strange that Rawls holds that political liberties, for example the right to vote, run for office, publish a newspaper, are less valuable than the right to think as I wish, which we have by nature, without needing permission from any government.

12 Cf. *Pol.* i.2.1252b28–29; iii.9.1280b39

13 Cf. *EN* vi.5.1140a25–28.

14 Mulgan (2000), 97 seems to have forgotten that Aristotle said "man is a political animal" in his comment that "the good life for the individual as Aristotle describes it is largely domestic and taken up with close, inter-personal relations and does not require membership of a political community directed toward its values."

15 So, contra Jackson (1990), Rawls is not apolitical.

16 Rawls (1999), 374.

17 Rawls (1999), 379.

18 Rawls (1999), 375, 379.

19 Rawls (1999), 374n20.

20 As Scruton (2010) argues.

21 *EN* x.4.1175a11–16; cf. esp. x.4, 5. Translation by Ross in Aristotle (1908b).

22 *EN* x.5.1176a26–29. Translation by Ross in Aristotle (1908b).

23 Rawls (1999), 374.

24 Rawls (1971), 62. Later in *Theory*, he adds self-respect to the list of social primary goods.

25 Subsequently, Rawls drops discussion of natural primary goods, so that in *Justice as Fairness: A Restatement*, he makes no mention of them; cf. Rawls (2001), 58–59.

26 The huge increase in inequality and in indulgence for luxury goods, unleashed by the return to free-market capitalism since the first publication of *A Theory of Justice* makes Rawls' principle ideal rather than real.

27 Rawls (1999), 88.
28 Cf. *Pol.* vii.10.
29 I thank David Konstan for making this point.
30 Rawls (1999), 87. Cf. also 63, 447.
31 *Rep.*, 370b.
32 *Rep.*, 369b.
33 *Rep.*, 369c.
34 *Rep.*, 369c. Strangely, Rawls (1999), 457 characterizes the community of the first city in Plato's *Republic*, 369–372, as one "in which the persons comprising it . . . have their own private ends which are either competing or independent, but *not in any case complementary*" (emphasis added), for complementarity is the core of the Greek idea. *Rep.* 369bc directly contradicts Rawls' claim.
35 Cf. *Pol.* ii.2.1261a22–24.
36 *EE* 1244a24, 27–28.
37 Cf. *EN* ix.6.
38 Cf. Rawls (1971), 75–80.
39 Cf. Rawls (1999), ¶13.
40 Cf. Rawls (1999), 66; Aris., *EN* v.3. 1131a28.
41 Cf. Rawls (1999), 68.
42 Rawls (1999), 68.
43 Cf. Rawls (2001), 42–43.
44 For an example, cf. ¶19.3 in Rawls (2001).
45 Cf. Rawls (1999), "Preface for the revised edition."
46 Cf. Rawls (2001), ¶21.
47 Cf. Rawls (1999), 67.
48 He says "This assumption is not emphasized sufficiently in *Theory*, ¶¶12–13." Cf. Rawls (2001), 61.
49 Cf. Rawls (1999), 68; Rawls (2001), 64.
50 Cf. Rawls (1999), 157.
51 For the original figure, cf. Rawls (1999), 66. In *Justice as Fairness: A Restatement*, cf. Rawls (2001), ¶18, Figure 1, which uses the terms MAG and LAG instead of x_1 and x_2.
52 The 45° slope in our Figure 3.1 corresponds to the line OJ in Figure 1 in Rawls (2001).
53 Cf. Rawls (1999), 66.
54 Cf. Rawls (1999), 66, 68; Rawls (2001), 63.
55 Or MAG and LAG in Rawls (2001).
56 Cf. Rawls (2001), 63. Note that Figure 3.1 is confusing. In the figure the x_1 value is highlighted (by being labelled *a*) rather than the tangent point. This is corrected in Rawls (2001), Figure 1, where the tangent point is labelled *D* and the abscissa value is unlabelled.
57 Following Rawls (2001), Figure 1, 63.
58 Cf. Rawls (1999), 66.
59 Cf. *EN* v.5.
60 Cf. Chapter 9.
61 Cf. Chapter 9.
62 Cf. Chapter 9; Rawls (1999), ¶12.
63 I am indebted to Leo Michelis for this suggestion.
64 Cf. Rawls (1999), §66–67.
65 Cf. Chapter 9; *EN* v.5; Rawls (1999), 88; cf. 88–90; Rawls (2001), 64, 76.
66 Rawls (1999), 90.
67 Cf. Rawls (1999), 225.

68 Cf. *Rep.* 617b–620e.
69 Plato seems not to share this view; cf. *Rep.* 618b–620d.
70 Rawls (1971), 92. Yet, in the same section of *Theory* he admits that "Greater intelligence, wealth and opportunity, for example, allow a person to achieve ends he could not rationally contemplate otherwise" (Rawls 1971: 93.)
71 Cf. Rawls (2001), 58–59.
72 Cf. *Grounding for the Metaphysics of Morals*, Indianapolis, 1993, section 2.
73 Cf. Rawls (1999), 157. I do not debate here whether Kant would agree with Rawls.
74 Cf. Part II.
75 Cf. *EN* v.5.1132b33–33a2.
76 Rawls (1999), 9. *Pleonexia* literally means "the state of having more" than others. Rawls' more advantaged qualifies.
77 Cf. *EN* 1163a26–27.
78 *EN* v.1.1130a4, cf. also 1134b5–6.
79 Cf. *EE* 1242b2–21; Gallagher (2012).
80 Cf. Chapters 8 and 9; Aris. *EN* 1163a26–27.

4   Amartya Sen

Amartya Sen first advanced the idea of "basic capabilities" to solve a problem in welfare economics in his 1979 Tanner Lecture on Human Values "Equality of What?" delivered at Stanford University.[1] For the next six years he independently developed his capabilities approach and justified it without any reference to Aristotle – up to and including his second Tanner Lecture "The Standard of Living," delivered at Cambridge University in 1985. But in revising that lecture for publication, Sen began to collaborate with Martha Nussbaum, as he notes, and, in the published version of the lecture, he includes a *footnote* crediting Aristotle for being an early proponent of "the perspective of 'functioning' in assessing social arrangements" and cites Aristotle's *Politics* Book iii. In the actual text of that lecture, however, he says that Adam Smith, William Petty, Antoine Lavoisier, Joseph Louis Lagrange, Karl Marx and A. C. Pigou are "the pioneers" who influenced him in developing the capabilities approach. He does not mention Aristotle there. He concludes that

> the system outlined here [i.e. the capabilities approach] seems to be both interesting in itself and well-related to the motivations underlying traditional concerns with the concept of the standard of living. The curiosity and interest that made Petty, Lavoisier, Lagrange, and others take up their investigations into real income and living standard were related to the assessment of the nature of people's lives. The view of the living standard taken here [i.e. the capabilities approach] seems to fit in fairly well with that motivation.[2]

Sen particularly credits Smith with the formulation of functionings of a social nature:

> Smith went well beyond the standard characterizations of living conditions and considered such functionings as "not being ashamed to appear in public," and analyzed the commodity requirements for this achievement – clothing, shoes, etc. – <which> varied with social customs and cultural mores . . . he also showed the social nature of these relationships between commodities (and opulence), on the one hand, and capabilities (and

achievements of living conditions), on the other. The same capability of being able to appear in public without shame has variable demands on commodities and wealth, depending on the nature of the society in which one lives.[3]

Even in his *On Ethics and Economics*, where Sen uses two pages to relate his theory of capabilities to Aristotle's ethics, he still spends much more time discussing Adam Smith than Aristotle. Sen has rehabilitated Smith from the reputation that he promoted "self-interest."[4]

Based on this brief review of Sen's work on capabilities up to the year 1987, it would seem that Aristotle was *not* a direct influence upon Sen in the early formulation of the capabilities approach to social welfare. Nonetheless, Sen, through his critiques of utilitarianism, welfarism and the primary goods approach of John Rawls, developed a number of concepts that distinguish him from his contemporaries, concepts that are distinctly Aristotelian in nature. Somehow he came to an Aristotelian perspective on these issues without studying Aristotle's treatment of them. These include: Sen's emphasis on need rather than desire,[5] his contention that people differ from each other[6] and his theory of value.[7] So, when Sen began to study Aristotle's ethical and political writings, he found much that was a natural fit with his own conceptions. By 1987, Sen was aligning himself with Aristotle in his *On Ethics and Economics,* particularly in his effort to bring ethics back into economics, his theory that economics has "two origins" – one in ethics and the other in engineering[8] – and his theory of motivation, that is, his view that "group associations . . . provide the focus of many actions involving committed behaviour" on motivational grounds other than mere self-interest,[9] that is "man is a political animal."[10] That said, at the same time, it is strange that Sen never makes any use of the principal texts of Aristotle's critique of political economy, *Politics* Book i and *Nicomachean Ethics* Book v.

The two "origins" of economics

Sen's Aristotelian departure from his contemporaries is seen especially in his argument that economics originated separately from ethics, on the one hand, and from engineering, on the other. In *Ethics and Economics* he says that "Economics relates ultimately to the study of ethics and of politics."[11] He adds that there is "no scope in all of this for dissociating the study of economics from that of ethics and political philosophy."[12] He credits Aristotle for developing this point of view in the *Politics.* Sen's assertions slap modern economic theory in its face, for a dissociation of ethics and economics is exactly what modern economics has pretended to achieve with its "self-consciously 'non-ethical' character,"[13] Sen charges. In contrast, he argues that "the historical evolution of modern economic theory largely [is] an offshoot of ethics."[14]

Sen says that there are "two central issues that are particularly foundational for economics." The first, he says, is "the problem of human motivation related to the broadly ethical question 'How should one live?'"[15] Sen calls this "the ethics–related view of motivation." The second issue that Sen identifies concerns "the judgment of social achievement." Again referring to Aristotle, he says the Philosopher "related this to the end of achieving 'the good for man.'" But, Sen explains, Aristotle noted "though it is worthwhile to attain the end merely for one man, it is finer and more godlike to attain it for a nation or for city–states."[16]

With the first issue, Sen continues to put aside the methodology of contemporary economics with the statement that fundamental for economics is the Socratic question "How should one live?" This is exactly the sort of question that contemporary economics for the most part ignores. With the second issue, concerning "the judgment of social achievement," Sen refers to Aristotle's notion of the human good as "to live well and do well." As discussed in Chapter 2, living well means to participate in the policy deliberation of one's state and to share in the social and culture riches of one's people. Sen labels Aristotle's notion of "the good for man" as the "judgment of social achievement" perhaps to appropriate Aristotle's theory as a foundation for his capabilities approach, for insofar as someone attains a set of functionings, s/he enjoys social achievement. (We discuss in Chapter 5 whether his use of Aristotle is valid.)

Sen concludes that ethics is vital for modern economics. He points out that "the importance of the ethical approach has rather substantially weakened as modern economics has evolved."[17] He explains that so–called positive economics has ignored ethical considerations by treating actual human behaviour as primarily matters of fact rather than of moral judgment, that is, the reality that people make moral judgments is set aside and instead emphasis in place on human behaviour as self–evident phenomena. He sums up his judgment of modern economics as follows: "the nature of modern economics has been substantially impoverished by the distance that has grown between economics and ethics."[18]

To draw the distinction between the ethics approach and the engineering one, Sen explains that the ethics–related view of social achievement rejects the metric of efficiency in justifying economic activity or policies.[19] Efficiency, however, is a focus of the engineering approach, the other origin of economics. This approach is concerned with logistics rather than with ultimate ends or such questions as what may foster "the good of man" or "how should one live." The ends are taken as straightforward, and the object of any undertaking is to find the appropriate means to serve them, argues Sen.[20]

Sen concludes that both approaches to economics "have cogency of their own."[21] Both have "much to offer to economics."[22] The engineering approach has made contributions "*despite* the neglect of the ethical approach, since there are important economic logistic questions which do call for attention and can be tackled with efficiency . . . even within the limited format of a narrowly construed non–ethical view of human motivation and behaviour."[23]

Sen does not draw the dividing line between ethical and non–ethical economics at the right place. Sen introduces confusion into the discussion of where to draw that line by conflating non-ethical economic thought, that simply does not discuss ethics, with unethical economics that involves considerations hostile to ethics, for example "positive economics."[24] Much, indeed most engineering is directed towards an ethical goal to provide housing, water, sanitation or transportation. But the engineer will usually not motivate engineering from ethical principles. Nonetheless, it accomplishes ethical results. Examples include the Tennessee Valley Authority and many others. Exponents of the ethical approach from Aristotle to Smith are deeply concerned with engineering issues as well, claims Sen.[25] Aristotle teaches us that the line between ethical and non-ethical economic activity should be drawn between activity that results in wealth accumulation in accordance with nature for the household or the city-state, and activity that results in wealth accumulation not in accordance with nature via commerce and merchandising.[26] For Aristotle engineering per se is part of "wealth accumulation in accordance with nature." Though we may debate whether merchandising is truly "not in accordance with nature," and whether financial manipulations are truly unethical, it is clear that civil and hydraulic engineering for the most part are in accordance with the ethical meeting of the needs of humans. Sen seems to have erred in dividing ethical economics from engineering in the way he does. Nonetheless, he follows Aristotle in attempting to divide ethical and unethical economic thought in some way.

Sen's theory of motivation

In several essays, Sen advances a theory of human motivation that bears some similarity to Aristotle's political thought. First, Sen is concerned to refute the modern view attributed to Adam Smith that "self-interest dominates the majority of men."[27] He discusses a passage from Smith where the classical economist says that

> [A]lthough the principles of common prudence do not always govern the conduct of every individual, they always influence the majority of every class or order.[28]

Stigler identifies prudence with self-interest and claims that the passage means that "self-interest dominates the majority of men."[29] But Sen argues that for Smith in *The Theory of Moral Sentiments*

> prudence is "the union of" the two qualities of "reason and understanding," on the one hand, and "self-command," on the other. The notion of "self-command" which Smith took from the Stoics, is not in any sense identical with "self-interest" or what Smith called "self-love."[30]

So Smith, Sen argues, does not adhere to Stigler's view. Sen has detached the self-interest view of human motivation and rationality from its pretense of a mooring in the thought of Adam Smith. Sen continues and argues that "The real issue is whether there is a plurality of motivations, or whether self-interest alone drives human beings."[31] Sen explains that

> the contrast is not necessarily between self-interest, on the one hand, and some kind of a general concern for all, on the other . . . groups inter-mediate between oneself and all – such as class, community or occupation groups – provide the focus of many actions involving committed behaviour. The members of each group may have partly congruent and partly conflicting interests. Actions based on group loyalty may involve, in some respects, a sacrifice of purely personal interests, just as they can also facilitate, in other respects, greater fulfillment of personal interests . . . The mixture of selfish and selfless behaviour is one of the important characteristics of group loyalty, and this mixture can be seen in a wide variety of group associations varying from kinship relations and communities to trade union and economic pressure groups.[32]

Sen argues that individuals are as often motivated by group interests as they are by self-interest. A striking worker may sacrifice his or her personal well-being for that of the union. In ancient Athens, an individual was first a member of a household, and then the household was part of a village. The individual was also a member of a tribe. Other associations also existed. With all this, Sen elaborates Aristotle's theorem that man is a political animal.[33] That is, the human is political not just in so far as as an individual he participates in the assembly or in juries or serves in a chorus. Rather, the individual is political in so far as his or her identity and interest is shaped by participation in such associations. The individual acts for the sake of the group, for the sake of his identity as a member of the group. Thus, the individual acts ethically, by acting out of an interest shared with others. The importance of Sen's thought here cannot be exaggerated, for it shows that individual interest is not mere "self-interest" and that individuals act in transactions from a shared social interest as much as from a self-interest. The modern sophism that an individual will never act contrary to what the economists conceive as his or her self-interest denies that humans act from shared social interests as well. The point here is *not* that people act altruistically, which, even if they do, is not relevant. The point is that people act from group-interests, often over and above any presumed self-interest. Thus, the ethics-based approach to economics has a foundation in human nature, while the self-interest view seems to conflict with human nature. Recall the passage above, where Smith himself says that "the principles of common prudence . . . always influence the majority of every class or order," that is members of classes or orders act from their group's interests. This means, says Sen, that they act ethically. In contrast, says Sen, "The self-interest view of rationality involves inter alia a firm rejection of the 'ethics-related' view of motivation."[34]

How people differ from each other

Sen formulated the capabilities approach out of his extensive study and criticism of utilitarianism, welfarism and Rawls' theory of primary goods. (A footnote briefly describes these theories for interested readers.[35]) Sen emphasized that those approaches to social welfare could be valid only if people were the same as each other. But, in fact, Sen argues, people differ in many respects; so, we must recognize "the fundamental diversity of human beings."[36] While arguing that Rawls ignores "the diversity of human beings,"[37] Sen discusses how people differ with respect to their needs:

> [I]n fact, people seem to have very different needs varying with health, longevity, climatic conditions, location, work conditions, temperament, and even body size (affecting food and clothing requirements). So what is involved is not merely ignoring a few hard cases [as Rawls does, claims Sen], but overlooking very widespread and real differences.[38]

Before we continue on this topic, it is important to note that Sen's interest in how people differ is very different from Aristotle's. Aristotle says that people "differ in kind" and he is concerned with functional differences, such as differences between a doctor and shoemaker or house builder.[39] He argues that such difference is essential to the formation and stability of a community or state.[40] Sen, on the other hand, says nothing about functional differences, but focuses rather on living conditions and environment. Such issues generally are of little interest to Aristotle. One place in which Aristotle's and Sen's interests in difference overlap, however, is in how people differ in their needs. For Aristotle, functional differences between persons imply differences in need: If I am particularly skilled in farming, I am in need of the skills of others in medicine, shoemaking and house building. Sen also is interested in differences that people have in respect of need, but the needs that he speaks of pertain to someone's individual situation rather than to their functional relationship to their community.

For its shock value, Sen discusses the example of a "crippled" person, who has greater needs (for mobility) than someone not handicapped, though meeting those needs is either ruled out or deemed unnecessary by conventional approaches to social welfare. In his 1979 lecture "Equality of What?" Sen argues:

> If it is argued that resources should be devoted to remove or substantially reduce the handicap of the cripple despite there being no marginal utility argument (because it is expensive), despite there being no total utility argument (because he is so contented), and despite there being no primary goods deprivation (because he has the goods that others have), the case must rest on something else. I believe what is at issue is the interpretation of needs in the form of basic capabilities.[41]

Sen focuses on the case of "the cripple" in order to develop the capability of moving about.[42] His interest here is to expose theoreticians who ignore the condition of those disabled with respect to self-movement. He argues that because reducing the handicap of the "cripple" will be very costly, the change in utility from doing so would be small relative to the cost, so that the marginal utility in doing it would be too small to be worthwhile according to utilitarianism. Because the "cripple" is otherwise "contented" there would be no increase in his total utility or well-being, so that welfarism would rule out reducing his handicap. Finally, because he already has the goods that others have, there is no deprivation in "primary goods," so Rawls' theory of justice as fairness would rule out reducing his handicap. This example and these arguments of Sen are the result of his investigating the limitations and shortcomings of utilitarianism, welfarism and the primary goods approach to social welfare. Sen found that they fail exactly in so far as they assume that people are all the same, for those contemporary approaches to social welfare cannot capture differences among human beings. Since utilitarianism evaluates all actions and transactions by their utility, it ignores difference among persons; because welfarism knows only total utility and ignores non-utility information that distinguishes people (such as immobility, in this case), welfarism treats "cripple" and non-"cripple" as though they were the same; likewise, Rawls' approach evaluates the well-being of all from the same standpoint of primary goods possessed, and so regards all persons as the same. In fact, Rawls deliberately sets aside the case of extremely disabled persons.[43] Sen elaborates:

> The primary goods approach seems to take little note of the diversity of human beings . . . utilitarianism could be rendered vastly more attractive if people really were similar. A corresponding remark can be made about the Rawlsian Difference Principle. If people were basically very similar, then an index of primary goods might be a good way of judging advantage. But in fact people seem to have very different needs . . .[44]

In so far as utilitarianism measures the value of any transaction by the same metric, its utility, utilitarianism assumes that people involved in such transactions are all the same, for example, in their needs. Hence, Sen's ironic comment that "if people really were similar," then "utilitarianism could be rendered vastly more attractive."

While Sen criticizes Rawls for neglecting social differences among people, Rawls is closer to Aristotle in recognizing the functional importance of difference in "natural talents" and "natural assets" (cf. Chapter 3). Subsequently, however, in formulating a basis of interpersonal comparison, Rawls puts aside natural assets, and, finally, drops discussion of them altogether.[45] This is the way that Rawls neglects difference. Sen, for his owns reasons, neglects natural differences among persons entirely, perhaps because of his liberalism, or perhaps because he was primarily thinking of India and the deep social incapacitations that the caste system and other primarily social factors create. But with his arguments that utilitarianism, welfarism and the primary goods approach all require that people be similar, Sen provides support for Aristotle's critique of political economy, especially his view that it is essential for a *polis* to be composed of people who differ in kind. Though Sen does not study functional difference, as does Aristotle, his critiques of utilitarianism, welfarism and the primary goods approach move us to consider more closely Aristotle's argument that people differ in kind.

Capabilities as a "set of vectors of functionings"

Sen proposes capabilities as a solution to the conceptual difficulty that he identifies in utilitarianism, welfarism and the primary goods approach insofar as they ignore difference. Sen models difference among people by representing differences in their capabilities (rather than their utility or their primary goods), and so invents an approach to social welfare more powerful than those approaches. In *Inequality Reexamined*, Sen attempts to represent difference among persons by advancing a geometric representation of inequality based on inequality of capabilities. That is, Sen decomposes inequality between persons into sets of inequalities in the functionings of those persons. Overall capability is a set of "vectors of functionings." "The relevant functionings can vary from such elementary things as being adequately nourished, being in good health, avoiding escapable morbidity and premature mortality, etc., to more complex achievements such as being happy, having self-respect, taking part in the life of the community, and so on."[46]

> Capability is, thus, a set of vectors of functionings, reflecting the person's freedom to lead one type of life or another. Just as the so-called "budget set" in the commodity space represents a person's freedom to buy commodity bundles, the "capability set" in the functioning space reflects the person's freedom to choose from possible livings.

> It is easy to see that the well-being of a person must be thoroughly dependent on the nature of his or her being, i.e. on the functionings achieved. Whether a person is well-nourished, in good health, etc., must be intrinsically important for the wellness of that person's being."[47]

Sen represents relative capability in his Fig. 3.1 in *Inequality Reexamined*.[48] The points in the figure represent human individuals, "the axes represent 'value-objects' (e.g. relevant functionings)." "[A]greement (viz. on the identification of value-objects) already precipitates a dominance ranking, e.g. *a* is superior to *b*."[49] Thus Sen models the relative social status of members of a community, as does Aristotle.

The differences that Sen represents are social rather than "natural," since he represents difference in a "person's freedom to live one type of life or another," rather than natural assets or talents. When Sen says that "Living may be seen as consisting of a set of interrelated 'functionings' consisting of beings and doings,"[50] he is not speaking about any metaphysical or ontological distinctions, but rather of states of which someone may be *predicated*, that is "being in good health" or "being happy" are examples of "beings"; "taking part in the life of the community" is an example of a "doing." Therefore, although Sen does emphasize that people differ, he does not seem to argue – unlike Plato, Aristotle and Rawls – that they differ in nature or kind or natural assets. Consequently, his theory of human difference represents largely socially determined distinctions among persons. When Sen speaks about "that person's being" (cf. above) he means it not in a metaphysical or ontological sense, but in a mere predicative sense, that is "that person is being educated". Sen's capability as a set of vectors of functionings represents a person's social status, not his or her being. Aristotle by contrast was interested in both differences in social status and differences in being qua being, and in his ethics and *Politics*, someone's function (*ergon*) in their community is determined by the difference of their individual kind (*eîdos*) from those of others, and therefore from his or her "being."

Sen's theory of goods

Sen's capability approach requires a shift in how we value goods: from valuing them in themselves as commodities with a price, to valuing goods for what they do for us. In his 1979 Tanner Lecture, "Equality of What?" Sen calls for "shifting attention from goods to what goods do to human beings."[51] He criticizes Rawls' "primary goods" approach:

> [T]here is in fact an element of "fetishism" in the Rawlsian framework. Rawls takes primary goods as the embodiment of advantage, rather than taking advantage to be a relationship between persons and goods.[52]

In other words, Rawls evaluates social advantage for a person by the amount and type of goods that the person possesses. His approach fetishizes goods, Sen claims. Sen explains: "Primary goods . . . is concerned with good things rather than with what these good things do to human beings." Sen argues that advantage is in the relationship between persons and goods, that is what these goods make me capable of being or doing. Thus, he shifts attention from goods in themselves to how goods support capabilities. In his 1985 Tanner Lecture "The Standard of Living," Sen argues that the usual measure of the standard of living as the income necessary to purchase a basket of goods, must be changed to necessary functionings and capabilities.[53] He explains:

> The standard of living . . . must be directly a matter of the life one leads rather than of the resources and means one has to lead life . . . the concern is not so much with food as such but with the type of life one succeeds in

living with the help of food and other commodities . . . The same applies to other types of commodities and other functionings or living conditions . . . Ultimately, the focus has to be on what life we lead and what we can or cannot do, can or cannot be . . . The main point here is that the standard of living is really a matter of functionings and capabilities, and not a matter directly of opulence, commodities, or utilities.[54]

Sen concludes that "The value of the living standard lies in the living and not in the possessing of commodities."[55] Sen's call for "shifting attention from goods to what goods do to human beings,"[56] and his claim that "advantage" is "a relationship between persons and goods,"[57] recall Aristotle's theory of living well, which we discussed in Chapter 2. For Aristotle, the aim of life activity is not the accumulation of wealth, but rather living well (*eû zên*). Goods are useful insofar as they support our capacity to live well. They have no value in themselves. Moreover, Sen's theory of goods recalls Aristotle's theory of value, in which the value of a good is proportional to the function it performs for the user. We will discuss Aristotle's theory of value in Part II.

Conclusion

We have seen that Sen applies Aristotle's philosophy to develop his capabilities approach. His theory of political economy is clearly influenced by Aristotle's, which again supports the argument that Aristotle himself articulated a theory of political economy. Following Aristotle, Sen argues that economics has an origin in ethics. He says that economics is concerned with the broadly ethical question "How should one live." Second, contrary to modern economic theory, he shows that people often act out of the interest of a group of which they are a member; they do not always act out of "self-interest," that is, as Aristotle says, "man is a political animal." Third, he formulates his capabilities approach in order to represent and respond to "the fundamental diversity of human beings," especially with respect to their needs (a concern of Aristotle's), which he shows is neglected by utilitarianism, welfarism and the primary goods approach. He develops a geometrical model of how people differ from each other in regards to capability, which he represents with "a set of vectors of functionings." Finally, he argues for a theory of value in which goods are valued for their function, as Sen says, for what they do for us. In the next chapter on the work of Martha Nussbaum, we discuss Sen and Nussbaum's claim that Aristotle's human function argument in *Nicomachean Ethics*, Book i, Chapter 7, supports and accords with Sen's theory of functionings,[58] for it is Nussbaum who defends that position.

Notes

1 Cf. Sen (1980).
2 Sen (1986), 38–39.
3 Sen (1986), 23.
4 Cf. Sen (1987), 22–28.

5 Cf. Sen (1973), Chap. 4; compare *EN v.5*.
6 Cf. Sen (1979), 202, 215, 219; compare *Pol*. ii.2; cf. also Sen (1992), 19–21, 85.
7 Cf. Sen (1979), 218–219.
8 Cf. Sen (1987), 2–10.
9 Cf. Sen (1987), 19–20.
10 Cf. *Pol*. i.2.1253a2–3.
11 Sen (1987), 3.
12 Sen (1987), 3.
13 Cf. Sen (1987), 2.
14 Cf. Sen (1987), 2.
15 Sen (1987), 3–4.
16 Sen (1987), 3–4; Aristotle (1908b), Book I, Chapter 1.
17 Sen (1987), 7.
18 Sen (1987), 7.
19 Sen (1987), 4.
20 Sen (1987), 4.
21 Sen (1987), 6.
22 Sen (1987), 6.
23 Sen (1987), 8. Emphasis in original.
24 Sen (1987), 7.
25 Sen (1987), 6.
26 Cf. *Pol*. i.9.1257b14–19.
27 Stigler (1975), 237, cited by Sen (1987), 22.
28 Quoted by Stigler (1975), 237, and cited by Sen (1987), 22.
29 Stigler (1975), 237, cited by Sen (1987), 22.
30 Smith (1790), 189, cited by Sen (1987), 22.
31 Sen (1987), 19.
32 Sen (1987), 19–20.
33 *Pol*. i.2.1253a2–3.
34 Sen (1987), 20.
35 Regarding *utilitarianism*, the *Stanford Encyclopedia of Philosophy* says: its "core insight . . . is that morally appropriate behaviour will not harm others, but instead increase happiness or 'utility'" (Driver, 2014). "*Welfarism*: The judgement of the relative goodness of alternative states of affairs must be based exclusively on, and taken as an increasing function of, the respective collections of individual utilities in these states" (Sen, 1979, 468). Regarding Rawls' theory of *primary goods*, the *Stanford Encyclopedia of Philosophy* says: "Like every theory of justice (for example those of Locke, Rousseau and Mill), justice as fairness requires an account of citizens' fundamental interests: what citizens need qua citizens. Rawls derives his account of *primary goods* from the conception of the citizen as free and equal, reasonable and rational. Primary goods are essential for developing and exercising the two moral powers, and useful for pursuing a wide range of specific conceptions of the good life. Primary goods are: 1) The basic rights and liberties; 2) Freedom of movement, and free choice among a wide range of occupations; 3) The powers of offices and positions of responsibility; 4) Income and wealth; 5) The social bases of self-respect: the recognition by social institutions that gives citizens a sense of self-worth and the confidence to carry out their plans (cf. Rawls, 2001, 58–59). All citizens are assumed to have fundamental interests in getting more of these primary goods, and political institutions are to evaluate how well citizens are doing according to what primary goods they have. It is equality and inequality of primary goods that, Rawls claims, are of the greatest political importance" (Wenar, 2012).

36 Sen (1980), 202.
37 Sen (1980), 215.
38 Sen (1980), 215–216.
39 Cf. *Pol.* ii.2; *EN* v.5.
40 Cf. Chap. 6.
41 Sen (1980), 218. Sen first discussed this case in Sen (1973).
42 Sen (1980), 218.
43 Cf. Sen (1980), 215: "Rawls justifies this [i.e., ignoring the plight of the "cripple"] by pointing out that 'hard cases' can 'distract our moral perception by leading us to think of people distant from us whose fate arouses pity and anxiety'." Cf. Rawls (1975), p. 96, cited by Sen.
44 Sen (1980), 215.
45 Cf. Rawls (2001), 58–59.
46 Sen (1992), 39.
47 Sen (1992), 40.
48 Fig. 3.1 from Sen (1992), 47.
49 Sen (1992), 48.
50 Sen (1992), 39.
51 Sen (1980), 218.
52 Sen (1980), 216. Cf. Marx (1962), 85–98 (section 4 of Chapter 1) on the fetishism of goods for the original treatment of this topic.
53 Cf. Sen (1986).
54 Sen (1986), 22–23.
55 Sen (1986), 34.
56 Sen (1980), 218.
57 Sen (1980), 216.
58 Cf. Sen (1993), Sect. 10.

5 Martha Nussbaum

Martha Nussbaum's version of the capabilities approach is a theory of social welfare that she developed out of Aristotle's theory of living "the good life" (*agathē zōē*), out of Aristotle's advocacy for redistribution, and out of Sen's capability approach. Here I discuss four papers she wrote that lay the foundation for her capabilities approach and her argument that it is Aristotelian (Nussbaum, 1987/1993, 1988, 1990a, 1990b).[1] In Part III, in motivating an Aristotelian Social Welfare Function, I will discuss the capabilities approach as a theory of social welfare.

In "Nature, function, and capability: Aristotle on political distribution," Nussbaum says that

(1) the Aristotelian lawgiver aims at enabling people to live well and do well [*to eû zên kai to eû prattein* – RG] . . . The aim of political planning is the distribution to the city's individual people of the conditions in which a good human life can be chosen and lived. This distributive task aims at producing capabilities.[2]

Nussbaum cites texts from Aristotle's *Politics* and *Nicomachean Ethics* which, she argues, support her claim that Aristotle advocates redistribution. For example, she cites and translates Aristotle at *Politics* vii.2:

(2) It is evident that the best *politeia* is that arrangement according to which anyone whatsoever (*hostisoûn*) might do best (*arista prattoi*) and live a flourishing life (*zōiē makariōs*).[3]

Nussbaum calls that passage "the Distributive Conception" (DC). Nussbaum's reasoning seems to be that if a constitution is best, the state orders affairs so that anyone "might do best and live a flourishing life," and as part of that arrangement, that state distributes to its citizens goods they need to accomplish that. Those goods may range from security, a good usually provided by governments, to a homestead or even food, as we will see below. I call attention to Nussbaum's translation of *zoiē makariōs* as "live a flourishing life," while the Greek would seem to read simply "live happily." As any reader of *Nicomachean Ethics* I.7–10 knows, Aristotle has a quite different concept of happiness than people do today. It is inappropriate to translate *makariōs* into twenty-first-century English as "happily." Reeve tries to make up for that with hyperbole; he renders: "live a blessedly happy life." All in all, Nussbaum's translation is a reasonable rendering of Aristotle's Greek.

Nussbaum also finds DC in the following passage, which she translates as:

(3) It is the job of the excellent lawgiver to consider (*theasasthai*), concerning a city and a class of human beings (*genos anthrōpōn*) and every other association, how they will partake in the flourishing living (*eudaimonia*) that is possible for them.[4]

Again, it is the job of the legislator to frame the laws of the land so that people will be able to live the good life. I point out that the Greek includes the phrase "the good life" (*zōēs agathēs*), which Nussbaum seems to include in her rendering "the flourishing living (*eudaimonia*)."[5] For Aristotle, the job of the lawgiver is to visualize (*theasasthai*) how those in his care will share in the good life and well-being. In light of her remarks in passage (1), it is strange that Nussbaum omits translating *zōēs agathēs* in this passage. Finally, Nussbaum produces a third passage which she argues is stating the Distributive Conception:

(4) For it is appropriate, if people are governed best (*arista politeuomenous*) that they should do best (*arista prattein*), in so far as their circumstances admit – unless something catastrophic (*paralogon*) happens.[6]

Again, if government does a good job, its people should live well.[7] Under passage (4), government is responsible for the conditions of life of the people it governs. This sounds rather like Franklin Delano Roosevelt. Note that "contrary to plan" or "unexpected" would be better renderings of *paralogon*, the point of which is that Aristotle concedes that it is not always possible to provide people with the circumstances with which one would like to provide them so that they can "do best." This statement of the Distributive Conception absolves the lawgiver from shortcomings in the programme.

From the starting-point of the Distributive Conception, Nussbaum constructs her capabilities approach by determining, in her view, just what capabilities individuals require, so that they "might do best and live a flourishing life." Those capabilities, she argues, are derivable from Aristotle's ethical and political writings.[8] Whether one has those capabilities, at least potentially, determines one's political status, for, Nussbaum argues,

(5) Citizenship is defined in terms of capability: it is "the authorization (*exousia*) to share in judicial and deliberative functioning" (1275b18–20).[9]

That immediately raises the question of whether farmers or labourers would have or ought to have those capabilities, whether they are to be so authorized "to share in judicial and deliberative functioning" and be included as citizens. Nussbaum acknowledges that in some texts in *Politics* vii Aristotle calls for excluding farmers or labourers from citizenship, but she argues that those texts express Platonic influence. Some scholars have identified this as a weak point in Nussbaum's argument that the capabilities approach is Aristotelian, for they see no way to combine Aristotle's texts disparaging the capability of workers to be citizens with Nussbaum's "Aristotelian Social Democracy."[10] They agree that there is a Distributive Conception in Aristotle's *Politics*, as Nussbaum claims, but that, despite Aristotle's inclusion of "anyone whatsoever (*hostisoûn*)" in its statement in passage (2), the Distributive Conception applies only to citizens, from the lists of which Aristotle would exclude those working the land, labourers and craftsmen.[11] Aristotle is said not to care whether working people "make it over the threshold" into "a flourishing life."[12] So, Mulgan says that "we should see [Aristotle] as someone who accepts with equanimity the unequal and accidental distribution of life chances," and so characterizes Aristotle as less compassionate than Rawls.[13] Mulgan argues that Aristotle is not concerned to extend full rights of citizenship and the good life to all men who are naturally capable of them, and that his principle of distributive justice does not extend as far as rectifying social disadvantage.[14] Furthermore, Wallach attacks the whole idea of turning to Aristotle for help in solving contemporary problems (as is attempted in this book).[15] He says that "the Aristotelian turn" in contemporary political philosophy "devalues the possibilities offered by contemporary politics and our fellow citizens in contributing to the understanding and realization of justice."[16] Wallach claims that "Aristotle's disagreeable, naturalistic prejudices," for example that slavery is "natural," are not "contingent features of his theoretical system" – they cannot be shorn from that system, as Wallach claims Nussbaum tries, "without eliminating its coherence or emptying its substance."[17] If I might translate Wallach, I believe what he means that if Aristotle truly believes that mass slavery is natural, that must somehow be part of the metaphysics that underlies his politics, so that if it is "shorn" from his system, his system becomes incoherent. That is an interesting argument.

But, first of all, Aristotle's description of the "natural slave" as those who lack the capacity to deliberate over their own lives, would pick out at most only a tiny minority from any population. Considering Aristotle's account, W. Fortenbaugh concluded that "there are no natural slaves in the world, so the view remains theoretical."[18] M. Schofield proposes, however, that privation of a deliberative faculty singles out "the feeble-minded," [19] that is those among us who lack ordinary cognitive capacities or suffer from serious neurological impairment, as in Down's syndrome. So Wallach errs. Aristotle does not argue that masses of humans are slaves by nature, and therefore natural slavery can be shorn from Aristotle's political thought without making it incoherent.[20]

Wallach may have committed this blunder because from the sixteenth century on, American classical studies bears a heritage of misinterpreting Aristotle in order to *justify* slavery. Based on that unfortunate tradition,

Wallach assumes the worst about Aristotle. Early in the sixteenth century Fernández de Oviedo, adventurer, New World settler and slaveholder argued in *Historia general y natural de las Indias* that American natives were slaves by nature and that it was therefore just to enslave them.[21] Charges brought against Oviedo led to an investigation. Although the Dominican Bartolomé de las Casas and his associates showed that Aristotle did not support natural slavery *en masse*,[22] and won the academic debate in Spain, Oviedo won the battle on the ground, in the New World, and in the American South.[23] When President Dew of William and Mary College (Virginia) declared that "it is the order of nature that the beings of superior faculties and knowledge, and therefore of superior power, should dispose of those who are inferior,"[24] he was reiterating the claim of Oviedo and the conquistadores that American Indians and Africans are "natural slaves." Wallach is simply repeating the distortion of Aristotle that was passed down to him from Oviedo, Dew and southern slaveholders. The terrible responsibility for the claim that Africans are slaves by nature lies with pro-slavery Spaniards and antebellum Americans, not Aristotle.

Moreover, the charge of Mulgan, Wallach and Charles and others is that Nussbaum's capabilities approach, her "Aristotelian Social Democracy," is not truly Aristotelian, that it differs from Aristotle's political thought in important ways, and that therefore her claim that her theory of social welfare is Aristotelian is unfounded. No one denies, however, that Nussbaum appropriately makes use of much of Aristotle's thought in constructing and defending her capabilities approach, much as Avicenna did in developing his metaphysics, and Averroes in articulating his psychology. Both Avicenna and Averroes departed from Aristotle in important ways, yet each is nonetheless called "Aristotelian." So even if Mulgan et al. are correct in saying that Nussbaum's theory differs from Aristotle's thought in important ways, Nussbaum's theory would remain nonetheless "Aristotelian."

Furthermore, Mulgan charges that Aristotle "accepts with equanimity the unequal and accidental distribution of life chances," a serious charge. I wonder how carefully Mulgan has read the *Politics*, for in the *Politics* and the ethical writings, there are grounds for holding that Aristotle supports including the working population in living the good life and in political participation as citizens. Moreover, he also recommended freeing slaves after so many years of service, and there is historical precedent that freedmen could then become citizens. Aristotle argues at length that "the multitude rather than the few best people should be in authority."[25] He argues that "A state in which a large number of people are excluded from office and are poor must of necessity be full of enemies."[26] Furthermore, Aristotle makes a variety of concrete proposals for correcting "the unequal and accidental distribution of life chances." Nussbaum – whom Mulgan is criticizing in making his remarks – describes at length Aristotle's plan for providing for the common meals out of the harvest of public lands so that required contributions by families are eliminated, thus enabling the poor to participate.[27] In addition, Aristotle urges

1) That the state provide block grants to the poor for the establishment of homesteads or for starting a trade or farming (1320a35–b2, 7–9); and
2) That the wealthy pay for the attendance of the poor at obligatory meetings of the assembly (1320b2–4).

Perhaps Aristotle's most radical proposal, however, is

3) That the well-off assist the needy by accepting terms of exchange through which they lose wealth (cf. *EE* 1242b15–21, Chapter 9).

Furthermore, Aristotle offers a path to citizenship for "all slaves." He says "it is better to hold out freedom as a reward to all slaves" for so many years of service,[28] and Charles adds that Aristotle "hence accepts that they are capable of being *free citizens*."[29] We will discuss proposal (3) further in Chapter 9.

Capabilities and Aristotle's human function argument

Finally, Nussbaum claims that Aristotle's human function argument in the *Nicomachean Ethics* and Aristotle's theory of functions in the *Politics* is the philosophical basis of "functionings" in the capabilities approaches. Before we discuss Nussbaum's claim, let us first review the conclusion of the human function argument. Aristotle says:

> We take the human function (*ergon*) to be a certain kind of life, and take that life to be activity and actions of a soul by means of reason (*meta logou*); and the good human does that well and finely. Now each <function> is fulfilled well in accordance with its proper virtue. And so the human good comes to be an activity of soul in accord with virtue, and indeed, if there are more virtues than one, with the best and most complete <virtue>.[30]

In her discussion of the human function argument, Nussbaum focuses on the first sentence of this conclusion, the statement that the human function is a certain kind of life, that is activity and actions of a soul by means of reason. For Nussbaum emphasizes correctly that "a life for a human being must be a life organized, in some fashion, by practical reason, in which all functionings are informed and infused by reason's organizing activity."[31] And in relating this to her list of "Basic Human Functional Capabilities,"[32] she says "there is a common notion at the core of all the functions we come up with. Reason is what all the functionings have in common; and this is, as well, the architectonic function that holds them all together."[33] But Nussbaum neglects the second half of the conclusion, where Aristotle says "the human good comes to be an activity of soul in accord with virtue, and indeed, if there are more virtues than one, with the best and most complete virtue." With his use of the phrase "comes to be" (*ginetai*) Aristotle indicates that he is about to state a more developed conclusion, for he has just added to his discussion the idea that any function is fulfilled well in accordance with its proper virtue. Nussbaum neglects this more refined conclusion. Moreover, Aristotle adds that the human good is activity of soul in accord with "the best and most complete virtue." At no time, does Nussbaum explore this second, more refined conclusion of the human function, or what this best and most complete virtue may be. Aristotle says that "the best and most complete virtue" is justice (cf. Chapter 7), and in his account of why justice is complete Aristotle defines justice as the only virtue that "seems to be another person's good, because it is in relation to another, for it does what benefits another."[34] If we add that to the conclusion of Aristotle's human function argument, we come up with something like:

> *The human good comes to be actions and activity of soul by means of reason and in accordance with justice as the virtue which "does what benefits another."*

Nussbaum does not discuss how justice, that is benefiting others, is an important part of the human function. Instead, human functioning for Nussbaum is concerned with such states as: "Being able to have good health," "having opportunities for sexual satisfaction," or "Being able to laugh, to play, to enjoy recreational activities."[35] Such "functionings" seem to have nothing to do with "activity of the soul in accord with virtue," in particular, in accord with justice. I propose that the reason for this is that the capabilities approach is only concerned with the well-being of the life of the individual, but justice for Aristotle is not concerned with the well-being of the individual who acts justly, but with whether that individual "does what benefits another."[36] If we have here provided a fair, if brief, account of Aristotle's conception of the human good, and if Aristotle does adhere to a distributive conception as Nussbaum claims, then that "distributive task" aims at providing citizens with the support that enables them to perform just acts that benefit their fellow citizens, *not* at producing Nussbaum's capabilities.[37] It would seem that the notion of "functionings" in the capabilities approaches does not pertain to Aristotle's human function argument. Nonetheless, this chapter has shown that Martha Nussbaum's capabilities approach is, in other respects, Aristotelian, as she claims. Moreover, since the capabilities approaches of Nussbaum and Sen has inspired the creation of the United Nations Development Programme's Human Development Index,[38] which has become a tool of contemporary political economy, it is clear that Nussbaum and Sen's theories are theories of political economy. That further supports my argument that Aristotle articulated a theory of political economy, since he influenced both Nussbaum and Sen in developing their own theories of political economy.

Notes

1 In Nussbaum (1990a) she lists these four papers as the ones articulating the basis of her theory and the Aristotelian foundation that she claims for it.
2 Nussbaum (1988), 160, 145.
3 *Pol.* 1324a23–25; Nussbaum (1988), 146; Nussbaum's translation. Compare Reeve in Aristotle (1998): "It is evident that the best constitution must be that organization in which anyone might be best and live a blessedly happy life."
4 *Pol.* 1325a7–10; Nussbaum (1988), 147; Nussbaum's translation.
5 The Greek for the indirect question reads ζωῆς ἀγαθῆς πῶς μεθέξουσι καὶ τῆς ἐνδεχομένης αὐτοῖς εὐδαιμονίας. Nussbaum's "the flourishing living that is possible for them" would be a fair translation of only τῆς ἐνδεχομένης αὐτοῖς εὐδαιμονίας. Reeve translates (cf. Aristotle, 1998): "The task of an excellent legislator, then, is to study how a city-state, a race of men, or any other community can come to have a share in a good life and in the happiness that is possible for them."
6 *Pol.* vii.1.1323a17–19; Nussbaum (1988), 147; Nussbaum's translation. In her paper, Nussbaum presents the Greek as if the text read πολιτευομένοις rather than πολιτευομένους.
7 This argument would perhaps run counter to contemporary neo-liberalism. Neo-liberalism would say: If people are governed the least, then they do best.
8 Cf. Nussbaum (1990a), 328–342. It is not relevant to our argument that we review those capabilities here.
9 Nussbaum (1988), 163; Nussbaum's translation. It seems that were this standard applied today in Western democracies, many people might fail to qualify, for, in the USA, for instance, citizens do not directly participate in legislative deliberation.
10 Cf. Charles (1988), Mulgan (2000), Wallach (1992), Knoll (2015).
11 Cf. Charles (1988), 190, 191. Charles' argument is philological, rather than philosophical. From select texts he constructs a narrow definition of *politeia* as an arrangement of offices (cf. Charles, 1988, 191). With such a philological exegesis, he misinterprets passage (2) as applying, not to citizens of the city, but to neighbours (cf. Charles, 1988, 192). This argument is not only strange, but false, for the reference to neighbours appears in a conditional clause in the text after passage (3) and is not the topic of the passage. (As Reeve translates the passage [*Pol.* vii.2.1325a10–14] in Aristotle, 1998: "There will be differences, of course, in some of the laws that are instituted, and if there are neighboring peoples, it belongs to legislative science to consider what sorts of military training are needed in relation to which sorts of people and which measures are to be used in relation to each.") So, Nussbaum's interpretation of the passage is correct, and Charles' incorrect. Moreover, in his brief discussion of *Pol.* ii.5 in which Aristotle is showing various inconsistences in the argument of *Rep.* v, Charles attempts to extract some Aristotelian doctrine about citizenship from this *peirastic* treatment of the *Republic*, a rather doubtful enterprise on his part. His references are so imprecise that he attributes the views of Plato discussed in *Pol.* ii.5 instead to Hippodamus (cf. Charles, 1988, 194).
12 Quoted phrases from Nussbaum (1990a), 229.
13 Mulgan (2000), 91. Cf. Wallach (1992), 618 on his allegation of "Aristotle's belief in the natural character of human and social inequality."
14 Cf. Mulgan (2000), 86.
15 Cf. Wallach (1992), 630–635.
16 Wallach (1992), 635.
17 Cf. Wallach (1992), 618.
18 Cf. Fortenbaugh (1977), 137.

19 Cf. Schofield (1990), 1–27. Schofield's interesting article strips Aristotle's account of slavery of much of its perceived offensiveness. Cf. also Gallagher (2011a), 382–384.

20 Thus Wallach's argument is refuted. But I conceive of a more powerful argument disputing Aristotle that Wallach failed to advance: If a "good life" for citizens relies for its support and sustenance upon the labour of slaves, it cannot be just in any real sense. How then do we judge Aristotle's remark in the *Politics* where he says that in the best state "the ones working the land should, if we can choose at will, be slaves that are neither drawn from the same race, nor spirited" (*Pol.* vii.10.1330a25–28, Reeve's translation in Aristotle, 1998). Aristotle faces a difficulty here: If the farmers are citizens, will they have sufficient leisure or education to view politics dispassionately and live the good life of citizens actively participant in their polis? This was a concern for Aristotle in his reflections on the disaster of the Peloponnesian Wars: A people's democracy triumphant over Persia adopted imperial ambitions, and, led by populist demagogues, imposed its dominion over small states, with the result that the smaller states took refuge in Sparta and brought the democracy down. By giving the franchise only to those with the education and leisure to view such matters dispassionately, perhaps Aristotle sought to save his best state from such a Peloponnesian disaster. But that problem is more complicated, for under Aristides' policies the Athenian citizens were relieved of the need to work the land, as they were provided with sustenance and government employment and therefore a certain degree of leisure (cf. *Ath. Res.* 24–25). Even with leisure Athenian citizens therefore failed to govern virtuously. But if to solve that issue, the farmers are excluded from citizenship and made slaves, what's the justice in that? The problem is this: Without a docile work force, the proposal of a leisurely body of citizens sharing in tragic festivals, philosophic dialogue and political activity would seem only a pipedream, for were they to support themselves, they would lack the leisure necessary for such *eû zên*. That is a difficult argument, for a cultured polity is hard to achieve as any glance at contemporary Western democracies shows.

21 Brading (1991), 40.

22 Las Casas argued that the Indians compared very favourably with the peoples of ancient times, were eminently rational beings, and in fact fulfilled every one of Aristotle's requisites for the good life. Anticipating the judgment of twentieth-century archaeologists, he compared the temples of Yucatan to the pyramids. Las Casas declared that Sepúlveda did not understand Aristotle and had absolutely failed to grasp Aristotle's theory of slavery. Like Schofield, Las Casas explained that Aristotelian slaves "by nature" are few in number and must be considered mistakes of nature (cf. Hanke 1949, 123–125). Separately, Las Casas declared that "it is as unjust to enslave Negroes as it is to enslave Indians, and for the same reasons" (cf. Hanke 1949, 125).

23 Cf. Brading (1991), 80–86, Hanke (1949), 28, 122–129.

24 Cf. Hanke (1935), 8–9.

25 Cf. *Pol.* iii.11.1281a39–40. Reeve's translation in Aristotle (1998).

26 Cf. *Pol.* iii.11.1281b28–29. Reeve's translation in Aristotle (1998).

27 Cf. *Pol.* 1330a; Nussbaum (1988a), (1990a).

28 Cf. *Pol.* vii.10.1330a32–3, *Oec.* 1344b15–17.

29 Charles (1988), 191.

30 *EN* i.7.1098a12–16.

31 Nussbaum (1988a), 182.

32 Cf. Nussbaum (1990a), 225.

33 Nussbaum (1988a), 182.

34 *EN* 1129b31–30a1, 3–5.

35 From Nussbaum (1990a), 225; cf. Sen's functionings such as "being adequately nourished, being in good health, avoiding escapable morbidity and premature mortality, . . . being happy, having self-respect," in Sen (1992), 39.
36 Only Nussbaum's basic human functional capability (7) pertains to others, but not even that communicates a clear idea of benefiting others. It reads: "Being able to live for and to others, to recognize and show concern for other human beings" (Nussbaum 1990a, 225).
37 Cf. Nussbaum (1988), 160, 145.
38 Cf. Anand et al. (2009); Dowding et al. (2009).

Part II

Aristotle's critique of political economy

Introductory note

Part II of *Aristotle's Critique of Political Economy* undertakes a systematic presentation of Aristotle's theory of political economy. In Chapter 6 we discuss the metaphysics of human nature that underlies his theory. Chapter 7 presents Aristotle's theory of "living well" (*eû zên*). The chapter discusses how the function of *oikonomia* is to sustain living well for the household and the *polis*. Some, however, out of anxiety, turn away from living well and towards unconstrained wealth acquisition, which divides the community. Chapter 8 presents Aristotle's theory of value, and refutes Marx's criticisms of it. The chapter presents the fundamental concept of Aristotle's theory of value: That the value of any product is proportional to the function of its producer in the community of the *polis*. Chapter 9 presents Aristotle's theories of reciprocity and of reciprocal justice. Reciprocity is a dialectic of producing in turn and being affected in turn in which sharers in a community participate. Reciprocal justice attempts to restore reciprocity that has been disrupted by injustice. Chapter 10 rounds out our discussion of Aristotle's critique of political economy with a presentation of the role to which he assigns *charis* (grace, kindness) in his theory of exchange.

6 The metaphysical foundations of Aristotle's critique of political economy

Aristotle's critique of political economy is founded on and develops out of his theory of community (*koinonia*), and that theory is based in turn on his metaphysics of human nature. Those who have failed to grasp the metaphysics behind Aristotle's theory of community, fail to comprehend that theory and his political economy.[1] But Aristotle's theory of community does not originate with Aristotle. Rather, he develops and elaborates the theory of community presented by Plato's Socrates in his discussion of the first city-state in the *Republic*, the one that Glaucon calls "a city-state of pigs."[2] There Socrates advances the view that (i) "each of us is born not quite like another, but differs in nature (*phusis*), one suited to the doing of one task (*ergon*), another to another."[3] In this one remark, Socrates immediately relates difference in the nature of human beings to different work that they perform in community. If differences in nature are metaphysical differences, as Aristotle would claim, then Socrates relates metaphysical differences to differences in the work that we perform, and so directly relates work and its function in the economy of the city-state to metaphysics. Furthermore, because we differ in nature and are not self-sufficient, we must form cities, for (ii) "A city comes to be because none of us is self-sufficient, but we all need many things."[4] (iii) Those different needs "will make the city,"[5] Socrates explains, "because people need many things, and because one person associates with a second because of one need, and with a third because of a different need, many people gather together in a single homeland to live together as sharers (*koinōnoi*) and helpers."[6] According to that passage, a citizen's different needs correspond to the different co-sharers who will fulfill those needs for him, co-sharers who each perform different tasks in the community, tasks suited to the differences in nature that they have from each other. The different members of a community, then, correspond to their manifold differences in nature, and also correspond to the various needs that they each have and have for each other. We can represent the city-state in the realm of metaphysics as a set of human natures, each of which is multiply related to all the other human natures in the set insofar as being different from it, they can provide something to it that it is not suited to provide for itself. That multiply connected set corresponds to a multiply connected set of sharers in the realm of the city/community. (iv) Quite naturally, then, the sharers "give shares (*metadidōmi*) to each other . . . or receive shares (*metalambanō*) from each other, thinking this better for themselves."[7] In other words, each sharer gives a share of his product to other citizens, and receives shares from them in turn. This is *metadosis*, "giving of a share." Later, in order to facilitate sharing of their goods with each other, the sharers establish a currency and a marketplace, and they buy and sell each other's goods.[8] (v) Socrates' interlocutor, Adeimantus, proposes that justice exists in the "need of these people for each other,"[9] that is, in the relation of their difference, for each sharer's individual nature makes him or her lacking in self-sufficiency: each needs what others can provide. Therefore, they all must cooperate in a community in which "each person does one thing in accordance with his nature,"[10] says Socrates.

That summarizes the Socratic conception of community as presented in the *Republic*. Aristotle develops and elaborates that. Following Socrates' first claim (i) that "each of us is born not quite like another, but differs in nature," Aristotle says in the *Politics*,

(1) A city-state (*polis*) is composed of people who differ in *eîdos*, for a city-state does not come to be from people who are similar (*homoioi*).[11]

The passage unambiguously asserts that the people who compose a city-state differ in nature, that is in *eîdos*, in metaphysical form, in "kind."[12] With passage (1), Aristotle advances what he considers a law of politics, that is, that a city-state *has to be* composed of people who differ in *eîdos*, a statement that clearly assumes that there are multiple *eidē* of humans.[13] To support that text, Aristotle advances a more general claim about the nature of unities: he says,

(2) Those things from which a unity (*hen*) ought to arise, differ in *eîdos*.[14]

Here Aristotle does not say that collections of things that differ in *eîdos* are *among* the collections of things from which a unity can arise. Rather, he says that for a unity to be formed, it must, it ought (*dei*) be formed out of things that differ in *eîdos*. In making his argument for passage (1), Aristotle contrasts a city-state with a military alliance. He says that a city-state is not the same as a military alliance because an alliance can be composed of states that are all alike in *eîdos*,[15] for example multiple democracies. Aristotle's point seems to be that a city-state is not an alliance of individual citizens who are the same in *eîdos*.[16] Aristotle means that a community is sustained by the circumstance that citizens who differ in *eîdos* produce essentially different *erga*, needed by their fellow citizens, who produce essentially different other *erga*. In the space of only eight lines of text, Aristotle three times employs the term *eîdos* a) to emphasize that a city-state must be composed of people that "differ in *eîdos*" and b) to distinguish the city-state from an alliance, whose members need not "differ in *eîdos*." For help in understanding what Aristotle means here, I turn to *Metaphysics* Book Z, where Aristotle discusses how a unity differs from a "heap" of identical individuals. In Chapter 17, he argues:

(3) That which is compounded (*suntheton*) out of something, so that the whole is a unity (*hen*), would not be like a heap (*sōros*), but like a syllable, and the syllable is not its elements, and the β and α are not the same as the βα, nor is flesh <the same as> fire and earth, for when these things are decomposed, the compounds no longer exist, for example, flesh and the syllable, but the elements exist, both fire and earth; therefore, the syllable is something, not only the elements, the vowel and consonant, but also something else, and flesh <is something>, not only fire and earth, or warmth and cold, but also something else . . . it would seem that this something, is not also an element, but that it is a cause which makes this thing flesh and that thing a syllable. And similarly in all others cases. And this is the substance of each thing; for this is the primary cause of its being; and since, while some things are not substances, as many as are substances are formed naturally and by nature, their substance would seem to be this nature, which is not an element but a principle.[17]

Here Aristotle makes multiple points: First, a composite unity is not an aggregate, or "heap" of identical individual elements: As in the syllable and flesh, the elements differ in kind from each other. In the syllable, β differs from α; in flesh, "fire" differs from "earth." In contrast, an ingot of gold is not a unity; it is rather a "heap," and an artifact of human technology. Applied to our present discussion, that point implies that a community is not a "heap" of similar (*homoioi*) individuals. Second, Aristotle argues that a composite unity is more than its elements: There is something else that makes up the composite, beyond the elements, that is "the cause" which makes them a unity, "which makes this thing flesh and that thing a syllable." There is something else in the syllable *ba* besides its phonemes *b* and *a*, and there is something else in flesh besides its elements "fire" and "earth," namely, the "substance" of the syllable or of flesh, respectively, "the primary cause of its being." In sum, the passage is telling us that the things which make a unity differ in *eîdos* in two ways: First, the elements differ in *eîdos* from each other. Second, the elements differ in *eîdos* from "the substance" of the composite, that which makes those elements a unity. In the passage, the elements in Aristotle's first example differ in *eîdos* insofar as one is a vowel, the other a consonant; in his second example, one element is earth, the other is fire. In conclusion, there are two significations of the phrase "those things" in the statement of passage (2) regarding "those things from which a unity ought to arise" (*ex hôn de deî hen genesthai*): 1) "those things" signify the elements, which differ in *eîdos*, for example the vowel and the consonant; 2) "those things" signify both the elements and whatever it is that makes those elements a composite, and those two sorts of things differ in *eîdos*, for example elements β or α differ in *eîdos* from the "substance" of the syllable. At least the first signification is invoked in passage (1), for the passage refers to difference in *eîdos* among the people of a city, whom in that text Aristotle seems to regard as "elements" of the city-state.[18] I draw the following conclusion from the foregoing discussion:

I) A city-state is composed of things that differ in kind, because: i) A city-state is a unity. (ii) It is the nature of a unity that it cannot be composed of things that are like one another (such as grains of sand in a heap).

To teach us further what he means by passages (1) and (2), Aristotle explains after passage (2) that the fact that "those things from which a unity ought to arise differ in *eîdos*" is the reason (*dioper*) why the practice of "reciprocal equality" (*to ison to antipeponthos*) among citizens preserves city-states.[19] For an explanation of reciprocal equality, Aristotle refers us to the *Nicomachean Ethics*. In Book v, Chapter 5, in discussing reciprocity (*to antipeponthos*) Aristotle treats a problem whose solution reveals a foundation for passage (1).[20] Aristotle says that reciprocity will exist among the citizens (*estai antipeponthos*) when, in exchanges, the different *erga* of the different citizens are set in fair relation to each other through proportion.[21] Via proportion, Aristotle states, we must relate both the *erga*, γ and δ (*deî oûn taûta isastênaî*[22]) of the persons involved in a transaction, and, surprisingly, the persons themselves, α and β (*toutous deî isastênaî*[23]). Aristotle specifies that the persons themselves appear in the proportions in his account of them (cf. passage (4), below), and in his use of the masculine gender (*toutous*) to refer to the persons, in distinction from the neuter gender (*taûta*) to refer to their *erga*. He represents two equivalent cases of exchange, of which one is the following:

(4) As farmer is to shoemaker, so the *ergon* of the shoemaker is to that of the farmer.[24]

Or, in the algebraic notation that Aristotle employs[25]:

(A) $$\frac{\alpha}{\beta} = \frac{\delta}{\gamma},$$

I am interested in what Aristotle says about the ratio *qualitatively*. Strikingly, in his commentary on passage (4) and proportion (A), Aristotle asserts that both the ratio of the persons and the ratio of the work (*erga*) in formula 1 are *incommensurable*.

(5) In reality, it is impossible for things that differ so much to be commensurable (*summetra*).[26]

That suggests that the persons and the *erga* "differ in *eîdos*," as we argue below. Incommensurability is attributed by Aristotle in passage (5) to the relation of those things to which the terms in Proportion (A) refer. Aristotle spoke of incommensurability often. His repeated example of incommensurability, in the ethical writings and elsewhere, is the ratio of the diagonal of a square to its side, that is $\sqrt{2}$.[27] That ratio cannot be expressed in rational numbers. It is a quantity, but an irrational one, which we approximate by the infinite decimal 1.141421 and so on.[28] Aristotle says that the diagonal and the side "have no common measure" (*asummetroi*).[29] They differ in kind: the diagonal and the side are two different *kinds* of quantities, one is rational, the other irrational. Thus for Aristotle, two entities that are incommensurable have no common measure or factor, and differ in kind. Commenting on passage (5), some writers have tried to remove the sharers from the problem by arguing that Aristotle means that only the *erga* are incommensurable.[30] But incommensurability refers to the *relation* of things – mathematically, to the nature of their ratio: For γ and δ to be incommensurable means that their ratio $\frac{\delta}{\gamma}$ is irrational.[31] If $\frac{\delta}{\gamma}$ is irrational, then so must be whatever Aristotle equates with it, that is, $\frac{\alpha}{\beta}$, the ratio of the sharers. If the ratio of the sharers is irrational, then the sharers must be incommensurable. So, in Aristotle's Proportion (A), if the *erga* are incommensurable, so also are the sharers. That conclusion is inescapable. Aristotle's aim here is not to reduce social relations to mathematical quantities, but to emphasize and highlight qualitative difference where he finds it to exist. He represents that with ratios of terms that he says are incommensurable. In mooting incommensurables to represent relations of human beings and of their *erga*, Aristotle emphasizes that human beings and their activities and products are "in reality" irreducible to scalar, "rational" magnitudes. Now, as we have said, things that are incommensurable have no common factor. They differ in kind. Thus, if the sharers who make up a community are incommensurable with each other, then the people who make up that community differ in kind. Here we have an independent argument for passage (1), on the condition that we accept Aristotle's assertion that different sharers *are* incommensurable with each other. We can solve that condition by referring back to passage (4): We note that *ergon* signifies not only a product or service provided by an artisan but also the artisan who provides it, for providing that product (*ergon*) is his function (*ergon*) in the community, a function he performs by applying his art (*techne*), for the *function* of a house builder in the community is to build houses for other sharers, and this is his *work* (*ergon*). The significance of that is shown in the *Politics* where Aristotle says that

(6) Everything is defined by its *ergon* and capacity.[32]

He says this in discussing the relation of the individual both to the community and to the city-state, for passage (6) is part of his argument for the famous statement that "a city-state is prior by nature to the household and to each of us, for the whole is necessarily prior to the part, for if the whole is destroyed, then there will not be a foot or a hand, except homonymously,"[33] for a dead hand cannot fulfill its function. Therefore, a human without a *polis* or household cannot fulfill his or her function and therefore does not exist qua human "except homonymously." Providing an illustration of how everything or everyone is defined by its *ergon*, Aristotle says that a doctor *is* the *ergon* he actualizes: It is easy, he says, to know about the various remedies for illness, but how one should dispense them and to whom and when, "that much a function (*ergon*) is what it is to be a doctor" (*tosoûton ergon hoson iatron eînai*).[34] In the *Politics* Aristotle offers another example in people who excel in the *ergon* of flute-playing. In arguing that only those who excel in an *ergon* should receive the tools or offices of that *ergon*, he says that different "goods," such as wealth or birth or skill in playing the flute, are not comparable.[35] So, the best flutes should be given to those who are superior in the function (*ergon*) of flute play-ing, to which wealth and birth contribute nothing.[36] Even though the rich man may be willing to pay more for the flute, it would be wasted with him, because he lacks superiority in the *ergon*. Aristotle again emphasizes the defining role of *ergon* in a thing's identity in the *Meteorologia*.[37] An eye that loses its capacity to see has lost its metaphysical status as substance, for it cannot perform the *ergon* of an eye. *Ergon* for Aristotle is non–accidental. In the *Politics, Ethics,* and the *Meteorologia*, Aristotle asserts a thesis of functional determination. In accordance with Aristotle's thesis of functional determination an individual will belong to a kind or class F if and only if it can perform the function of that kind or class.[38] The import of this thesis is that a human being is defined by his or her *ergon*, which is both individual and universally human. For as Aristotle says in the *Nicomachean Ethics*, "we take a human's *ergon* to be a certain life, and this life is a soul's activity (*energeia*) and actions in accordance with reason,"[39] and Aristotle introduces that remark and his human function argument of which it is a part, by stating that individual human beings have individual functions (and he names carpenters, leather workers, harpists and others).[40] The signification of *ergon* as product is dependent on the signification of *ergon* as work that pro-duces that product, and both depend on the signification of *ergon* as function of the human being who performs that work and produces that product.[41] Each signification refers to a distinct entity with a distinct essence.[42] Accordingly, *ergon* is a case of what Shields calls "*core-dependent homonymy.*" The significa-tions of homonyms "product" and "work" are dependent on the signification "function," qua human function, for the product (*ergon*) is produced through human work (*ergon*). Thus, in formula (A), α, β invoke one signification of *ergon* (function), and γ, δ invoke another (product). This relation among the significations of *ergon* is metaphysical: It arises from the "essence," that is, the what-it-was-to-be (*to ti ên eînai*), succinctly put, the "whatness," of the human being who fulfills the function and produces the product.

In accordance with this understanding of the homonymy of *ergon*, Aristotle's proportions (for example formula (A)) are derivable *by analogy* from such analysis of producers and products, for as shoemaker is to shoes, so are doctor to health, farmer to nourishment, carpenter to bed and house builder to house, which analogies lead to the following proportion for any two producer/product pairs:[43]

(P) $$\frac{\alpha}{\gamma} = \frac{\beta}{\delta}.$$

Proportion P serves as a rule for distribution by function, as in the flute example.[44] Moreover, via a simple transformation, Proportion P is the source for Proportion B, Aristotle's proportion for distributions[45]:

(B)
$$\frac{\alpha}{\beta} = \frac{\gamma}{\delta}$$

As I show in a later section of this book, Aristotle says that Proportion A arises from Proportion B through the way social relations affect exchange.

Of what sort is the incommensurability of sharers? Consider whether Aristotle means only the following:

(a) α in respect to *ergon* is incommensurable with β in respect to *ergon*.

In other words, (a) says that the parties differ only in respect to *ergon*, that is not in *eîdos* or kind. That suggestion seems to fall short of the import of passage (6), which states that the *ergon* of a thing *defines* it, and thus *ergon* is not just an attribute of someone, such as we conceive of "occupation." Moreover, claim (a) surely falls short of the import of Aristotle's passage (1). For if, as that passage says, sharers differ in *eîdos*, sharers would be incommensurable not only in respect to *ergon* but also in respect to *eîdos*, since they would not be reducible to a common *eîdos* as a common factor or element. Therefore, it seems that Aristotle holds to more than (a), namely,

(b) α in respect to *eîdos* is incommensurable with β in respect to *eîdos*.

It is because the people of a city-state differ in *eîdos* that, Aristotle says, "reciprocal equality" (*to ison to antipeponthos*) among citizens preserves city-states.[46] As he says elsewhere, if the sharers did not differ, they would have nothing to offer each other. For an explanation of reciprocal equality, Aristotle refers us, as noted above, in the text immediately following passage (1), to *Nicomachean Ethics* v.5, to the very text under consideration here, where he discusses reciprocity (*to antipeponthos*) among sharers who are incommensurable.[47] That relationship between passage (1) and *EN* v.5 suggests that Aristotle's view that sharers in a community are incommensurable is interrelated with his view that sharers must differ in *eîdos*.

Now things that are commensurable are comparable, and things that are not comparable are not commensurable. Thus comparability is an indispensable ingredient of commensurability.[48] In *Physics* vii.4 Aristotle explores what movements or changes (*kinēsis*) are comparable. A circular motion and a rectilinear motion can cover the same distance in the same amount of time and have the same speed, and hence be considered comparable; similarly, an alteration can occur at the same speed as a displacement, so that a "pathos" is comparable to a length; but this, he says, is impossible.[49] For speed is a homonym and refers to different things in rotational and rectilinear motion, and in alteration and displacement.[50] These cases are therefore not really comparable.[51] The reason is that *kinēsis* has forms (*eídē*),[52] that is, the movements are produced by differing processes. We can compare the speed of alterations if what is altered is the same, for example becoming healthy: This seems to be comparable, for one person can become healthy quickly, another slowly, but others at the same time, so that that alteration will occur at the same speed. For they are altered in the same amount of time.[53] But if we take a case where the changes are different, for example one subject becomes pale and another becomes healthy, then we cannot compare them, for they are neither the same, nor equal, nor similar.[54] We cannot compare them because alteration has forms.[55] Aristotle concludes by stating reasons why changes would not be comparable: 1) If the things being changed differ in form, and 2) if the changes are with respect to the things themselves and not accidental, then the changes differ in form.[56] Accordingly, the alterations of seed, earth and other elements, which the farmer superintends, differ from the alterations of leather and other elements, of which the shoemaker is the agent. They are not comparable, *even*, as Aristotle points out, *if they are measured per unit time*, for the things being changed differ in form, for the farmer superintends given processes of reproduction and growth of plants and animals to provide plants, animals and their by-products to others, while the shoemaker transforms, at best, dead natural things into artifacts of human skill. So, while it is valid to compare farmer A and farmer B and the wheat produced by farmer A and the wheat produced by farmer B, it is not, however, valid to compare farmer and shoemaker, or the *ergon* of the farmer with the *ergon* of the shoemaker, for they are not comparable, and so Aristotle says in *EN* v.5 that they are incommensurable.[57]

Aristotle's treatment of comparability in *Physics* vii.4 clarifies why in *EN* v.5 he regards the *erga* of different sharers to be incommensurable, and why he regards also the sharers themselves to be incomparable and hence incommensurable: Differences in function (*ergon*), such as those of which he speaks in *Pol.* ii.2, signify not mere differences in occupation, but formal difference in the nature of their action. As Meikle states: "as natural activities, weaving and mining are no more commensurable with each other than, as natural entities, their products, cloth and coal, are."[58] Aristotle's view is incompatible with a labour-time theory of value, for if the *erga*, the "function" or "work," of different sharers is incommensurable, then so is the labour, since in his view there is no common factor between the labour of differing sharers.

In conclusion, different types of citizens in Aristotle's city-state are incommensurable with each other, for they perform distinct functions, which define their whatness, for the types of action that they carry out in performing those functions are incomparable, and, therefore, incommensurable. Because the citizens differ in function, they differ in *eídos*. Consequently, we have an independent demonstration of passage (1), which we summarize as follows:

(II) Everything is defined by its function and capacity. Those sharing in a community differ in function and produce goods that differ in function. Therefore, both the sharers and the goods they produce are incommensurable.[59] Things that are incommensurable differ in *eídos*.

Some will find the Socratic-Aristotelian claim that people differ in nature or kind unsettling, for it conflicts with the Enlightenment idea of the equality of all humans. But difference does not necessarily entail political or social inequality. We shall see that Aristotle uses the Socratic claim that people are different, to argue that the community protect the weak from the strong, for Aristotle proposes safeguards for the less advantaged against the exploitation of the more advantaged. That is the signification of the phrase "reciprocal equality," as will be discussed in Chapter 9. Through the use of proportion, Aristotle argues that we can meet the needs of all. The Greek view coheres with Nussbaum's criticism of the modern social contract tradition for its assumption that "contracting parties are rough equals."[60] An assumption of that sort of equality is a subterfuge for the exploitation of the weak by the more powerful – for example of unemployed worker by employer, or of tenant by landlord, or of developing by advanced nation, for none of the "partners" in any of those pairs is truly equal to the other.

Aristotle elaborates the Socratic proposal that people differ in nature, by showing how its elements are interdependent. Aristotle argues that people that make up a community must differ in kind (*eídos*) (point (i) as argued by Socrates at the beginning of this chapter), for if they did not, they would not have anything to offer each other, for they would possess the same skills (points (i) and (ii) argued by Socrates).[61] Since sharers differ in kind, the different needs that sharers have, can be met (points (ii) and (iii)), through mutual sharing (*metadosis*) of their different goods (point (iv)). As Aristotle says, "Useful things are exchanged for other useful things . . . to fill a lack in a natural self-sufficiency."[62] Like Socrates, Aristotle makes use of the concept of "giving of a share" (*metadosis*), but he goes further and names the socio-economic process of mutual giving of a share *reciprocity* (*to antipeponthos*), the process to which Socrates refers in points (iii) and (iv), but does not name. Because a community is founded on reciprocity, it is preserved by its practice;[63] the practice of reciprocity is the ground of its continued existence, for reciprocity is what preserves a union of things that differ in kind,[64] for "it is by giving-of-a-share (*metadosis*) that the sharers remain together."[65] Here, we have mainly focused on showing how Aristotle elaborates Socrates' statement (i) in *Republic* ii that people differ in nature. Subsequent chapters show his development of the other points of Socrates' analysis of the *polis*.

Notes

1 For example, Booth (1993), Meikle (1997), Miller (1998), and others.
2 *Rep.* i.369–372. Glaucon's comment is at 372d5.
3 *Rep.* 370b.

4 *Rep.* 369b.
5 *Rep.* 369c.
6 *Rep.* 369c.
7 *Rep.* 369c.
8 *Rep.* 371b–d.
9 *Rep.* 372a.
10 *Rep.* 370c.
11 Cf. *Pol.* ii.2.1261a22–24. The statement is the second half of a period, which reads: οὐ μόνον δ' ἐκ πλειόνων ἀνθρώπων ἐστὶν ἡ πόλις, ἀλλὰ καὶ ἐξ εἴδει διαφερόντων. οὐ γὰρ γίνεται πόλις ἐξ ὁμοίων.
12 Clearly, passage (2) challenges the modern rendering of *eîdos* as "species." Gallagher (2011a) provides an extensive discussion of that issue.
13 Commentators on passage (2), including this author, have said that Aristotle speaks of multiple "kinds" or "types" of humans but have not expressly considered any metaphysical implications of the text. The issue is whether the differences to which Aristotle refers in (2) are essential or accidental. We do not escape from this problem by rendering *eîdos* as "type" or "kind" (rather than "form") since those terms can also refer to essential differences. Cf. notes on 1261a23 in Newman (1887); by Aubonnet in Aristote (1960); by Saunders in Aristotle (1995); in Simpson (1998). This writer worked with passage (2) for several years before study of passage (1) in connection with other texts brought the metaphysical implications of (2) into focus. Cf. Gallagher (1998).
14 *Pol.* ii.2.1261b29–30.
15 Cf. *Pol.* 1261a24–27.
16 Cf. *EN* 1133a16–18.
17 *Met.* Z.17.1041b11–31. My revision of Ross' translation in Aristotle (1908a). In the elided text, Aristotle refers to another example, of flesh compounded out of fire and earth.
18 Alternatively, in *Pol.* i, he regards households as elements of villages, and villages as elements of city-states.
19 *Pol.* ii.2.1261a30–31. "Reciprocal equality" is the translation of *to ison to antipeponthos* by C. D. C. Reeve in Aristotle (1998). Jowett in Aristotle (1984) renders it as "the principle of reciprocity." Barker and Stalley in Aristotle (1995) paraphrase the whole clause as "the stability of every city depends on each of its elements rendering to the others an amount equivalent to what it receives from them." The rational for Reeve's translation is straight-forward: *to ison* is a typical case of an article plus an adjective expressing a substantive, in this case "equality," and *to antipeponthos* is in the attributive position, hence Reeve's translation. Jowett's rendering ignores *to ison*. Perhaps he worried over Aristotle's phrase in *EN* v.5 where he said *to antipeponthos kat' analogian kai mē kat' isotēte*, that is "reciprocity in accordance with proportion, not in accordance with equality" (1132b32–33). Reeve's translation satisfies Aristotle's caveat. Barker and Stalley's paraphrase is simply incorrect, since Aristotle emphasizes that goods exchanged are usually not equivalent, as we discuss in the main text. (Nonetheless, my thanks to Barker and Stalley for their translation, which I found useful when working on my dissertation before Reeve's translation was available.)
20 Cf. esp. *EN* v.5.1132b21–1133b28. The passage and one other to be discussed below appear in texts that A. Kenny has shown belong to the *Eudemian Ethics*, which, following Kenny, is the text as it appears in Aristotle (1991), plus the text of Books V–VII in Aristotle (1894). In *The Aristotelian Ethics* (1978), Kenny has presented considerable textual evidence that those three central books of the *Nicomachean Ethics*

were transplanted from the *Eudemian Ethics*. J. Barnes agrees in his Introduction to Aristotle (2004).

21 Cf. *EN* v.5.1133a31–32.
22 *EN* v.5.1133a13–14.
23 *EN* v.5.1133a18.
24 *EN* v.5.1133a32–33.
25 He says: "Let a farmer be α, nourishment γ, a shoemaker β, his ergon that is equalized δ" (*EN* v.5.1133b4–5).
26 *EN* v.5.1133b18–20.
27 Cf. *EN* 1112a23, *Met.* 983a16; *Phys.* 222a5; *GA* 742b28.
28 Cf. Courant (1937), I, 7; Klein (1945), 31–37.
29 *EN* 1112a23.
30 Heath (1949), 274–5; Meikle (1997); Gauthier and Jolif (1970) cite 1194a7–27 in *Magna Moralia* (the authenticity of which is seriously doubted) in support, but their use of the passage is refuted by Finley (1977).
31 See n. 28.
32 *Pol.* i.2.1253a23.
33 *Pol.* i.2.1253a18–22.
34 *EN* v.9.1137a16.
35 *Pol.* iii.12.1283a3–11. Cf. Nussbaum's discussion of this passage in Nussbaum (1988a).
36 *Pol.* iii.12.1282b33–83a3.
37 Cf. 390a10.
38 Cf. Shields (1999), 31–35. For further discussion of functional determination in Aristotle, cf. Shields (1999), 240–244 and Shields (1990), 19–33. Deslauriers (2013), 132 says that "the fundamental difference that Aristotle advocates is a difference in virtue." This interesting idea is not supported by the text of *Pol.* ii.2. Rather, the text asks the reader to consult *EN* v.5 for explanation of ii.2, and there the reader finds argument that people differ in function.
39 *EN* i.7.1098a12.
40 For the human function argument, cf. *EN* i.7.1097b25–98a8, and Irwin (1988), §133, 135, 194 and note 16n37.
41 Cf. Shields (1999), Chap. 4.
42 Regarding homonymy based on multiple significations, cf. *Top.* 107a3–18 and Shields (1999), 52, 54–56 and Chap. 3.
43 For discussion of Aristotle's use of analogy, cf. Hesse (1965), Olshewsky (1968).
44 For discussion of distribution by function, cf. Jackson (1985).
45 Cf. *EN* v.3.
46 *Pol.*1261a30–31.
47 Clearly, passages (1), (2), (3), (5) and (6) suggest metaphysical issues of interest. Those issues are discussed in Gallagher (2011a).
48 Shields (1999), 261–262 even renders *sumblēta* as "commensurable." I explain the significance of "reciprocal equality" in subsequent chapters.
49 Cf. *Phys.* vii.4.248a15.
50 Cf. *Phys.* vii.4.248b10–12.
51 For homonymy based on non-comparability, cf. *Top.* 107b13–18 and Shields, (1999), 52n18; for that based on multiple significations, cf. note 43.
52 Cf. *Phys.* vii.4.249a11–12.
53 Cf. *Phys.* vii.4.249a29–b1.
54 Cf. *Phys.* vii.4.249b7–9.
55 Cf. *Phys.* vii.4.249b9–10.

56 Cf. *Phys.* vii.4.249b11–14.
57 The same treatment applies to the other case which Aristotle offers us: The relationship between a house builder and a shoemaker (1133a22–23).
58 Meikle (1991), 174. Cf. Judson (1997), 171 on houses and shoes, and Burnet (1900), 225 on nutrition and health care, who make similar points. Of course, Aristotle would disagree with Meikle's assertion that products of human art, for example weavings, cloth, are "natural."
59 Cf. *Pol.* ii.2; *EN* v.5.
60 Cf. Nussbaum (2006), 69, 71, and Chapter 5 herein.
61 369b–370b; cf. *EN* v.5.1133a16–19; *Pol.* ii.2.1261a24, 29–30.
62 *Pol.* 1257a25–31.
63 Cf. *EN* v.5.1132b31–33a2; *Pol.* ii.2.1261a29–31.
64 *Pol.* ii.2.
65 Cf. *EN* v.5.

7 Living well versus mere living

The bifurcation of the community

Both Plato and Aristotle were interested in establishing an account of why the Peloponnesian War occurred and how society could be organized so that such a disaster would not revisit the Greek world. Plato represents the problem early in the *Republic*: After outlining the first city-state (*polis*) in which "many people gather together in a single homeland to live together as sharers (*koinōnoi*) and helpers,"[1] Socrates concludes: "And so they'll live in peace and good health, and when they die at a ripe old age, they'll bequeath a similar life to their children."[2] That peace and good health are interrupted by the demand of Glaucon, Socrates' interlocutor, for "couches" from which to dine, and "delicacies and desserts" to satisfy the appetites.[3] In response, Socrates enlarges the first city into "a luxurious city," which indulges in pleasures, and which *goes to war* to expand its territory to support its expanding appetites.[4] Socrates gives no political or sociological account of how the first "healthy" city becomes the luxurious city, "a city with a fever," but arbitrarily expands the first city by listing a variety of objects of desire that the inhabitants now want to include in it, from couches to pastries and perfumed prostitutes.[5] He only says that the expansion and the war that results originate from "those same desires that are most of all responsible for the bad things that happen to cities and the individuals in them."[6]

Aristotle, however, investigates this problem in a scientific fashion. In the ninth chapter of the first book of the *Politics*, he concludes that the anxiety that people feel that they may not have enough of the goods for life, together with the desire for gratification (*apolauseis*), prompt some to engage in a form of property acquisition that is "not by nature" (*ou phusei*),[7] one that employs a form of exchange that is contrary to nature (*para phusin*),[8] for the sake of "unconstrained (*mē anagkaia*) wealth acquisition."[9] The development of "unconstrained wealth acquisition" divides the community and produces discord.

Living well

Aristotle's analysis of the origin of "unconstrained wealth acquisition" in *Politics* Book i is based on his account of the origins of the city-state (*polis*), which we now review. As Aristotle says, to get the best view of things, we must see how they develop naturally from the beginning.[10] He says that a city-state originates from households that develop into villages, as the children of an original household establish their own.[11] These villages can form a city-state if they satisfy the following conditions:

(1) The community (*koinōnia*) composed of several villages that is complete, that has already attained a limit of near total self-sufficiency (*autarkeia*), so to speak, is a city-state (*polis*). It comes to be for the sake of (*heneken*) living (*zên*), but continues to exist for the sake of living well (*eû zên*).[12]

The community of villages must be complete among themselves, that is, must contain all skills necessary for a city-state, and therewithal must have attained near total self-sufficiency, to become a city-state. That much is clear. (Why that is a "limit" (*peras*) is discussed below in connection with passage (6).) One unusual idea in the passage is that the community that has attained self-sufficiency *exists for the sake of living well*. That means that the point of self-sufficiency is cultural as much as economic, that is self-sufficiency permits the full development of human culture in living well (*eû zên*), in experiencing the culture of one's *polis* and participating in its political life.[13] In other words, according to Aristotle, were a community of villages not self-sufficient, but were dependent on other city-states for sustenance, then its people could not experience living well. Perhaps the idea here is that *if a community is rather dependent on other states, then it cannot deliberate on its future, for it does not command the parameters that affect its future,* for Aristotle says that we cannot deliberate over matters that are out of our control.[14] So, if we cannot deliberate on our future, we cannot live well. If that is true, then very few people in our contemporary world can "live well," for most states, for example the USA, are not self-sufficient. Thus living well is an experience beyond the grasp of most of us, and in studying it we learn of the culture of a bygone age.

For the sake of living well, even when people do not need each other's help, they nonetheless choose to live together.[15] As Aristotle says later in the *Politics,* a city-state is "a community of living well" for households and extended families (*genē*) for the sake of a complete and self-sufficient life.[16] Aristotle's definition of a city-state as "a community of living well for households and families" suggests that living well is an experience not just for the master of the household, the *oikonomikos*, but also for his entire household. By contrast, anyone who cannot form a community with others or who is self-sufficient without others and does not need a community, is either a beast or a god,[17] and cannot experience living well (*eû zên*). Living well is a social experience. Other animals are also gregarious,[18] but what's unique about humans is that they form communities of perception of what is good and bad, just and unjust, and other social values. Aristotle explains:

(2) It is peculiar to human beings alone, in comparison to the other animals, to have perception (*aisthēsis*) of what is good and bad, just and unjust, and the rest. And it is the community in these things that makes a household and a city-state.[19]

What "makes a household," according to Aristotle, is "community," that is agreement, of its members in the "perception of what is good and bad, just and unjust" and so on.[20] Efforts to reduce Aristotle's theory of political economy to a few pages in the *Nicomachean Ethics* and *Politics*[21] miss the point of this definition of the household, the primary unit of the economy of the *polis*, for the fact that Aristotle's conception of the household is dependent on shared ethical or "phronetic" perceptions shows that his entire moral and metaphysical philosophy informs his political economy. That community and agreement in ethical perceptions is the basis of the friendship (*philia*) which holds the household (and *polis*) together.[22] On one level, Aristotle's first point in passage (2) is that unless people agree on fundamentals it is hard for them to cooperate in a common effort. More importantly, the passage underscores the fact that for Aristotle, the household, its master or *oikonomikos*, and his practice of *oikonomia* are not primarily "productive" (*poiētikē*), but rather oriented towards moral action (*praktikē*). Because community in ethical perceptions makes a household or city-state, Aristotle says that household masters (*oikonomikoi*) and statesmen are among those who have practical wisdom (*phronēsis*) and are concerned with *prakta*,[23] the results of moral action,[24] for practical wisdom is concerned with what is good and evil for human beings,[25] and it is "practical" because it is concerned with action (*praxis*),[26] rather than (primarily) production (*poiēsis*).[27] Therefore, the end of the household is not production, though it does engage in it.[28] Rather, the end is the exercise of practical wisdom in regards to what is good or evil for its members. Based on the agreement of their members on the "perception of what is good and bad, just and unjust and the rest," multiple households form villages, and groups of villages form city-states based on their mutual agreement concerning such ethical perceptions.[29] These city-states exist for the sake of living well (*eû zēn*) (cf passage 1). In order to live well, they must have formed community in "what is good and bad, just and unjust, and the rest" and practise *phronēsis* in managing their households and city political affairs.

Problems arise, however, when people become confused about the distinction between mere living (*zēn*) and living well (*eû zēn*). "Living well" does not simply mean that an individual's household is provided with enough goods to live comfortably, for if that were true, they would not need a city-state. But a city-state is "the *community of living well* (*hē toû eû zēn koinōnia*)."[30] Without community, *eû zēn* is not possible. I cannot *eû zēn* by myself.

Aristotle sketches out what "living well" signifies at the beginning of the *Nicomachean Ethics*. There he is asking, what is the human good? Both the masses and the educated, he recounts, say that the human good is happiness, which they suppose to be "the same . . . as living well and doing well" (*to d' eû zēn kai to eû prattein*).[31] They disagree, however, about what happiness signifies.[32] A few chapters later Aristotle gives his answer to the question, what is the human good? His answer in his famous "human function" argument is that we achieve the good – "living well and doing well" – if we fulfill our human function, which he defines as follows:

(3)   We take the human function (*ergon*) to be a certain kind of life (*zōē*), and take that life to be activity and actions of a soul by means of reason (*meta logou*); and the good human does that well and finely (*eû kai kalôs*). Now each <function> is fulfilled well in accordance with its proper virtue. And so the human good comes to be as activity of a soul in accord with virtue, and indeed, if there are more virtues than one, with the best and most complete <virtue>.[33]

To live well and do well, we must engage in activity of soul by means of reason and in accord with "the best and most complete virtue." This is why Aristotle says that "the city-state . . . must be concerned with virtue,"[34] for it must be concerned with whether its members live well and do well. Now, Aristotle explains elsewhere that "the best and most complete virtue" is justice. He gives two arguments for this. First, he says that insofar as the law (*nomos*) prescribes that we act in accordance with virtue, that is that we do the deeds of the courageous and not flee from battle, that we be temperate and not commit adultery, that we be mild-mannered and not verbally abuse others, in that way the law prescribes just behaviours that add up to complete virtue.[35] Moreover, justice is also complete virtue in another sense, insofar as it is "with respect to another":

(4)   Justice is complete because the one who has it is able to use the virtue in relation to another, not just in relation to himself. For many are able to use the virtue in their personal affairs, but are unable in matters pertaining to another . . . For the same reasons, justice alone among the virtues seems to be another person's good, because it is in relation to another, for it does what benefits another, whether a ruler or a fellow member of the community.[36]

Accordingly, to live well, we must live justly in relation to the other. We cannot live well if we are unjust to the other, if we exploit the other for our personal gain. If we exploit the other, we violate the common "perception of what is good and bad, just and unjust," and the community of living well of which we are members. In conclusion, for Aristotle,

> We achieve the human good – living well and doing well (*to eû zên kai to eû prattein*) – through actions and activity of soul by means of reason and in accordance with justice.

Sources of division

Domestic economy (*oikonomia*) provides the support and infrastructure for living well (*eû zên*) for both the city-state and the household, for living well requires goods. Aristotle explains:

(5) One form of property acquisition (*ktētikē*) in accordance with nature is a part of domestic economy (*oikonomikē*) because it must either possess or acquire enough so that it possesses a storehouse of goods necessary for life and useful for a community of a city–state or of a household. It even seems that true (*alēthinos*) wealth is from those goods.[37]

Oikonomikē must produce or have in store enough goods so that the household or city-state achieves a level of self-sufficiency (*autarkia*).[38] In producing that self-sufficiency, the object is to enable *eû zên*, and the exercise of practical reason, the purposes of *oikonomikē*, on the one hand, and within that, to preserve *philia*, the common bond of householders and citizens in preserving their culture, on the other hand.[39] That self-sufficiency is necessary to support leisure for citizens and householders, "for leisure is necessary both for the development of virtue and for political actions (*tas praxeis tas politikas*),"[40] both parts of living well (*eû zên*). Thus, as Aristotle says, the household, as a locus of the practice of *phronēsis*, is the end (*hou charin*) of *oikonomikē*."[41] Likewise the city-state. Thus, household and city-state qualify as *prakton* goods, for "if something of all the things to be done (*prakta*) is an end (*telos*), then this would be the *prakton* good," says Aristotle.[42]

Aristotle's inclusion of the city-state as an object of *oikonomikē* in the above passage shows that *oikonomikē* signifies more than "household management," the usual translation of the term.[43] That is why Liddell and Scott's rendering of *oikonomikē* as "domestic economy" is better, for "domestic economy" captures both significations of *oikonomikē*: both national economy and the economy of the household.[44] So, *oikonomikē* (economics) is inseparable from politics; consequently, Aristotle devotes Book i of the *Politics* to the topic.[45] Is *oikonomia* a craft (*technē*)? Aristotle does not say so. His use of the feminine gender for its adjective, *oikonomikē*, suggests it is described by some feminine noun. I suggest action (*praxis*), for to say that *oikonomia* is an action is consistent with his emphasis that managers of domestic economy (*oikonomikoi*) have practical wisdom (*phronēsis*) and are concerned with *prakta*,[46] the results of moral action,[47] and with his view that the purpose of *oikonomia* is to enable us to live well, that is, to deliberate on our future as citizens of a *polis*.

Aristotle's claim that "goods necessary for life and useful for a community" are what constitute "true wealth" suggests that there is another sort of wealth that is not genuine. Indeed, Aristotle's use of the alpha-privative *alēthinos*, signifying "true" as opposed to the merely "apparent" wealth, implies that what is ordinarily or often considered wealth is not true wealth, for the root of *alēthinos*, *alēthēs*, signifies the "*unconcealed,* and so *true, real,* as opposed to *false,* or *apparent.*"[48] Aristotle's conception of "true wealth" is normative, as Natali points out.[49] Aristotle measures other notions of wealth against his concept of true wealth. He explains "it is strange for something to be wealth if someone who has a lot of it will starve, as is said of Midas . . . That is why those who seek a different wealth and wealth acquisition (*chrēmastistikē*), seek rightly, for natural wealth and wealth acquisition are different. The first is *oikonomikē*, and the other is merchandising (*kapēlikē*), which is productive of goods (*poiētikē chrematōn*) not generally but through exchange of goods."[50] For Aristotle, there is natural wealth and wealth acquisition (or rather "money making," as Marx translates *chrēmastistikē*), and another form of *chrēmastistikē*, which Aristotle identifies with merchandising. Natali calls these two forms "chrématistique[1]" for the natural kind, and "chrématistique[2]" for the kind practiced by merchandising.[51] What is the point of *chrématistique*[1] if *oikonomikē* already has a subsidiary function that acquires property (*ktētikē*)? The point is that even *oikonomikē* needs cash, money, to settle necessary exchange to support self-sufficiency. Thus household managers sell their surplus product for cash that they need for necessary exchange. Marx is therefore right to translate *chrēmastistikē* as "the art of money making." But subordinated to *oikonomikē*, it is money making for the sake of the self-sufficiency of the household or *polis*. In the case of merchandising (*kapēlikē*), however, *chrēmastistikē* is money making for its own sake.

In order to distinguish the two types of wealth acquisition, Aristotle turns his critique of political economy towards substantiating the idea that there is both "apparent" wealth and "true wealth" by discussing "limits" to *oikonomikē*. There is disagreement over the central concept of his critique. The dispute manifests itself over the meaning of a noun phrase of the lead clause of his analysis following passage (5). Jowett, Barker and Stalley and Reeve agree on the basic meaning of the phrase. Reeve's translation says: "For the amount of this sort of property that one needs for the self-sufficiency that promotes the good life is not unlimited."[52] The clause reads in transcribed Greek:

hē gar tês toiautēs ktēseōs autarkeia pros agathēn zōēn ouk apeiros estin.[53]

Published translations have inverted the syntactic relations in the noun clause *hē gar tês toiautēs ktēseōs autarkeia*, and have subordinated the subject-noun *autarkeia* to the genitive phrase *tês toiautēs ktēseōs*.[54] Instead of translating something like "the self-sufficiency of that sort of property acquisition," as the Greek says, Reeve says "the amount of this sort of property that one needs for the self-sufficiency." Jowett and Barker and Stalley are even more off the mark. The difference is significant, for in the published translations it is the amount of property that is not unlimited, but in the Greek it is the self-sufficiency that is not unlimited. That is a strange and difficult concept, but one that lies at the heart of Aristotle's critique of political economy. He hints at the concept as early as Chapter 2 of the *Politics* in passage (1), above. Aristotle's claim is that past the point at which a household or city is providing for itself from its own production combined with a modicum of trade, a higher level of self-sufficiency – for either a household or a city-state – is not achievable by accumulating more wealth. That is counterintuitive: How could having more money not make one more self-sufficient? The answer is that making that extra money makes one more dependent on markets and other entities beyond one's household or city-state. A household becomes dependent on the market, so it produces for the market, no longer just for itself, and to continue to exist at its current size it must continue to produce for the market. If the market encounters problems, the household suffers from those problems; it is no longer independent. A city-state becomes dependent upon foreign sources of income, for example through trade, or in case of Athens, tribute extracted from allies, so that to sustain itself, it must somehow accumulate more such income. Aristotle implicitly condemns the Athenian city-state's pursuit of wealth as a practice that destroyed their experience of *eû zên*, and of rational praxis in politics. Let us now review the entire passage:

(6) The self-sufficiency (*autarkeia*) achievable from that sort of property acquisition, for a good life (*agathēn zōēn*), is not unlimited, contrary to what Solon says in his poem that "No boundary to wealth is established for human beings." For a boundary exists just as in other crafts. For no instrument of any craft is unlimited, either in multitude or in size, and wealth is a multitude of instruments for household managers (*oikonomikoí*) and for statesmen (*polītikoí*). It is now clear that there is some craft of property acquisition (*ktētikē*) in accord with nature for household managers and statesmen, and why. But there is another kind (*genos*) of craft of property acquisition, which they in particular call – and are right to call it – money making (*chrēmastistikē*), through which there seems to exist no limit to wealth or property, and which many believe to be one and the same as the one we have discussed because of their proximity, but it is neither the same as the one discussed, nor far from it. And one of them is by nature and the other is not, but rather comes to be through some experience and craft.[55]

Note that in this passage (which continues passage (5)), Aristotle repeats his assertion that *oikonomikē* names the art of management of the economy of the city-state as well as that of the household, for he concludes "there is some craft of property acquisition in accord with nature for household managers and statesmen."[56] He thereby confirms that "domestic economy," in the sense of both the economy of the state and that of the household, is the preferred meaning for *oikonomikē*.

The principal message of the passage, however, is that for a Greek citizen, further wealth accumulation beyond what is needed to support the household and its political and cultural praxis is only possible by involvement in mercantile trade, and that makes one dependent on markets when before one was independent of them. It means expanding production on the household farm for the market. That makes the household dependent on market sales to maintain its production at that higher level. Therefore, there is a limit to achievable self-sufficiency. After making that point, Aristotle then turns to criticize Solon, the reformer who banned chattel slavery in Athens,[57] but who, in the poem quoted by Aristotle, asserts that there is no limit to wealth for human beings, a popular belief today, but one for which Aristotle criticizes the statesman. It would seem that Aristotle is wrong, for why cannot someone accumulate billions and billions without limit? Indeed, many seem to do just that. Aristotle's point is that wealth accumulation has a natural limit, beyond which further accumulation is both unethical and a perversion of the function of economic activity. Wealth accumulation beyond one's needs destroys one's ability to experience *eû zên*. Wealth is only a tool (*organon*) or rather a multitude of tools (*organōn plêthos*) for the use of the household manager or politician to support the good life for members of the household or citizens of the *polis*. If we obsess on the tool, we interfere with living well. A tool is not an end, but only a means. The true end is living well (*eû zên*). The fitting use of wealth "was to liberate its owner from economic activity and concern," Finley wrote.[58] I add one other fitting use: To "benefit another," under Aristotle's definition of justice described above. As discussed in Chapter 10, it is a function of "superior" members of a community to support the existence, the being, of weaker ones.[59] In this way, such a superior sharer uses wealth the best,[60] and in doing so, he fulfills a communal function, for wealth is one of the qualities of the community,[61] and its use consists in spending and giving.[62] It is not possible for me to acquire wealth beyond what I need to practise *eû zên* if I give away such excess wealth in practising *eû zên*.[63] But if I procure more wealth than I need to enjoy *eû zên* and spend that on my own household, I violate both the doctrine of the *Politics* described here *and* Aristotle's theory of reciprocal justice expressed in *Nicomachean Ethics* v.5, for in acquiring excess wealth and hoarding it, I violate the *Ethics* requirement that I "benefit another."

Wealth acquisition, money making, becomes "unlimited" only when wealth is erroneously treated as an end in itself, rather than a means. It is this to which Aristotle refers with the phrase "unconstrained wealth acquisition," that we discussed earlier in this chapter, for unlimited wealth acquisition is certainly without constraints. But unlimited wealth accumulation is not the task (*ergon*) of *oikonomikē*. Rather, living well is its end, that is, the *praxis* of the household, the participation of the members of household in the cultural and political life of the *polis*.[64] Since goods are necessary to support the good life, however, some people become confused and devote all their time to acquiring wealth and neglect the good life itself.[65] Aristotle explains:

(7) Some people (*tisi*) believe that increase of property is the function (*ergon*) of *oikonomia*, and thinking it necessary, they persevere in saving their store of money or increasing it without limit. Anxiety for living (*to spoudazein peri to zên*),[66] rather than living well (*eû zên*), is a cause of this disposition. Since that desire is unlimited, they desire also that the things productive (*poiētika*) of it be unlimited. Whoever aim also at the good life seek what is conducive to physical gratification; as a result, since this appears to lie in acquisition of property, there is every concern about making money (*chrēmatismon*), and from this arose the second form of wealth acquisition. Since gratification lies in excess, they seek what is productive (*poiētikē*) of this gratifying excess.[67]

Here Aristotle proposes a psychological explanation for the obsession with making money (*chrēmatismon*). Some people (*tisi*) are anxious (*spoudazein peri*) whether they will have the means to live and to physically gratify themselves, come what may.[68] (How well Aristotle characterizes the syndrome of modern man!) They concern themselves with attending to that imagined problem, rather than with living well in political and cultural activity in the community of their city-state. They are not concerned with action (*praxis*), but rather production (*poiēsis*): From this arose the craft of wealth acquisition that is not in accordance with nature, which Aristotle names "commerce" (*to kapēlikon*), by which he means profit-seeking mercantile trade.[69] Through commerce, which is "productive of goods (*poiētikē chrematōn*),"[70] they seek what is productive (*poiētikē*) of the means of life and of a gratifying excess. Such commerce, however, subverts civic friendship and community. In *Politics* i.9 Aristotle outlines how commerce arose out of the barter of surplus goods by members of a community with each other and with other communities: Exchange to "make money" arose out of simple commodity exchange.[71] Aristotle says that at first people exchanged useful things for useful things "in order to complete natural self-sufficiency."[72] Exchange starts between members of different households, and then between villages and cities.[73] That kind of exchange is an instrument of the form (*eidos*) of property acquisition (*ktētikē*) that is in accordance with nature.[74] That kind of exchange (*metablētikē*), he says, is not contrary to nature and is not a form of wealth accumulation (*chrēmastistikē*).[75] But wealth accumulation arose out of it after the invention of money for the purpose of settling exchange transactions.[76] At first, people used money to settle transactions in which one party did not have anything of interest to the other. The first party would have to pay money to obtain something needed for self-sufficiency. As a result of that practice, as a matter of course, people would trade some of their own produce to obtain money, so that they could obtain what they needed to complete self-sufficiency. That was wealth accumulation ("money making") in accordance with nature.[77] But when it was understood thereby that money could be accumulated through exchange, some decided to devote themselves to doing that exclusively.[78]

Some modern scholars report that "a large proportion of Athens' trade was in the hands of non-citizens," and that there was a long-standing prejudice against the occupation.[79] But Aristotle's account of the development of commerce as a part of the development of the city suggests that to his mind, commercial traders are not in general foreigners but rather citizens who succumb to psychological weakness. Although he hints elsewhere that trading is incompatible with citizenship,[80] nonetheless, in the entire discussion of commerce in *Politics* Book i, Chapter 9, there is not one reference to a commercial trader as a foreigner or metic. In passage 7, he refers to those who develop into commercial traders only as "some people" (*tisi*) out of the people who make up the city-state, that is some of the citizens. Elsewhere in the *Politics* Aristotle says four times that the people comprise a farming part, a trading part (*agoraîon*) and a crafts part; there is no hint in the passages that any of these people are foreigners.[81] Moreover, in Book vi Aristotle proposes that poor citizens be given assistance so they can obtain a plot of land or at least get a start in farming or trade (*emporia*).[82] At the very least, it is fair to assume that in the fourth century, a significant number of those involved in merchandising were citizens. Polanyi reflects on this in his comments on Aristotle's evaluation of the commercial trader:

> Commercial trade, or, in our terms, market trade, arose as a burning issue out of the circumstances of the time. It was a disturbing novelty, which could neither be placed nor explained nor judged adequately. Money was now being earned by respectable citizens through the simple device of buying and selling. Such a thing had been unknown, or rather, was restricted to low-class persons, known as hucksters, as a rule metics [resident aliens], who eked out a living by retailing food in the market place. Such individuals did make a profit by buying at one price and selling at another. *Now this practice had apparently spread to the citizenry of good standing*, and big sums of money were made by this method, formerly stamped as disreputable. How should the phenomenon itself be classified? How should profit, systematically made in this manner, be operationally explained? And what judgment should be passed on such an activity? . . . By calling commercial trade *kapēlikē* – no name had been given to it – [Aristotle] intimated that it was nothing new, except for the proportions it assumed. It was hucksterism writ large. The money was made "off" each other (*ap' allēllōn*), by the surcharging methods so often met in the marketplace.[83]

How can we better understand these phenomena? First, as Polanyi puts it, how should profit, systematically made in this manner, be operationally explained?

Is merchandising "contrary to nature"?

In necessary exchange, people exchange surplus goods (C), which they produced via their household for money (M) and then that money for the surplus goods (C) of others which they need,[84] a process representable by the schema C—M—C. In such exchange people receive the goods they need, and no one makes a profit, for the aim is not to make money, but to acquire the goods necessary to maintain self-sufficiency and to support *eû zên*. Necessary exchange mediated by currency gave rise to commerce, which became a craft concerned "with *how, and from what, something exchanged will produce the greatest profit*."[85] As Xenophon writes, merchants "find out where corn is at the highest value, and where the inhabitants will set the greatest store by it, and there they take and deliver the dear article."[86] The craft of commerce eventually led in Athens to what Lysias reports in "Against the corn dealers," that the dealers bought up all the available corn and then resold it at six times the legally allowed profit.[87] That kind of exchange is an instrument of the form of property acquisition that is contrary to nature,[88] which form of property acquisition is itself also contrary to nature.

Aristotle gives several reasons for why exchange to make money is contrary to nature

First, *every piece of property has two uses: a proper use and an improper use*. Aristotle gives the example of a shoe. I can wear a shoe, or I can exchange it for something else. But it is not the proper use of the shoe to exchange it. If I exchange the shoe for money or food, I am not using it in accordance with its proper use (*tēn oikeian chrêsin*), "for it did not come to exist for the sake of exchange" (*ou gar allagês heneken gegone*).[89] Many will object that, in fact, manufacturers and others make shoes and many other products precisely "for the sake of exchange," and Aristotle acknowledges that.[90] Aristotle means that the shoe was invented for the sake of protecting the human foot, not for the sake of exchange. So, exchange to make money is contrary to the nature of the items exchanged.

Second, in the type of exchange that is contrary to nature, *the purpose of the exchange is* not to exchange some goods for others, but *to make a money profit*. For the purpose of exchange in accord with nature is to obtain the goods necessary for "the filling-up of the natural self-sufficiency" of the household and not to 'make money,'[91] for the ancient Greek household produces much of what it needs through the family farm and household industry and exchange was only needed to obtain some items.[92] Some will argue that those who "make money" via exchange also do so in order to complete the natural self-sufficiency of their households, but this is wrong-headed for two reasons: 1) Contemporary urban households are not self-sufficient in any respect, but entirely dependent on income earned outside the household through wage-paying or salaried employment. (Obviously, agricultural households are an exception to this urban rule.) That earned income is the entire support of the household in most cases. 2) The aim of modern manufacturing or merchandising is not to make the households of the employees self-sufficient, and then stop work at that point, so that the employees can enjoy *eû zên*. Rather, the aim is single: to maximize profit for the enterprise.

Third, according to Aristotle, *merchandising transforms production as well so as to make it not in accordance with nature*, for merchandising, he writes, "is productive of goods (*poiētikē chrematōn*) not generally but through exchange of goods."[93] What Aristotle means is that the growth of commerce comes to drive production, so that where there previously used to be production only for use, under the influence of commerce there often is production only for the market. So, merchandising is productive of goods, but not generally, not for the use of the producers, but for the market, for exchange.

In exchange "not in accordance with nature, a merchant exchanges money for goods and then exchanges those goods for more money than she or he originally expended and so garners a profit, in a process representable by the schema M—C—M'.[94] Clearly, Aristotle regards that form of property acquisition as reprehensible, for he says in the *Eudemian Ethics* that "If someone makes a profit, we can refer it to no other vice than injustice,"[95] and in the *Nicomachean Ethics* he explains, "it is not possible at the same time both to make money from the commons (*chrēmatizesthai apo tōn koinōn*) and be honoured,"[96] for exchange to make a mercantile profit acts as a drain on the community, for in the C—M—C exchange, equivalents are exchanged for equivalents, and no one is exploited. But into such a community of exchange enters the commercial trader, who does not exchange equivalents for equivalents, but trades a commodity C (purchased earlier with money M) for more money M' than he or she originally expended, to garner a profit M' − M through "making money from the commons."[97] That profit-seeking trade is judged unjust by the "phronetic perception" of the commons, and it can lead to civil strife, as one portion of the community − traders − separates itself from the rest.[98] Aristotle notes of the two types of wealth acquisition that:

(8) The use of each type of wealth acquisition (*hekatera tē chrēmatistikē*) − being of the same thing [i.e. goods] − is entangled. For the use is of the same property, but not with respect to the same end.[99]

Because the two types of wealth acquisition are "entangled" insofar as they use the same property, they are in "proximity" to each other and are not "far" from each other, as says passage (6). But their ends differ. One kind aims at achieving self-sufficiency through necessary exchange; the other aims at profit-making. The co-existence of these two types of exchange, of these two types of wealth acquisition, at first divides the community into wealthy traders and everyone else. It causes civil strife because there is no reciprocity between traders and other citizens.[100] We have already noted an example of mercantile profiteering in the case of the Athenian corn dealers, prosecuted by Lysias. In that case, the value of the income of an ordinary Athenian artisan or labourer is devalued as a result of the corn dealers grabbing control of the corn supply and then jacking up the price to guarantee a huge (illegal) profit. The artisan must expend more of his income in order to feed his family. The corn dealers "make money from the commons" and are hated. But Aristotle says that this practice comes to pervert all other activities in the *polis*. If people cannot procure the excess they want for gratification, they try to make money in some other way by using their powers in an unnatural way,[101] by turning medicine, generalship, even bravery, into ways to make money in the belief that acquiring wealth is the end, and that everything ought to be oriented to that end.[102] In this way, Aristotle perceived and anticipated the mores of modernity, as Polanyi notes.[103]

To illustrate the divisiveness of commercial trading, I cite a contemporary example: Wage earners, following the C—M—C paradigm, sell their labour to an employer for money income (C—M) and then use that income to purchase goods and services for their households (M—C). The merchandisers from whom they purchase goods, however, follow the M—C—M' paradigm, for they use their capital to purchase commodities (M—C), which they then sell at a mark-up (C—M'). Wolff argues that when wage earners so depart the realm of production and enter into the realm of circulation to purchase goods that they need for their households, they must purchase those goods "at prices that are driven up above their labor value by the positive rate of return on the capital invested throughout the economy."[104] This striking claim has the retail market exploiting the wage-earning consumer in every transaction. The result, Wolff argues, is that a portion of the value of wage income is transferred to retail income outside the terms of fair exchange. That is a contemporary example of a contradiction between the practice of simple commodity exchange and chrematistics in merchandising.

We have answered Polanyi's questions: How profit, systematically made through merchandising should be operationally explained, and what judgment should be passed on such activity. As a result of the practice of intensive wealth acquisition ("making money"), wealth comes to be concentrated in the hands of a few. That there is inequality in wealth in Greece in Aristotle's time is confirmed by features of community life that Aristotle notes.[105] Such division in the community separates us into "self" and "other" as it wears away at the civic friendship upon which the community rests. As we shall see in Chapters 9 and 10, Aristotle argues that graciousness, sacrifice, forgiveness and restitution are needed to bring the community together again. Chapter 8 presents Aristotle's theory of value and the model by which he studies exchange.

Aristotle's evaluation of the merchant

Before we go on to those topics, we return to study Aristotle's psychological analysis of those who, due to anxiety whether they will have the means to live and to physically gratify themselves, turn away from *eû zên* and towards the accumulation of wealth, a syndrome we notice is at least as common today as it was in the ancient world. We might even congratulate Aristotle for discovering this modern neurosis in its bud in the ancient world when the individual was not left to his own resources to support his household, in comparison to our current age when he or she largely is so. Aristotle argues that the obsession with making money is not confined to mercantilists and commercial traders, but perverts many throughout the city-state. Aristotle says that those who are not commercial traders engage in "making money" by turning every human capacity into a means for making money, and destroy its natural purpose.

(9) They use each of the capacities but not in accordance with nature (*ou kata phusin*). For to make money is not the purpose of manliness, but courage, nor of generalship or medicine, but victory for the first, and health for the second. They make everything into money making, as if that were its end, and it were right to approach everything for that end.[106]

It is as if Aristotle were writing about the twenty-first century where health care has become big business and unnecessary surgeries are commonplace, where retired generals earn hundreds of thousands of dollars as consultants. His concern, however, is with his own era, where the tendencies that now run rampant first manifested themselves. His point again is that insecurity over one's means of living drive some, today most, into an obsession with money making. How do we account for this "disposition" (*diathesis*), as Aristotle calls it, within his theory of mind?[107] According to passage (2), all members of the community share in the common "perception of what is good and bad, just and unjust, and the rest," even those who end up obsessed with money making. How and why do they depart from that common ethical perception that judges their money making negatively? One explanation that I offer, following the *Politics*, is that those people suffer from a deficiency in their deliberative capacity. We reject in anger what Aristotle writes when he says that in general women and slaves suffer from some incapacity in the deliberative capacity, that "natural slaves" lack the deliberative capacity altogether, and that the deliberative capacity of women is *akuron*, that is "without authority."[108] Putting that aside, let us consider whether those who succumb to anxiety for money are not in fact better examples of some sort of weakness in the deliberative capacity, according to Aristotle, some condition in which the irrational part of the soul, manifested in *eros* and other passions, interferes with reason.[109] In other words, while putting aside Aristotle's specific and disturbing comments about women and slaves, let us take the point of his remarks in *Pol.* i.13 to be rather that there exists variation in the deliberative capacity of human beings and apply that to the case of those obsessed with money making, whom he regards as confused in regards to the purpose of life, for they are preoccupied with "living (*to zên*), rather than living well (*eû zên*)." For within Aristotle's social psychology, *all* members of a community share in a common perception of what is good and bad, just and unjust, and so on. In other words, they share in the perception that exchange of equivalents for equivalents is just, and that exchange not in accordance with nature in which a merchant makes an unfair profit, as in the case of the corn dealers, is exchange of non-equivalents, and is unjust. How is it then that the individual turns against that consensus and towards exchanging non-equivalents and making unfair profits? Through a kind of weakness of will, through which he sacrifices his life qua *eû zên* for the sake of money, for the one who is "anxious about living" destroys the leisure by which he can *eû zên* through an obsession with making money.[110] For as de Tocqueville says, the end result for the merchant is lack of leisure and mental disturbance:

(10) He who possesses a small commercial fortune (*une petite fortune mobilière*) almost always depends, more or less, on the passions of another person. He must bend either to the rules of an association or to the desires of a man. He is prey to the smallest changes in the commercial and industrial fortunes of his country. His existence is perpetually upset by the alternatives of well-being and distress, and it is rare that the turmoil that rules

his destiny does not also introduce confusion into his ideas and instability into his tastes.[111]

De Tocqueville's comments well portray how the anxious businessperson suffers from "confusion <in> his ideas." Socrates in Xenophon's *Oeconomicus* argues that such people are "slaves" to "unseen masters."[112]

(11) Slaves are they to luxury and lechery, intemperance and the wine-cup along with many a fond and ruinous ambition. These passions so cruelly belord it over the poor soul whom they have got under their thrall, that so long as he is in the heyday of health and strong to labour, they compel him to fetch and carry and lay at their feet the fruit of his toils, and to spend it on their own heart's lusts.[113]

Such people are deficient in the deliberative capacity, for they know what they should do, but anxiety and intemperance undermines their knowledge, and they act differently.[114] I propose that such a person is an example of one whose deliberative capacity is *akuron*, that is "without authority."[115] For Aristotle says of the intemperate, "To the one corrupted by pleasure and pain, no principle appears for the sake of which or by which it is necessary to choose or do any thing."[116] When it comes to acquiring the wherewithal to satisfy their lusts, they throw reason to the wind, and abandon *eû zên* for the sake of wealth accumulation. In the *Nicomachean Ethics*, Aristotle gives wealth accumulation (*chrēmastistikē*) as an example of matters about which we deliberate,[117] and therefore of matters about which we err in our deliberation. If we move from natural wealth acquisition (Natali's "chréma-tistique¹") to unnatural ("chrématistique²"), we make such an error.[118] The anxious ones err in their deliberation about what sort of activity they should engage in to support themselves, and how much time they should devote to that activity.

For Aristotle, the ancient community followed a model of life activity in which the goal is non-economic: happiness as living well and doing well (*to eû zên kai to eû prattein*). Intermediate goals are self-sufficiency (*autarkia*) and leisure, "for leisure is needed both to develop virtue and to engage in political actions."[119] By contrast the merchant is confused about the nature of happiness, and as Aristotle (with Xenophon's Socrates) says "seeks what is conducive to physical gratification." Those obsessed with making money believe happiness lies in the satisfaction of lusts, and "Since gratification lies in excess, they seek what is productive of this gratifying excess."[120] As Polanyi says, "*Money is an end in itself, the craving for it is therefore limitless. Once accepted as the means of acquiring more and more enjoyable things the idea of the good life is perverted.*"[121] For that reason, their intermediate goal is *pleonexia*, getting and acquiring more wealth than others. The merchant's activity is not leisured and does not lead to self-sufficiency since s/he is dependent on the activity, commerce and trading of others.[122] Lysias says they have forsaken their fatherland for another, their fortune, their wealth:

(12)   But those who, though citizens by birth, adopt the view that any country in which they have their business is their fatherland, are evidently men who would even abandon the public interest of their city to seek their private gain, because they regard their fortune, not the city, as their fatherland.[123]

The merchants move the community to endulge in luxury and go to war to expand that wealth that gratifies their excesses. In that way, Aristotle and his contemporaries answer Socrates' question in the *Republic* as to the origin of injustice.

Notes

1   *Rep.* ii.369c.
2   Plato (1992), 372d.
3   Cf. *Rep.* ii.372c–d.
4   Cf. *Rep.* ii.372d–373e.
5   Cf. *Rep.* ii.373a–c.
6   Cf. *Rep.* ii.373e.
7   Cf. Liddell and Scott (1897), *spoudazō* I.2 for the signification I use ("be anxious about"). On "not by nature," cf. *Pol.* i.9. 1257a4; cf. 1257a 17.
8   Cf. *Pol.* i.9.1257a28–b7.
9   Cf. *Pol.* i.9.1258a15; cf. Liddell and Scott (1897), *anagkaîos* II.1 for the signification I use ("constrained"), which is consistent with Aristotle's representation of this wealth acquisition as "without limit" (*apeiron*) (cf. Pol. 1.9.1257b40). This translation best represents Aristotle's thought.
10 Cf. *Pol.* i.2.1252a24–25.
11 Cf. *Pol.* i.2.1252b16–18. In contrast with Plato, for Aristotle, "Household becomes to city not stumbling-block, but building-brick" (cf. Price, 1990, 193).
12 Cf. *Pol.* i.2.1252b27–30. For a city-state comes to be whenever a community is large enough to become self-sufficient (cf.*Pol.* ii.2.1261b11–14; cf. also iii.9.1280b39). By Aristotle's account, city-states need not be as large as the Athens of the Peloponnesian Wars, argues Nagle (2006). He says that Athens is quite misleading as an example of the cities considered by Aristotle. Of the roughly 1,500 Greek cities, the average city would have been 25 to 100 kilometres square with 230 to 910 male citizens, according to Nagle, whereas Athens was 2,580 square kilometres with 25,000 to 40,000 citizens at the beginning of the war. On this basis Nagle argues that Aristotle's ideal city was only 2 percent to 3 percent the size of Athens and that this smaller size would have facilitated a substantially higher degree of citizen familiarity and civic participation. But I agree with Carmichael that "The fact that Athens was anomalous [i.e. atypical – R G], then, doesn't show that it was irrelevant or even marginal in Aristotle's thinking about human well being."
13 Gigon (1965), 272 says that "in *eû zên* man fulfills his destiny (*Bestimmung*)."
14 Cf. *EN* iii.3, vi.9
15 Cf. *Pol.* iii.6.1278b19–22.
16 Cf. *Pol.* iii.9.1280b33–35.

17 *Pol.* i.1253a28–9.
18 *Pol.* i.2.1253a8: *agelaiou.*
19 *Pol.* 1253a16–18. Cf. Rawls' rejection of this principle discussed in Chapter 2.
20 The slave's inclusion in the household challenges us to ask: Does the slave share
    in the "perception of what is good and bad, just and unjust, and the rest" with
    the free members? I argue that Aristotle holds that s/he does. Putting aside our
    anger at the suggestion that some are "natural slaves," let us consider Aristotle's
    text. If the slave is a slave "by nature," that is, if the slave lacks the deliberative
    capacity (cf. *Pol.* i.13.1260a12), and cannot successfully deliberate over his or her
    own future, we might wonder whether such a person could share in the ethical
    perceptions of the rest of the household. First, slaves who are not "natural slaves,"
    that is, those who have the souls of the free and are enslaved unjustly (cf. *Pol.*
    i.5.1254b33–34), as Aristotle puts it, clearly can share in the "perception of what
    is good and bad, just and unjust, and the rest," and these comprise the vast major-
    ity of slaves. Second, Aristotle defines a natural slave as "he who shares in reason
    enough to understand it, but does not possess it himself" (*Pol.* i.5.1254b22–23).
    A natural slave could therefore share in the "perception of what is good and
    bad, just and unjust, and the rest." Moreover, the rather different view of Dobbs,
    Depew and Nagle that natural slaves "are not . . . born but created," that natural
    slaves are "the product of environment rather than genetics" (cf. Nagle, 2006,
    111–112; Depew, 1981), that is through habituation, certainly implies that they
    have the capacity to share in the "perception of what is good and bad, just and
    unjust, and the rest." In conclusion, it is clear from Aristotle's text that all slaves
    can share in the "perception of what is good and bad, just and unjust, and the
    rest" with the free members of a household. Cf. Gallagher (2011a) for further
    discussion of Aristotle's theory of natural slavery.
21 That is, *EN* v.5 (3 pages) and *Pol.* i.8–10 (5½ pages). Cf. Meikle (1997). That
    limitation is false on its own face as all of *Pol.* i is devoted to political economy
    as is much of *EN* v, for example Chapters 1, 3, 4 and 6, as well as much of the
    Eudemian Ethics.
22 *Philia* signifies both friendship (or affection) and belonging to (or membership in)
    the household. Cf. Booth (1993), 517.
23 Cf. *EN* vi.5.1140b10–11. I agree with the comment of Gauthier and Jolif (2002),
    v. 2, 472 that masters of *oikoi* and statesmen are "sages purement et simplement," as
    they are concerned for the good life, in its totality, of those under their direction.
24 For discussion, cf. Kontos (2011), Chap. 1.
25 Cf. *EN* vi.5.1140b5–6.
26 Cf. *EN* vi.5.1140b5.
27 Cf. *EN* vi.5.1140b6. Murphy (1993), 91 interestingly expresses concern that
    Aristotle's distinction between *praxis* and *poiēsis* "has profound and disturbing
    implications for the dignity of work." I think Aristotle's distinction could be under-
    stood with a modern example: A machinist engages in production when s/he
    produces a machine tool, and engages in action (*praxis*) when s/he organizes a
    union meeting.
28 Contrary to Booth (1993), 36.
29 Moreover, Aristotle argues, sometimes there is also mutual benefit and friendship
    between master and slave (cf. *Pol.* i.6.1255b12–14; cf. 1255b4–15), but this is an
    experience for the minority of slaves (cf. 1255b14–15). Strangely, Booth (1993)
    36–37 asserts that the common perception of ethical values is not a common
    ground between household and city, despite Aristotle's statement that it is.
30 *Pol.* iii.9.1280b33

31 *EN* i.4.1095a19–20.

32 Cf. *EN* i.4.1095a20–22.

33 *EN* i.7.1098a12–16.

34 Cf. *Pol.* iii.9.1280b6–7.

35 Cf. *EN* 1129b11–26.

36 *EN* v.1.1129b31–30a1, 3–5.

37 Cf. *Pol.* i.8.1256b26–31. *Ktētikê,* the craft of property acquisition of a household or city-state, must be strictly distinguished from *chrēmastikē,* the craft of "making money." Booth (1993), 49 confuses them. Cf. *Pol.* i.8.1256b26–30.

38 Booth (1993), 37 says "autarky means the greatest possible independence from external forces: a way of life or a city which can stand largely on its own."

39 Cf. discussion limited to the household in Booth (1993), 31–32.

40 Cf. *Pol.* vii.9.1329a1–2, cf. also 34a15ff, 38a10ff. As Booth (1993), 8, 27 puts it, "Autarky and leisure . . . are the principal goods of the household to which its productive activities are subordinated . . . The governing purpose of the oikos: the unconstrained life, the leisure of the free . . . the object of work is to create a space in the world for beauty and leisure."

41 *EN* i.7.1097a20.

42 *EN* i.7. 1097a22–23. Cf. Kontos (2011), Chap. 1.

43 As by Booth (1993), 35 and many others.

44 Cf. Liddell and Scott (1897), *hē oikonomikē technē* under *oikonomikos.*

45 Cf. Booth (1993), 35.

46 Cf. *EN* vi.5.1140b10–11.

47 For discussion, cf. Kontos (2011), Chap. 1. Saunders in Aristotle (1995), 84 says that household managers "need time to be statesmen."

48 Cf. Liddell and Scott (1897), *alēthinos,* 2; *alēthēs,* I; cf. also Heidegger (2010), 33, 219 on *alēthēs.*

49 Cf. Natali (1990), 303–304.

50 Cf. *Pol.* i.9.1257b14–19.

51 Cf. Natali (1990), 307.

52 Cf. Aristotle (1998), i.9.1256b30–32. Jowett: "for the amount of property which is needed for a good life is not unlimited" (Aristotle, 1984). Barker and Stalley: "for the amount of household property which suffices for a good life is not unlimited" (Aristotle, 1995, i.9.1256b30–32). Jowett drops the idea of self-sufficiency from his translation. Barker and Stalley degrade the concept self-sufficiency to the mere verb "suffices." Both omit to translate *toiautēs.*

53 Cf. *Pol.* i.9.1256b31–32.

54 The translators violate *lectio difficilior potior,* the principle of textual criticism that "the more difficult reading is preferable." Though articulated by Erasmus and others as a rule in choosing which textual variant to include in the principal reading of a text, it also applies to reading content. In this case, however, the translators have gone off the deep end and chosen a non-existent reading, roughly: *hē gar toiautē ktêsis pros agathēn zōēn ouk apeiros estin.*

55 Cf. *Pol.* i.8.1256b31–57a5.

56 Cf. *Pol.* i.8.1256b37–39.

57 The verse is from Diehl (1925), I.21, f. 1.71, cited by Reeve in Aristotle (1998), 15. In *The Constitution of Athens,* Aristotle praises Solon for liberating the people by cancelling all debts for which the freedom of the borrower was the security, and prohibited future lending secured by the person of the borrower. Cf. *Ath. Resp.* 6; *Pol.* ii.12.1273b37; Howatson (1989), "Solon."

58 Finley (1982), 72.

59 Cf. *EE* 1244a24, 27–30.

60 Cf. *EN* 1120a6–7.
61 Cf. *Pol.* 1296b18.
62 Cf. *EN* 1120a8.
63 So I believe Natali (1990), 308–309 errs in arguing that it is possible to make an exchange which is at the same time just for *EN* and bad from view of "*Pol.*", if we procure for ourselves (without making dishonest gains) more wealth than would serve well the good life, for if I benefit others with that "more wealth," it serves the practice of *eû zên*.
64 Cf. *EN* i.1, *Pol. i.4*.1254a1–8.
65 Cf. *Pol. i.9*.1257b38–58a2.
66 Cf. Liddell and Scott (1897), *spoudazō* I.2 for the signification I use ("be anxious about"). Reeve translates *to spoudazein peri to zên* as "preoccupied with living" (Aristotle, 1998, 17), Barker and Stalley as "concern about living" (Aristotle, 1995, 28), and Jowett as "intent upon living only" (Aristotle, 1984, v. 2, 1996), but none of these translations, except Jowett's, provides a distinguishing mark for the one who seeks accumulation of wealth, for everyone is "preoccupied" or "concerned" with his or her own life. But those people who "persevere in saving their store of money or increasing it without limit" are appropriately called "anxious."
67 Cf. *Pol. i.9*.1257b38–58a8.
68 Cf. Pack (2010), Chap. 2, "Aristotle on the relation between capital (chrematistics) and character," for a very useful discussion.
69 Cf. *Pol.* i.9. 1257a41–b2.
70 Cf. *Pol.* i.9.1257b14–19.
71 Cf. *Pol.* i.9.1257a25–b10.
72 Cf. *Pol.* i.9.1257a30.
73 Cf. *Pol.* i.9.1257a19–34.
74 Cf. *Pol.* i.8.1256b26–30.
75 Cf. 1257b19–21.
76 Cf. *Pol.* i.9.1257a31–b2.
77 Cf. *Pol.* i.9.1257a35–41; Natali (1990) calls it "chrématistique[1]."
78 Cf. *Pol.* i.9.1257b1–8; "chrématistique[2]."
79 Cf. Saunders in Aristotle (1995), 90; Pecirca (1967) and Polanyi (1957a), 100–101 on involvement of foreigners in trade; and Lys. 22 and Polanyi on prejudice against traders. Humphreys (1978), 144 summarizes some of these reports.
80 Cf. *Pol.* 1278a25–26 and 1319a24–37, highlighted by Saunders in Aristotle (1995), 90.
81 Cf. *Pol.* iv.3.1289b32–33, 4.1290b39–91a8, 4.1291b17ff., vi.7.1321a5–6.
82 Cf. *Pol.* vi.5.1320a39.
83 Cf. Polanyi (1957a), p. 100–101; emphasis added.
84 Cf. 1257a31–41.
85 Cf. 1257b1–4; emphasis added.
86 Xen. *Oecon.* i. 20.
87 Lys. 22, ¶12. In the same speech, he says of the corn dealers: "For their interests are the opposite of other men's: they make most profit when, on some bad news reaching the city, they sell their corn at a high price. And they are so delighted to see your disasters that they either get news of them in advance of anyone else, or fabricate the rumor themselves; now it is the loss of your ships in the Black Sea, now the capture of vessels on their outward voyage by the Lacedaemonians, now the blockade of your trading ports, or the impending rupture of the truce; and they have carried their enmity to such lengths that they choose the same critical moments as your foes to overreach you. For, just when you find yourselves worst off for corn, these persons snap it up and refuse to sell it, in order to prevent our disputing about the price: we are to be glad enough if we come away from them

with a purchase made at any price, however high. And thus at times, although there is peace, we are besieged by these men. . .if you condemn these men to death, the rest will be brought to better order; while if you dismiss them unpunished, you will have voted them full licence to do just as they please. . . . far rather ought you to pity those of our citizens who perished by their villainy" (¶14–21). Booth (1993), 58–59 says: "Lysias . . . points to the powerful ethos against the exploitation of necessity and of wealth acquiring that is contrary to the needs of the city." Measures taken by Athens against "the exploitation of necessity" include placing limits on the size of corn purchases and on the profit that can be made on a sale, which were both enforced to keep the price low.

88 Cf. *Pol.* i.9.1257a4
89 Cf. *Pol.* i.9.1257a12–13.
90 Cf. *Pol.* i.9.1257b20–22.
91 *Pol.* i.9.1257a21–30.
92 Cf. Booth (1993), 34–93.
93 1257b20–22. Cf. Polanyi, 1944, 54 and Chap. 2.
94 Cf. Chap. 1.
95 Cf. *EN* 1130a32.
96 Cf. *EN* 1163b8–9.
97 Cf. 1163b1–14.
98 *EN* v.5.1132b33–33a1. On phronetic perception, cf. Kontos (2011), Chap. 1.
99 *Pol.* i.9.1257b35–38.
100 Cf. *EN* v.5.
101 Cf. *Pol.* i.9.1258a8–10.
102 Cf. *Pol.* i.9.1258a12–14.
103 Cf. Chap. 2.
104 Cf. Wolff (1982), 86–87; cf. Wolff (1981).
105 Cf. *EN* v.2.1130b30–32, 3.1131a25-29, *Pol.* iii.12.1283a3–11, *EN* iv.1.1120a6–7.
106 Cf. *Pol.* i.9.1258a10–14.
107 Cf. *Pol.* i.9.1257b41.
108 Cf. *Pol.* i.13.1259b18–60a24, esp. 1260a12–14. Interestingly, Nagle (2006, 169) argues, as in the case of the "natural slave," that the alleged "Women's deficient deliberative capacity" was not genetic but environmentally determined: it "was simply the result of a lack of opportunity," that is limited education or experience with responsibilities that required deliberation. He adds that "It was compensated for only partially by women's important role in public religious affairs."
109 Cf. *Pol. i.*13.1260a6–7 on *alogon* part of soul.
110 As Booth (1993), 9 notes, the commercial trader pursues a "not leisured" existence. Garver (2011), 24 says he should be denied citizenship in the *polis*: "People who organize their lives around acquiring wealth are slavish, even if not slaves, because to aim at wealth is to aim at satisfying the ends of people other than oneself . . . Organizing one's life around living rather than living well produces slavishness that goes deep enough to disqualify one from Aristotelian citizenship. To this extent, then, slavishness is a permanent practical problem . . . The irony of history is at work here. Slavery was finally abolished in part due to the triumph of slavishness, that is, lives of unlimited acquisition produced a new economic order that made slavery seem anachronistic, and made it possible for modern economies to flourish without slave labor. While most people have to be coerced into being slaves, no such compulsion is necessary for living slavishly . . . Capitalism abolished slavery by making slavishness universal." According to Garver's reasoning, today's stock broker, real estate agent,

CEO, attorney and so on would not qualify for Aristotelian citizenship, for they "organize their lives around acquiring wealth."
111 De Tocqueville (1988), 67–68. Trans. from Booth (1993), 53.
112 Cf. Xen. *Oecon.* 1.18ff.
113 Cf. Xen. *Oecon.* 1.20.
114 Unfortunately, such people acquire responsibility over those devoted to *eû zên*.
115 Cf. *Pol.* i.13.1260a12–14.
116 *EN* vi.5.1140b17–19.
117 Cf. *EN* iii.3.1112b4.
118 Cf. Natali (1990), 307.
119 Cf. *Pol.* vii.9.1328b38–29a2.
120 Cf. *Pol.* i.9.1257b38–58a8.
121 Cf. Polanyi (1959), 6.
122 Booth (1993), 9 offers contrasting models of *oikos* and trader, but he imagines *pleonexia* is goal of trader's activity rather than some notion of happiness.
123 Lys. 31.6.

8   Incommensurability and Aristotle's theory of value

Aristotle develops a theory of value that is able to represent exchange between members of a community who are unequal, such as those who differ in function, wealth or power.

Near the outset of his discussion of reciprocal justice in the *Nicomachean Ethics*, Aristotle states what he considers to be the central problem of the exchange of goods between two different parties, that those who are "different and not equal" (*ouk isoi*) must somehow "be made equal."[1] He emphasizes that such individuals and their work or products (*erga*) "in reality" are not "commensurable" (that is, there is no common factor between them), but they can nonetheless be made "sufficiently" commensurable with respect to "need."[2] With these statements, Aristotle identifies difficulties in the subject matter of reciprocal justice, for things that are unequal can never be made equal, and things that are incommensurable can never be made strictly commensurable.[3] Critics, however, have put aside the difficulties posed by Aristotle and deny that parties to an exchange are unequal and incommensurable. One concludes that Aristotle's claim of incommensurability "is tantamount to an admission that he does not know what is equalized in fair exchanges of food, shoes and houses," and amounts to an "admission of failure" in the task he sets out for himself in Chapter 5 of Book v of the *Nicomachean Ethics* (hereafter called "*EN* v.5").[4] Critics have also set aside Aristotle's view that the inequality of the exchangers must figure in an exchange. One has objected that "Private property could not conceivably be exchanged in anything like this way. The idea is absurd."[5] Aristotle's claim of commensurability via "need" is also rejected.[6] We are thus presented with two kinds of difficulties, one that Aristotle identifies in the subject matter, and another in our attempts to understand the way he views exchange relations, for a rejection of Aristotle's views may reflect a failure to understand those views. Such difficulties impede progress. As Aristotle explains, if there is a difficulty in our thinking in regards to an investigation, what we suffer resembles the condition of those who are tied up, for it is impossible to go forward.[7] Accordingly, our efforts to understand Aristotle's thought will fail, until we come to terms with the difficulties identified here. I believe that it is the absence of proper attention to the difficulties of inequality and incommensurability that accounts for much of the confusion and puzzlement over *EN* v.5, and in particular, over interpretation of the proportions that Aristotle introduces there, and over the meaning of "diagonal pairing" (*hē kata diametron suzeuxis*).[8] It is the task of this chapter and the following one to confront and resolve those problems. I defend Aristotle here. To do that, in this chapter and the next, I attempt to explain: 1) What Aristotle means when he says that it is impossible for two sharers or their *erga* to be commensurable; 2) the extent to which the variables in Aristotle's proportions can be quantified; 3) what diagonal pairing is; 4) how need makes sharers and their *erga* "sufficiently" commensurable; and, finally, 5) Aristotle's theory of what is just in exchange. In doing that, I try to synthesize the useful contributions of other authors with my own research. To define Aristotle's terminology, I refer to passages outside the *Nicomachean Ethics*, in the *Eudemian Ethics*, the *Politics*, the *Physics* and elsewhere.

In this chapter and the next, I represent Aristotle's thought with a series of algebraic formulae. These simply represent mathematically what I already express in words. It is not necessary to understand the mathematics to understand what this book is saying. Why then include the mathematics at all? The answer is that the mathematics compels us to grapple with Aristotle's ideas.

Incommensurability

Investigators have disagreed whether Aristotle holds that only the products (*erga*) of the members or sharers (*koinōnoi*) of a community (*koinōnia*), as he calls them, are incommensurable, or also the sharers themselves who produce the *erga*, or neither.[9] So, it is first necessary to determine what things, if any, Aristotle regards as incommensurable. Aristotle raises the issue of incommensurability in his discussion of fair exchange in *EN* v.5. Much of the chapter is devoted to examining the relation among pairs of sharers who exchange their different *erga* with each other to satisfy each other's needs, an act fundamental to Aristotle's conception of the *polis*, an act that manifests the interdependency among the different types of individuals upon which the *polis* is based, for the sharers need each other's *erga* − a house (*oikia*), nourishment (*trophē*), shoes (*hupodēma*), health (*hugieia*) − as part of the necessary ingredients of life for their households. That is why they come together and that is why they stay together. As Aristotle says: "need holds a community together as if it were a single entity, for whenever people do not need each other . . . they do not exchange,"[10] and without exchange there is no community.[11] Aristotle presents the problem of exchange as follows:

(1) It is not from two doctors that a community arises, but from a doctor and a farmer, and in general from those who are different and not equal (*ouk isoi*); nonetheless, these people (*toutous*) must be made equal (*isasthēnai*). That is the reason that everything − of which there is exchange − must somehow be comparable (*sumblēta*).[12]

That passage puts before us the problem: How can the unequal be equalized, the incomparable be compared? Passage (1) breaks down into the following antinomy:

a)   A community arises from people who are *not equal*, but
b)   Those same people must somehow *be made equal* for there to be exchange, and *that* is necessary for the community to stay together.

Formally speaking a) is incompatible with b). Practically speaking, Aristotle says we must find a way to resolve that formal incompatibility. That is one difficulty that Aristotle sees is inherent in communal reciprocal exchange. He emphasizes that what is just in exchange is proportional, for the *polis* stays together through proportional reciprocal action.[13] He expresses the problem in algebraic symbols, which he places into proportion with each other. "Let a farmer be α, nourishment γ, a shoemaker β, his *ergon* that is equalized δ."[14] He proposes for consideration the following proportion:

(2)   As farmer is to shoemaker, so the *ergon* of the shoemaker is to that of the farmer,[15]

or restating (2) with the symbols he assigns:

(A)
$$\frac{\alpha}{\beta} = \frac{\delta}{\gamma}$$

Proportion A represents, for examination, the described relation of pairs of sharers exchanging their *erga*. Aristotle has built into the terms of this proportion the very incomparability with which he is trying to reckon. In doing so, he demonstrates the truly scientific character of his thought, for he does not attempt to reduce an incommensurable quantity to a rational one, but builds such qualitative difference into his analysis, which becomes, as a result, rather powerful.

Aristotle introduces the ratio $\frac{\alpha}{\beta}$ in *EN* v.3 when he is presenting a general introduction to his treatment of distributive, corrective and reciprocal justice. He says that since the unjust person is unequal and the unjust thing is unequal, clearly there exists a mean of the unjust and this is the equal, for in whatever action there is a more and a less, there is also the equal. Aristotle concludes that justice must be a mean between "the more" (that is profit) and "the less" (that is loss) with respect to two persons and two objects of interest (*pragmata*), that is goods.[16] Because of that, justice must be represented by four terms, two for the persons involved and two for the objects.[17] Parties to a transaction are usually "unequal" (*anisou, mē isoi*),[18] as represented in the ratio $\frac{\alpha}{\beta}$; in the language of the *Eudemian Ethics* one party is "superior" (*huperechōn*),[19] the other "lesser" (*elattō*)[20] or "outdone" (*huperechomenos*).[21] Aristotle concludes his introductory remarks in *EN* v.3 by saying that "justice is something proportional" in at least four terms,[22] as in Proportion A, above.

Note that in his determination of the number of terms necessary in formulae representing justice, Aristotle calls parties to a transaction "unjust" (*adikos*).[23] Clearly, someone who claims more than his due (*pleonektēs*) and uses superior wealth or power to exploit an exchange partner, is unjust.[24] But Aristotle also means that the party exploited is unjust, for the just is a mean between profit and loss,[25] and the exploited party suffers from character defects as well, for example subservience.

By including the ratio $\frac{\alpha}{\beta}$ in formula A, Aristotle makes possible a certain social criticism. The exchange, though proportional, is not equal, for the quantity of the *ergon* each sharer receives is determined not only by the relative value of the *erga* but also by the ratio $\frac{\alpha}{\beta}$, which does not equal 1 because the sharers are not equal.[26] According to Aristotle, some comparison of the parties traditionally played a role in distribution and exchange. Aristotle indicates in *EN* v.3 and viii.14 that the ratio $\frac{\alpha}{\beta}$ signifies the relative worth or merit of the parties to a transaction (*to kat' axian*).[27] It represents the initial social conditions prior to an exchange. Therefore, what Aristotle calls *metadosis* ("the giving of a share"), what we have come to call exchange, is a "status transaction."[28] Merit, Aristotle says in *Nicomachean Ethics*, Book v, Chapter 3, signifies different things to different people: "wealth" to oligarchs, "freedom," that is the status of being a free citizen, to democrats,[29] "virtue" to aristocrats. Wealth seems easily quantifiable.[30] In reality all three can be operative at the same time to varying degrees, as they were in the Athenian democracy, and are also today in many nations. (Aristotle evaluates worth with respect to the function [*ergon*] that a sharer fulfills in a community, as discussed in Chapter 6.)

In *EN* v.4, Aristotle presents a quantitative illustration of one use of $\frac{\alpha}{\beta}$: "the just distribution from common assets (*chrēmata*) will accord with the very same ratio [$\frac{\alpha}{\beta}$] that deposits have to one another," where α represents the deposit of party α, β that of party β, γ the distribution to α, and δ the distribution to β, so that[31]

(B) $$\frac{\alpha}{\beta} = \frac{\gamma}{\delta}$$

This is the same proportion that we derived in Chapter 6 from Proportion P, Aristotle's universal producers-to-products proportion. When Proportion B represents distribution from common assets, the relative positions of α and β are unchanged by such a distribution, so that[32]

(B') $$\frac{\alpha}{\beta} = \frac{\alpha + \gamma}{\beta + \delta}$$

Note that the quantities in Proportion B could be commensurable with each other if the deposits were made in comparable assets (e.g. both in currency or both in grain, for example). So, though α and β may be unequal, they need not be incommensurable. That is not the case in regards to the proportions treated in *EN* v.5, however, for there Aristotle presents a second antithesis in two contrary passages, one of which affirms quite the contrary. In the first, he says:

(3) Everything must be measured by some one thing, just as was said earlier. And that, in reality, is need (*chreia*), which holds everything together.[33]

Aristotle says, need holds a community together and, by custom, currency represents need and as a measure makes things commensurable and equalizes them, for there would be no community unless there were exchange, and no exchange unless there were equality, and no equality unless there were commensurability.[34] But then, he seems to contradict passage (3) in saying:

(4a) In reality, it is impossible for things that differ so much to be commensurable (*summetra*).

And then rephrasing his assertion of passage (3), he adds:

(4b) but they admit of becoming sufficiently so with respect to need.[35]

Aristotle does not explain in *EN* v.5 why the terms of Proportion A are incommensurable, or how "need" measures incommensurable quantities and make them "sufficiently" commensurable. In Chapter 6, I explain what Aristotle means by incommensurable and why different sharers in a community are incommensurable with each other. Below I outline Aristotle's concept of need and its role in his theory of value.

Need and function

After stating that in reality, it is impossible for the terms of Proportion A to be commensurable, Aristotle says, in the second half of the passage that "they admit of becoming sufficiently so with respect to need," a comment that accords with passage (3) where he says that need measures all things. But if need measures all things, on what grounds does he say at the same time that the terms of Proportion A are incommensurable? Either they are incommensurable or they are not, and if they are incommensurable, they have no common measure,[36] whether that be need or anything else.

Regarding Aristotle's term, *chreia*, it is clear that it "means 'need' and not 'demand' in the modern economists' utilitarian sense of 'demand and supply.' Nor does the term have anything to do with modern utilitarian theories of subjective preference."[37] But one critic rejects Aristotle's claim of commensurability through need on the grounds that "need . . . inheres in the exchangers rather than the products."[38] That argument is inconsistent with Aristotle's theory of goods (*ktēma*) in *Pol.* i.9, where Aristotle says that a shoe "does not come to be for the sake of exchange" but for someone "who needs a shoe" to protect the foot, for this is its *telos* and its "proper use" (*hē chrēsis . . . hē men oikeia*).[39] At the same time as it is a property of exchangers to have needs (for health, nutrition, shoes, housing), it is a property of *erga* to satisfy those needs, and that is the reason for the existence of those *erga*.[40] Thus need relates *erga* and exchangers to each other. It is common to all things to which the terms in Proportion A refer.

Chapter 6 contains a thorough discussion of the homonymy of *ergon*, which we summarize here. *Ergon* signifies not only a product or service provided but also the artisan who provides it, for providing that product (*ergon*) is his function (*ergon*) in the community, a function he performs by applying his art (*technē*), for the *function* of a house builder in the community is to build houses for other sharers, and this is his *work* (*ergon*). Accordingly, *ergon* is a case of what Shields calls *core-dependent homonymy*, for the definition of *ergon* as product is dependent on the definition of *ergon* as work that produces that product, and both depend on the definition of *ergon* as function of the human being who performs that work and produces that product.[41] Each signification refers to a distinct entity with a distinct essence.[42] Thus, α, β refer to one signification of *ergon* (function), and γ, δ refer to another (product).

Aristotle's proportions are derivable by analogy from the relations of producers and products, for as shoemaker is to shoes, so are doctor to health, farmer to nourishment, carpenter to bed, and house builder to house, which analogies lead to the following proportion for any two producer/product pairs:[43]

(P)
$$\frac{\alpha}{\gamma} = \frac{\beta}{\delta}$$

Proportion P represents the fundamental concept of Aristotle's theory of value: The value of any product is proportional to the function of its producer in the community of the *polis*, so that any two different products can be put into relation with each other through the fundamental social relation of sharer-producer to sharer-producer. Via Proportion P, the value of a good is understood in relation to its producer and in relation to any other good for which it is exchangeable and produced by another producer. It is then not surprising to see that Proportion P is the source for Proportion B via a simple algebraic transformation. Through that, Proportion B is revealed to be a rule for *distribution by function*, as in the flute example discussed in Chapter 6.[44] As I show in the next chapter, Proportion A arises from Proportion B through the way social relations affect exchange.

Thus Aristotle replaces conventional Greek signifiers of worth, "wealth," "freedom" and "virtue" with function (*ergon*) as his signifier.[45] I have drawn "function" out of Aristotle's text. It subsumes previous suggestions for what Aristotle means by "worth," that is "skill", "quality of labour" and "social value" of work.[46] We can say, to a first approximation, that in Aristotle's economic thought, $\frac{\alpha}{\beta}$ signifies the relative worth of the functions of two sharers in a community. Yet Aristotle does not separate the human being's function from the human being itself. His reasoning is this: The functions of doctor and farmer differ (cf. passage (1)). Therefore, their worth differs. In passage (4) Aristotle compares persons of different *erga* and asserts, in accordance with his functionalist views, that they are incommensurable. I refer the reader to Chapter 6 for discussion of the type of incommensurability of the sharers, and of the incomparability and incommensurability of the alterations they carry out to produce their products.

Quantifying Aristotle's incommensurables

There is no difficulty in performing calculations with incommensurable quantities. But what Aristotle challenges us to do raises special difficulties, for the problem is not only that *erga* and sharers are incommensurable but that quantifying those terms relative to each other is problematic. It is literally akin to comparing apples with oranges, or, rather, with houses. Such difficulty arises when we try to compare shoes (the *ergon* of the shoemaker) with health (that of the doctor) or nourishment (that of the farmer). Health is a *condition* that a doctor seeks to restore to a patient with treatment that the doctor administers based on a diagnosis of the patient's condition of illness.[47] How is that comparable with a house or shoes, which are objects, not conditions? At first glance, nourishment seems easily quantifiable, for it appears reducible to agricultural commodities that the farmer chooses to produce and bring to market. But, for Aristotle, "nourishment" (*trophe*) is a homonymous term that signifies 1) nourishing food (I call this *trophe*$_1$),[48] and 2) a state produced in the body by the soul (*trophe*$_2$)[49] from the nutritive capacity acting upon *trophe*$_1$. Aristotle seems to hold that a farmer has a vital mission to his community, to provide *trophe*$_1$ as raw material to sustain *trophe*$_2$. Thus the farmer provides things needed for sustaining the very being of his fellow sharers, for "whatever is deprived of nourishment cannot exist."[50] We could say that about health also, but we cannot say that, at least not in the same way, for shoes, beds, or houses. Moreover, examples of *trophe*$_1$ are themselves substances (i.e. fruits, vegetables, grains, etc.) in contrast to the artifacts produced by the shoemaker and house builder.[51] We can certainly analyse *trophe*$_1$ into so many tomatoes, heads of lettuce or kilos of fish. Yet, it is defined by its essential relation to *trophe*$_2$.

We can begin to quantify these *erga* by organizing them as members of an ordered set, of which we can say whether $x_i < x_j$ but we do not yet know, or are even yet able to estimate $\frac{x_i}{x_j}$. An example of such a set would be all *genē*, that is invertebrates < vertebrates < mammals, or the set of feudal identities, that is peasant < manor lord < knight < king. Aristotle discusses such ordered sets in other works.[52] In *EN* v.5 he orders the *erga* that he discusses by making the γ term refer to the more valuable *ergon* of the superior party α. Here we can say, therefore, that the *erga* form an ordered set E, in which shoes < houses < health, and shoes < nourishment, but we do not know the value of $\frac{\delta}{\gamma}$ for any pair of those *erga*.[53] In passage (2) presenting Proportion A and in his definition of its terms,[54] Aristotle does not define quantities but only speaks of "nourishment" and the "*ergon* of the shoemaker" or the "*ergon* of the farmer." His first mention of quantities in *EN* v.5, "however many shoes," is indefinite. With that indefinite quantity he presents a case of Proportion A: "Just as house builder is to shoemaker, so must so many shoes be to a house or nourishment."[55] Again, he presents us with an indefinite quantity, and that is emphasized with the inclusion of the alternative "nourishment" in the formulation. The point of the text there is that we must find some way to quantify *erga* relative to each other even though, as he says later, they are incommensurable, for if we do not, "there will be neither exchange nor a community."[56] Aristotle's example of an exchange of beds and a house is an illustration of the sufficient commensurability of which he speaks in passage (4b) and elsewhere in *EN* v.5. I restate Aristotle's antinomies of passages (4a) and (b) in the following formulae.

Since, as Meikle has shown, shoes, houses, nourishment and health are incommensurables, we cannot arrive at an exact exchange ratio of those *erga*. Therefore,

(A₁)
$$\frac{\delta}{\gamma} \neq \frac{N_\delta}{N_\gamma}$$

where N subscripted is the quantity of *ergon* δ or γ. Aristotle does not say that so many shoes or five beds "in reality" equals one house, for that would mean that shoes and houses are commensurable. Rather, he says that we can have only sufficient commensurability: we can only approximate their relative value, that is

(A₂)
$$\frac{\delta}{\gamma} \approx \frac{N_\delta}{N_\gamma}$$

where we use $\approx$ to indicate the reduction involved in expressing $\frac{\delta}{\gamma}$ as a rational number. It is the need of the sharers that brings them to settle upon five beds or so many shoes for a house. Such proportions are not based on any intrinsic characteristic of the *erga*, except the fact that they satisfy needs of the exchangers. As Irwin comments, Proportion A "suggests that α and β achieve equality when the price that α pays for the shoes corresponds to his need for them."[57] Insofar as the *erga* are shoes, houses, nourishment and health, the proportions are arbitrary.[58] Agreement on those proportions, however, is what makes it possible to express the exchange in money. We do that with the following rule: The quantity of one good exchanged for the quantity of another is the inverse ratio of their unit prices.[59] Thus

(A₃)
$$\frac{N_\delta}{N_\gamma} = \frac{P_\gamma}{P_\delta}$$

where P as subscripted is the unit price of *ergon* δ or γ. For Aristotle's example of the exchange of five beds for one house:

(A₄)
$$\frac{N_{beds}}{N_{houses}} = \frac{5\,beds}{1\,house} = \frac{P_{house}}{P_{bed}} = \frac{5\,minae}{1\,mina} = 5.$$

Difficulties also arise in attempts to compare the persons involved in an exchange, as is suggested in the ratio $\frac{\alpha}{\beta}$. I consider first whether it is possible to arrive at a value of the ratio if the terms signify worth of function of the persons. Aristotle has left us an example of persons who differ in worth of function in his contrast between the activities of doctors and house builders in respect to nature and form in the *Parts of Animals* (*PA*). Since he refers to both doctors and house builders in *EN* v.5 it is useful to bring the *PA* text into this discussion. Aristotle says that a doctor determines how to bring a patient to health by thought (*dianoia*), while a house builder determines the house he builds by perception (*aisthēsis*).[60] That is, the doctor deduces the patient's internal physiological condition by evaluating various observable signs of health and illness: he must draw inferences to determine diagnosis and treatment. By contrast, the house builder conceives of a house via his faculty of perception and his memory of past perceptions of houses. The activity of the doctor differs in form from that of the house builder: What the doctor does is not as self-evident as what the house builder does. For those reasons, both they and their *erga* differ, and are incommensurable. They differ in "worth." Because the doctor uses the faculty of thought in producing his *ergon*, his *ergon* is worth more than goods produced only with the use of the faculty of perception, such as houses. We may disagree with Aristotle here, but his own view is clear. The doctor and his *ergon* are worth more in Aristotle's estimation.[61] Combining these observations with passage (1) and Aristotle's use of the α term to represent the superior party, we can say that Aristotle's sharers constitute an ordered set K in which shoemaker < house builder < doctor, and shoemaker < farmer < doctor, but we do not know the value of $\frac{\alpha}{\beta}$ for any two members of the set. Let us now consider a relation suggested by A and A_2, that is

(A$_5$) $$\frac{\alpha}{\beta} \approx \frac{N_\delta}{N_\gamma}$$

Using A_5 to interpret Aristotle's example of the exchange of beds and a house, $\frac{\alpha}{\beta} \approx \frac{N_\delta}{N_\gamma} = \frac{P_\gamma}{P_\delta} = 5$. If we accept A_5, the worth of the house builder is estimated as five times that of the bed maker. That would seem to be disturbing, for suppose the bed maker made seven beds in the same amount of time that the house builder produced a single house? Would that circumstance not make him worth more than the house builder, or at least worth as much? But, as Meikle has argued, no concept of labour time plays a role or even exists in Aristotle's economic thought.[62] Rather, Aristotle seems more concerned with the need that is met by a sharer's work than with the amount of time required to complete the work. A doctor restores patients to health, a farmer provides nourishment, house builders build houses, and shoemakers and bed makers produce shoes and beds. The worth of function depends on the worth of the produced good that satisfies a need. It is fine that a bed maker produces 20 beds in the time that the house builder completes a house, but my need for a bed is satisfied by one. The need-satisfying unit of the bed maker's work is one bed, not two, not five. Likewise, the need-satisfying unit of the house builder's function is one house, for a sharer in Aristotle's hypothetical community needs only one house. The point here is that, given two skills, if the need-satisfying unit of one is greater than the other, as a house is to a shoe, then the first skill is worth more than the other. Moreover, house building and bed making differ in scale. Building a house is generally a considerably larger enterprise than making a bed. Multiple persons may be involved, which immediately raises the need for supervision of some, so that the function of the house builder in part involves organizing others, for example carpenters. A variety of other skills and materials may also be required. But for bed making, a single carpenter working with wood will suffice in most cases. It is therefore not unreasonable to say that the worth of the house builder is greater than that of the bed maker. We have thus, for one case, drawn out of Aristotle's text a quantification of $\frac{\alpha}{\beta}$.

Yet a caveat is in order here. This treatment has considered the comparatively easy case of the relative worth of function of artisans who produce artifacts. What do we say of the worth of the doctor or the farmer, however? The *ergon* of the farmer is nourishment. What is the unit of nourishment? One potato? A bushel? Or a basket of agricultural goods sufficient to sustain *trophe*$_2$, and for how long? And how much compares with a house? An amount that would nourish me for the life of the house? The only answer to these questions in Aristotle's text is that sharers barter with each other to arrive at the in fact arbitrary quotient $\frac{N\delta}{N\gamma}$ so that they can meet their needs.[63] So, yes, the doctor will trade with the house builder and the farmer with the shoemaker, despite their incommensurability. When the operative worth of a sharer is based on function, such a transaction can produce a fair result.

Exploitation

But where conventional Greek (and contemporary) notions of worth (e.g. wealth, status as a free citizen, virtue) are invoked, matters external to the production of the *erga* determine the exchange, for the conventional measures each express one or other Greek social system, that is oligarchy, democracy, and aristocracy. An estimation of worth based on any of these three amounts to social status or relative power, which as an externality introduces arbitrariness into the exchange, so that prices would be *skewed* to the advantage of the sharer superior in whatever external respect is deemed important. Then, the point of $\frac{\alpha}{\beta}$ is to state a reality through which to interpret transactions, that is, that all exchange is overshadowed by the social relations between the exchangers.[64] This becomes more evident upon further consideration of Proportion A to ascertain whether either expression in it determines the other, that is, to what extent Proportion A, taken as an identity statement, represents the determination of $\frac{\delta}{\gamma}$ by $\frac{\alpha}{\beta}$ or of $\frac{\alpha}{\beta}$ by $\frac{\delta}{\gamma}$. To clarify the issue, we first consider the application of Proportion B to determine distributions from a common fund, an example of how one expression in an equation represents a state or condition that determines the value of another expression. In the case of proportionate withdrawals from a common fund, $\frac{\alpha}{\beta}$ determines $\frac{\gamma}{\delta}$, since the amounts of the original deposits of the parties set how much each party can withdraw in relation to the other. Returning to Proportion A, we consider whether $\frac{\alpha}{\beta}$ determines $\frac{\delta}{\gamma}$ or vice versa. It seems that $\frac{\alpha}{\beta}$ represents an external condition that exists prior to the exchange, and even prior to the production of the *erga*, insofar as it refers to the relative socio-political standing of the two exchangers. Again, it seems that a pre-existing condition represented by the expression $\frac{\alpha}{\beta}$ skews the value of the ratio $\frac{\delta}{\gamma}$ to the advantage of the stronger. (Case studies illustrating the impact of $\frac{\alpha}{\beta}$ in contemporary exchange appear in Chapter 12.)

With that in mind, I investigate situations where $\frac{\alpha}{\beta} > 1$. Such situations will vary depending on which signification of α and β is in effect, that is whether α and β signify one of the conventional Greek notions of worth (e.g. wealth, status as a free citizen, etc.), that is in one form or another, "status," or whether they signify worth of function (Aristotle's notion of worth), for function differs from the conventional measures of worth insofar as it signifies a sharer's activity in providing useful *erga* to other sharers.

On the one hand, if $\frac{\alpha}{\beta}$ signifies the relative status of two sharers, and $\frac{\alpha}{\beta} > 1$, then party β hands over to party α more of his product than the product of party α is worth by the factor $\frac{\alpha}{\beta}$, for in accordance with A₅,

(A₆) $$N_\delta \approx \frac{\alpha}{\beta} N_\gamma$$

That means that party α is materially rewarded through the transaction due to possessing a higher status. That higher relative status skews the exchange ratio. The result is that the price of the *ergon* of party α is higher than its value, that is

(A₇) $$\frac{P_\gamma}{P_\delta} > \frac{V_\gamma}{V_\delta}$$

where V is the unit value of *ergon* δ or γ. Party α exploits party β. Here with Aristotle we distinguish between the proper use of a good and its use as an item for exchange,[65] and take into account the fact that prices as exchange-values may not always reflect the use value of a good.[66]

On the other hand, if $\frac{\alpha}{\beta}$ signifies the relative function of two sharers, and $\frac{\alpha}{\beta} > 1$, then party α may be materially rewarded through the transaction due to performing a function that is more essential to, or more highly valued within the community. In that case, one possibility is

(A$_8$)
$$\frac{P_\gamma}{P_\delta} \approx \frac{V_\gamma}{V_\delta}$$

that is sharer α is rewarded directly in proportion to worth. Then, the higher relative worth determines the exchange ratio. Another possibility is:

(A$_9$)
$$\frac{P_\gamma}{P_\delta} < \frac{V_\gamma}{V_\delta}$$

that is the price that sharer α receives for *ergon* γ is less than its value, that is the compensation is not in proportion to worth. An example of A$_9$ might be a doctor's compensation for saving the life of a patient, for the patient cannot truly pay the doctor for what the doctor has done, for "what could a man give in exchange for his life."[67] Aristotle comments that "friendship seeks what is possible, not that <strictly> in accordance with worth."[68] In such a case, $\frac{\alpha}{\beta} > \frac{N_\delta}{N_\gamma} = \frac{P_\gamma}{P_\delta}$, for example the doctor is not fully compensated in proportion to worth.

In conclusion, Aristotle's theory of value states that the value of a good is a relationship between the good, its producer-exchanger, and any other good for which it is exchanged and the producer-exchanger of that good, so that from (A),

(A$_{10}$)
$$\delta = \frac{\alpha}{\beta}\gamma$$

where δ is the product of superior party α, and γ the product of party β, or

(A$_6$)
$$N_\delta \approx \frac{\alpha}{\beta} N_\gamma$$

Then by (A$_3$) and (A$_5$), the price of δ is

(A$_{11}$)
$$P_\delta \approx P_\gamma \frac{\beta}{\alpha}$$

Marx's criticisms of Aristotle's theory of value

Karl Marx, however, in his critique of Aristotle in *Capital*, claims that Aristotle's theory of political economy suffers from "the absence of any concept of value."[69] Aristotle, Marx says, "gives up the further analysis of the form of value" when he says of exchanged *erga* that they cannot be commensurable.[70] Few scholars have dared challenge Marx's assessment.[71] Even those sympathetic with Aristotle accept his argument.[72] Following Marx, one scholar asserts that Aristotle "does not know what exchange value is in his technical sense of 'what x is'."[73] One reason for such aping of Marx's reading of Aristotle may be that Marx is the only modern political economist to take Aristotle's economic thought seriously.[74] It may come rather as a surprise, therefore, to discover that it does not take much to call into question, and even refute, Marx's claim that Aristotle "gives up" the analysis of the form of value. One need only check the passage from Aristotle's text that Marx cites. We find that Marx elided the conclusion of Aristotle's *men . . . de* construction, which is our passage (4b), reprinted here:

> But they [e.g. the *erga*] admit of becoming sufficiently so [i.e. commensurable] with respect to need.

That conclusion appears to overturn Marx's claims regarding Aristotle's economic thought, for Aristotle says that *erga* can be sufficiently commensurable. Furthermore, our entire discussion in this chapter shows that Aristotle does not "give up the further analysis of the form of value," but rather develops a highly elaborate theory, which I argue has more explanatory power than those of modern economists, including Marx. Marx's differences with Aristotle are best understood in relation to three points: Marx's argument for the strict commensurability of goods, Marx's inability to represent the effect of inequality in exchange, and Marx's rejection of Aristotle's view that people differ in kind.

Marx's argument for the commensurability of goods

Though Marx agrees with Aristotle that different work and different products are qualitatively different,[75] contrary to Aristotle he also asserts that commodities are strictly commensurable because they all contain a common ingredient, which he calls *menschliche Arbeit* ("human work").[76] His argument that commodities contain a common ingredient appears early in *Capital*. He says:

> Let us take two commodities, *e.g.*, corn and iron. Whatever their exchange proportion (*Austauschverhältnis*) may be, it is always representable in an equation in which a given quantity of corn is set equal to some quantity of iron: *e.g.*,
>
> (D₁)   1 quarter corn = 1 cwt. iron.
>
> What does this equation tell us? That there exists in common something of the same quantity in two different things, in 1 quarter corn and also in 1 cwt. iron. The two things must therefore be equal to a third, which in itself is neither the one nor the other. Each of the two, so far as it is exchange value, must therefore be reducible to this third.
> A simple geometrical example illustrates this. In order to determine and compare the area of any rectilinear figure, one decomposes them into triangles . . . In the same way the exchange values of the commodities are reducible to something common, of which they represent a greater or less quantity.[77]

In this passage, Marx claims that exchange relations, such as (D₁), are equalities like the equation

(D$_2$)   *2 cm * 15 cm = 3 cm * 10 cm*

stating that two rectilinear areas are equal. Each of the two areas can be reduced to the same number of right isosceles triangles with unit sides. Marx claims that, in the same way (*ebenso*), the two commodities of (D$_1$) are reducible to a common factor. But the areas on the right and left of (D$_2$) are decomposable into triangles *by definition*, as are all rectilinear areas. There is, however, nothing common by definition between iron and corn. Iron is composed of an inorganic material, elemental iron. Corn is the fruit of a plant, of a biological process of growth and reproduction. The work involved is also very different. In the first, workers tend a blast furnace. In the second, a farmer superintends the living processes of nature, which produce the product for him. The sort of formal mathematics that reduces rectilinear areas to so many triangles cannot relate goods that are so different.

Commodity exchanges are arrived at by negotiation, as in a market, not from any formal properties shared by the commodities. Formulae like (D$_1$) are not strict or formal equalities but approximations to which exchanging parties arrive through the negotiation implicit in all exchange. Rather, what is truly evident, is that if two parties arrive at agreement to exchange quantities of each other's goods, it is because they are satisfied that their needs are fulfilled by that exchange, at least as well as they are able to negotiate that. It is need that brings the sharers to settle upon so many shoes for a house. Such proportions as (D$_1$) are not based on any intrinsic characteristic of the *erga*, except the fact that they satisfy needs of the exchangers. Insofar as the *erga* are shoes, houses, nourishment and health, or iron and corn, the proportions are arbitrary. If different goods are of different quality, as Marx argues otherwise in *Capital*, then they are incommensurable; in formulae, they can only approximate each other's value.

Marx argues that the third thing to which 1 quarter corn and 1 cwt. iron are "reducible" is "abstract human work" (*abstrakt menschliche Arbeit*), which he also names "undifferentiated human work." It is the presence of "abstract human work" in both iron and corn that makes it possible to equate so much iron to so much corn, and therefore makes them exchangeable. How then is "abstract human work" defined? we ask. Significantly, Marx admits in *Capital* that the reduction of which he speaks occurs only insofar as one commodity is exchanged for another and thereby has an exchange value, as he says in connection with an exchange of linen for a coat.

> [I]t is true that the tailoring, which makes the coat, is concrete work of a different sort from the weaving which makes the linen. But the act of equating it to the weaving, *reduces* the tailoring to that which is really equal in the two kinds of work, to their common character of human work.[78]

Marx says elsewhere, "that expression of equivalence [i.e. the exchange proportion, e.g. (D$_1$)] reduces the different kinds of work embodied in the different kinds of commodities to what they have in common, human work in general."[79] That is, before exchange, there is no commensurability. As Dixon and Kay argue, "value does not pre-exist exchange, but is constituted by it."[80]

Thus, as one scholar suggests, Marx's "argument is in fact circular."[81] Therefore, Marx's argument for a strict commensurability of goods fails. If he argues that goods are commensurable in exchange because they possess a common factor, he cannot properly argue that that same common factor is determined by the process of exchange.

Marx seeks strict commensurability of goods in order to render the summing of currency values of corn, iron and other qualitatively different goods a valid operation in calculating rates of profit, of exploitation and of capital intensity. Aristotle is not the only figure who argues that such goods cannot be so added. In questioning the validity of contemporary methods of economic calculation, W. Leontief has charged that in "adding pounds or tons of steel and yards or meters of cloth" to calculate "index numbers," "the reduction in qualitative variety is attained at the cost of increasing quantitative indeterminacy."[82] Marx's failure to establish strict commensurability would seem to be shared by contemporary economists who seek to sum amounts of qualitatively different goods, or who share the same model of exchange as Marx (see below).

Marx's inability to represent the effect of inequality in exchange

Marx's theory of political economy is incapable of representing the effects of inequality upon exchange. It was Marx, not Smith, not Ricardo, who first formulated algebraically the Modern Exchange Model in the following:[83]

(D₃)   x commodity A = y commodity B,

where x, y are quantities of commodities A, B. Formula (D₃) expresses the theories of value and of exchange of Smith, Jevons, J. S. Mill and others.[84] It is shared by contemporary economists. Any demonstration of inadequacy or falsehood in (D₃) is of considerable importance.

(D₃) can be restated, following (A₆), as

(D₄) $N_\delta \approx \frac{\alpha}{\beta} N_\gamma$

where $\frac{\alpha}{\beta} N_\gamma$ = x commodity A, and N_δ = y commodity B. For example,[85]

(D₅)   5 beds = 1 house.

Aristotle teaches us to interpret such a relation as a simplification of formula A₆, where the effect of $\frac{\alpha}{\beta}$ is *concealed* in the exchange relation, as in (D₃). The general representation of formulae of the sort as (D₃) and (D₅) is (A₆). So, (D₅), for example, is analysed as

(D₆)   5 beds $\approx \frac{\alpha}{\beta} N_\gamma$ houses where $\frac{\alpha}{\beta} N_\gamma \approx 1$ and $\frac{\alpha}{\beta} > 1$. The import of (D_6) is that the carpenter gets a house that is worth less than his five beds. Party β hands over to party α more of his product than the product of party α is worth by the factor $\frac{\alpha}{\beta}$. That is, even if *four* beds are equivalent to a house *as use values*, that is as *erga* that satisfy roughly equivalent need, the house builder receives five beds from the carpenter because of his superiority. Making use of his position to make money off the lesser, the one superior in the traditional marks of worth makes a profit and the lesser party suffers a loss. The ratio $\frac{\alpha}{\beta}$ inflates the value of the house, so that $\frac{\alpha}{\beta} N_\gamma$ comes to the value of five beds. The Modern Exchange Model (formula (D_3)), stripped as it is of Aristotle's factor of social difference between persons $(\frac{\alpha}{\beta})$, is not capable of representing exploitation.

Let us apply this analysis to the case of merchandising discussed by Wolff.[86] Workers purchase goods that they need for their households. Let us represent the transaction as follows:

(D_8)
$$N_\delta \approx \frac{\alpha}{\beta} N_\gamma,$$

where $N_\delta \approx$ a worker's expenditures in dollars, $N_\gamma \approx$ a quantity of goods valued in dollars before any retail markup, $N_\gamma < N_\delta$, $\frac{\alpha}{\beta} = 1 + \zeta$, where $\zeta =$ "the positive rate of return on the capital invested throughout the economy;"[87] then $\frac{\alpha}{\beta} > 1$. The formula means that the worker-consumer receives goods less in value than the money s/he pays. The ratio $\frac{\alpha}{\beta}$ represents the transfer of a portion of wage income to retail income without a corresponding transfer of goods of equivalent value to worker-purchasers.[88] Again, the Modern Exchange Model is not able to represent such cases, but Aristotle's theory of value does.

In conclusion, not only does Aristotle have a "concept of value" – contrary to Marx's criticism cited above – but he has one that directly represents social injustice. Indeed, in his formulation of the terms of (A), he says at least one party is "unjust" (*adikos*).[89] A transaction that follows Proportion A maintains the superiority of party α, so that party β cannot improve in wealth or position. That would seem to be the situation that Aristotle describes in which the inferior party's circumstances "seem to be slavery."[90] Thus Aristotle too writes about class antagonisms. Proportion A, therefore, casts light upon the problem of the oppression of the weak by the strong that is often concealed in day-to-day social relations. Aristotle's concern in his ethical writings is to solve that difficulty, so that communities remain together and do not degenerate into civil conflict between the rich and the poor, where each tries to avenge themselves of the other, as they did in the civil wars that ravaged Greek city-states during the Peloponnesian War.[91] Aristotle's theory of exchange includes more dimensions of variability than Marx's, namely, the terms α, β. One result of that is that Marx's exchange model can be considered a simplification of Aristotle's, namely, for the unreal case where $\frac{\alpha}{\beta} = 1$. Not only does Aristotle have a theory of value, but he has one with greater explanatory power than Marx,[92] for it takes into account the effect of social relations on prices. Aristotle understands "what exchange value is" far better than his critics.

Marx's rejection of Aristotle's view that people differ in kind

Marx rejects the view that people differ in kind, and therefore abandons Aristotle's Proportion A, for he regarded differences among individuals to be only an effect of the division of labour "which is forced upon [them] and from which [they] cannot escape,"[93] even though forms of that division of labour develop naturally (*naturwüchsig*). But even if Marx's view is correct that differences result from the division of labour, those differences still must be brought into economic analysis. Marx's view stems from his immersion in the Enlightenment culture in which, as he says, "the idea of human equality already possesses the fixity of popular opinion,"[94] under which it was believed that all humans are the same in nature and possess identical capacities. In his enthusiasm for Enlightenment equality, however, Marx stripped economic theory of Aristotle's device for representing social injustice, the ratio $\frac{\alpha}{\beta}$.

Issues in Marx's theory of value

Marx argues that commodities are composites of matter and the work that informs that matter. For any commodity, the work that produces it is always of a specific sort, qualitatively different from other forms of work, for "all work is an expenditure of human work-power in a particular purposeful form,"[95] and Marx does indeed use the word form in his German text.[96] Commodities that differ in form, differ qualitatively, for example a house, shoes, nourishment and medical treatment, to name examples from Aristotle, all differ in form, and if they differ in form, then the work that produces them differs in form, and if that work differs in form, it cannot be reduced to something undifferentiated, that is "abstract human work," or "undifferentiated human work." At best, "the expenditure of human work-power without regard to its form of expenditure"[97] would seem to refer simply to the time worked without regard to the form of the work, and if that is fair, then Marx's "reduction" eliminates all qualitative difference, and, as noted above, falls into the same error as conventional economics that is criticized by Leontief.[98] In reducing work to a scalar, of which we can measure how much, Marx blurs the distinction between what something is produced *out of*, and what something is produced *by*, for if work is quantifiable and is measured in units,[99] it becomes something "out of which" things are made and such is matter.[100] It ceases to be the activity of an agent, and becomes just another ingredient of commodities rather than that which forms matter into commodities. Then it can no longer serve as the foundation of a theory of value, for work was a foundation of a theory of value insofar as it was the activity of an agent, rather than a material. In reducing work to a scalar, Marx treats it as a universal, and contradicts the metaphysics underlying his own theory of value. Work is not a material constituent. "Undifferentiated human work" does not exist. Rather, work, as Marx himself says, is the manifestation of mind, for "Besides the exertion of the bodily organs which do the work, there is the effective will of the worker, which manifests itself as attentiveness."[101] Marx cannot consistently base his theory of value on hylomorphism but then abandon it when it is inconvenient. Of course, Marx does not consider his adoption of "abstract human work" or "undifferentiated human work" to mean that he abandons concrete work and hylomorphism. Rather he treats concrete work and "abstract human work" as contraries of an antinomy which recurs and echoes throughout *Capital*, for he says their nature is "conflicted" (*zwieschlächtige*) as is that of value itself, which is "conflicted" between use-value and exchange-value.[102] But that conflict is simply the social one between capital and the real communities it exploits.

In conclusion, Marx erred in saying that Aristotle's theory of exchange suffers from "the absence of any concept of value," and in claiming that Aristotle "gives up the further analysis of the form of value" in *Nicomachean Ethics* v.5. Marx's criticism of Aristotle does not hold up under examination, for not only does Aristotle have a concept of value, but that concept is representable mathematically and has greater explanatory power than Marx's. Aristotle's theory of value is compatible with Marx's overall theory of political economy and could be incorporated into it, but that is a topic for another time and place.

Notes

1 Cf. *EN* v.5.1133a16–19.
2 Cf. *EN* v.5.1133b18–20.
3 Also noted in Meikle (1997), 34. Cf. also McNeil (1990), 60.
4 Meikle (1997), 25–26, 35, 41.
5 Meikle (1991), 194. Cf. also Meikle (1997), Chap.7, esp. 140–142; Judson (1997), 162, 168–169; Heath (1949), 274–275. Danzig (2000), 399–424, is one exception, as discussed below.
6 Meikle (1997), 25.
7 Cf. *Met.* 995a31–33.
8 H. Joachim (Aristotle, 1951, 150) states, "How exactly the values of the producers are to be determined, and what the ratio between them can mean, is, I must confess, in the end unintelligible to me." M. Finley (1977): "I do not understand what the ratios between the producers can mean."
9 Although Meikle has made the incommensurability of *erga* a focus of his treatment, he denies that the sharers are incommensurable as well (cf. n. 5 for others). He is to be praised, however, for beginning to uncover the philosophic issues at the heart of *EN* v.5. Cf., for example, Meikle (1997), Chap. 6. So as not to jar the reader too much, I give "community" for *koinōnia*. But "communion" is the first rendering given for *koinōnia* in Liddell and Scott (1897), and better represents the close bonds that exist among sharers in an Aristotelian *koinōnia*.
10 Cf. *EN* v.5.1133b7.
11 Cf. *EN* v.5.1133a24; cf. also *Pol.* 1261a23–24.

12 *EN* v.5.1133a16–19. The passage undermines the claim of Meikle (1991), 194 that "persons are irrelevant." He erred in stating that all "what have to be equalized are referred to by a neuter plural pronoun."
13 Cf. *EN* v.5.1132b34, 1132b31–33, 1133a6.
14 Cf. *EN* v.5.1133b4–5.
15 Cf. *EN* v.5.1133a32–3.
16 Cf. *EN* 1131a10–18.
17 Cf. *EN* 1131a18–20.
18 Cf. *EN* 1131a11, 24.
19 Cf. *EE* 1242b7.
20 Cf. *EE* 1242b8.
21 Cf. *EE* 1242b15.
22 Cf. *EN* 1131a29.
23 Cf. *EN* 1131a10.
24 Moreover, the exploited party also manifests vice insofar as he accepts the exploitation of the other and his own loss, and exhibits the character defect of subservience (cf. Chapter 10).
25 Cf. *EE* 1221a4.
26 *Ergon* is the singular of *erga*. I disagree with Scaltsas (1995), 258 who says that the value of the *erga* determines the value of the sharers. For if that were true, there would be only two independent variables in Proposition A, not four, and the transaction would not be determined by relative worth, as shown in this chapter, though Scaltsas acknowledges it should be (p. 257).
27 Cf. *EN* v.3.1131a24, viii.14.1163b11–12.
28 For discussion of status transactions, cf. Polanyi (1957a), 82–84, 91–93.
29 The point of "freedom" in *EN* v.3 is that before Solon's reforms, a citizen who defaulted on debt could be enslaved. Such enslaved Athenians could hardly be called full citizens.
30 As is freedom: either one has it, as in the case of the citizen (freedom = 1), or one does not, as in the case of a slave (freedom = 0).
31 Cf. *EN* v.4.1131b29–31, cf. 3.1131b5–7.
32 Cf. Heath (1949), 272. H. Jackson (1879), 82 constructs a comparable example of distribution of war booty in a plutocracy.
33 *EN* v.5.1133a25–27.
34 Cf. *EN* v.5.1133a29–31, b16–18.
35 *EN* v.5.1133b18–20.
36 Cf. *EN* 1112a23.
37 *Kudos* to Meikle for proving that. Cf. Miller (1998), 387–398; Meikle (1997), 28–42, 110–128. Irwin in his notes to Aristotle (1999), 346–347 agrees that, as a translation of chreia, need "seems more suitable than 'demand,' since need may be expressed in any actual demands."
38 Meikle (1997), 37.
39 Cf. *Pol.* 1257a5–17. Marx credits Aristotle for first distinguishing between the use value and the exchange value of a good, despite denial of that in Miller (1998). Cf. Marx (1904), 20.
40 Noticed by Soudek (1952), 60 and reiterated by Miller (1998), 392.
41 Cf. Shields (1999), Chap. 4.
42 Regarding homonymy based on multiple significations, cf. *Top.* 107a3–18 and Shields (1999), 52, 54–56 and Chap. 3.
43 For discussion of Aristotle's use of analogy, cf. M. Hesse (1965) and Olshewsky (1968).

44 For discussion of distribution by function, cf. Jackson (1985).

45 Cf. *EN* v.3.1131a25.

46 Cf. Meikle (1991), 193, which notes "'As builder to shoemaker,' on the standard view, measures some property in which the two are unequal. Williams thought the property to be 'the worth of the architect as compared with the worth of the cobbler,' and Grant the 'quality of the labour.' Rackham considered that 'different kinds of producers have different social values and deserve different rates of reward.' Burnet, following Jackson, thought unequal friendship to be the key, and that 'the *huperechōn* is apt to expect to get more services from his friend than he gives in proportion to his own superiority.' Meek suggests that a producer is measured for his status and skill, and Soudek that he is measured for his skill alone." For references, cf. Meikle (1991), 193n6. Danzig (2000), 421 argues that Aristotle means "cost" of the producer, but that notion also does not appear in Aristotle's text, and Aristotle holds that doctors are worth more, while, in ancient Greece, they were actually paid less. Cf. remarks of de Ste. Croix in n. 79 of Chapter 9.

47 Cf. *PA* 639b17.

48 Cf., e.g. *EN* 1104a31.

49 Cf. *An.* ii.4.416a9–15.

50 Cf. *An.* ii.4.416b18–19.

51 Cf. *Phys.* ii.1. Thus, contrary to Meikle (1991), 194, not "all the things in question are artifacts," for neither nourishment nor health are such.

52 Cf. Hesse (1965), 332, who says that in *De anima* and *De Sensu* Aristotle "analyzes sensory qualities – colours, sounds, odors, flavours and tactile sensations – in terms of an ordering on a numerical scale." Hesse cites Ross' commentary in Aristotle (1955), 206 on Aristotle setting a "one-to-one relation" of colours and flavours.

53 For the case of health and houses, cf. *PA* 639b17, discussed below.

54 Cf. *EN* v.5.1133b4–5.

55 Cf. 1133a22–24.

56 Cf. 1133a24.

57 Cf. Aristotle (1999), 232.

58 As argued by Meikle.

59 Samuelson (1948), 58 notes the same, which is cited by Soudek (1952), who does not exhibit a full understanding of its applicability to explaining Aristotle's economic thought.

60 Cf. *PA* 639b17. W. Ogle's translation of *PA* 639b17 in Aristotle (1984) is misleading since he renders the exclusive "or" of the participial clause independently of the *men . . . de* construction of the clause it complements. Better is A. L. Peck's Loeb translation in Aristotle (1937). Consideration of R. Kühner's discussion of disjunction recommends linking the disjunction with the *men . . . de* construction; cf. Kühner et al. (1898), v. 2, pt. 2, §536, pp. 295–296.

61 Aristotle similarly contrasts the doctor and grammarian in *EE* 1226b33f.

62 Cf. Meikle (1991), 194.

63 Cf. passages (3) and (4b).

64 I noticed while editing the final draft of this chapter that Danzig (2000), 420–421 expresses an idea of how "status" could affect exchange.

65 Cf. *Pol.* i.9.

66 Danzig (2000), 420–421 makes a contrast between "inherent value" and exchange value a foundation of his treatment, and in doing so, re-introduces the metaphysical issues that Meikle has raised.

67 Cf. Mark 8.37. Other examples: The compensation for the soldiers who repelled the Persians at Marathon, an example of someone's worth being evaluated in

relation to "virtue" (*aretē*), i.e. courage on the battlefield (cf. *EN* 1163b14); the compensation for a parent for raising a child (cf. 1163b15–18).

68 Cf. 1163b15. The insertion of "strictly" in the translation should be credited to Thomson and Tredennick in Aristotle (2004), though they did so only in a note.

69 Marx (1962), 74. Translations are mine.

70 Cf. passage (4a).

71 One exception is Johnson (1939).

72 E.g. Scott Meikle; cf. also: Becker (1977), 123: Aristotle "did not succeed in providing the formula expressing the equalization of unequal work, the formula of what he called proportionate requital or, simply, reciprocity." McCarthy (1990), 69: "Aristotle never really does explain how commodities for exchange are made compatible."

73 Cf. Meikle (1997), 26, 35, 41.

74 Cf. Chapter 1.

75 Cf. Marx (1962), 56: "Were these things not qualitatively different use-values (*qualitativ verschiedne Gebrauchswerte*) and therefore products of qualitatively different useful work (*qualitativ verschiedner nützlicher Arbeiten*), then they could not in general confront each other as commodities"; 59–60: "The formative elements of the use-values coat and linen are tailoring and weaving precisely because of their different qualities (*ihre verschiednen Qualitäten*)"; Aris. *EN* v.5.1133b18–20; cf. Meikle (1991), 174.

76 Marx (1962), Chap. 1, Sec. 3A3, 74. I explain in Gallagher (2014a) why I translate *arbeit* as "work" rather than "labour." Ben Fowkes in Marx (1976), I, 271 agrees.

77 Cf. Marx (1962), Chap. 1, sect. 1, 51. A UK hundred weight (cwt.) is 112 lbs.

78 Marx (1962), Chap. 1, sect. 3A2. 65.

79 Marx (1962), Chap. 1, sect. 3A2. 65.

80 Discussing Williams' argument, Dixon and Kay (1995), 513 write: "Until commodities are exchanged, [Williams] argues, the labours which produce them have nothing in common and therefore do not count as abstract labour ... In other words, value does not pre-exist exchange, but is constituted by it. "If monetary exchange relations constitute the social character of value, then value constitutes, only *ex post*, what private labours have in common. The systematic problem of any "substance" of value pre-existing universal exchanges then disappears." The argument is compelling and delivers a deadly blow to the traditional labour theory of value." Cf. Williams (1992), 441.

81 T. Carver, "Marx's Two-fold Character of Labour," *Inquiry* 23 (1980): 349–352, 350.

82 Cf. W. Leontief (1966), 55–56. Leontief argues (631): "The operation of determining the magnitude of such artificial aggregative objects – the economic statistician calls them index numbers – involves, in other words, adding pounds or tons of steel and yards or meters of cloth. The final result thus necessarily depends on the arbitrary choice of units in which one measures the magnitude of each one of the component parts. If one speaks of the 'output of consumers' goods' instead of the outputs of bread, shoes, and books, or of the 'price of agricultural commodities' instead of the price of wheat, the entire economic system can indeed be described in fewer words. However, the reduction in qualitative variety is attained at the cost of ever increasing quantitative indeterminacy; as we have seen, the more general the contents of an index number, the more vague and arbitrary will its measure be."

83 From Marx (1962), 63, though Marx's only innovation here is to state in an equation what others say in prose.

84 The latter include Smith, Jevons and J.S. Mill. Smith (1776), i.4.¶13 says that "value in exchange" is "the power of purchasing other goods which the possession of that

object conveys," that is from D_3, $A = \frac{y}{x} B$. Jevons (1924), 78: "the value of the ton of iron is equal to the value of the ounce of gold," which statement is equivalent to D_3; and J. S. Mill (1848), bk. iii, Chap. 6: "The value of a thing means the quantity of some other thing, or of things in general, for which it exchanges," as cited in Jevons (1924), 77; again, $A = \frac{y}{x} B$. As Pack (2010) 50–51, 52 emphasizes, Smith also expresses multiple labour theories of value.

85 Cf. Marx (1962), 73, where D_5 is Marx's representation of Aris. *EN.* v.5.1133b23–28.
86 Cf. Chapter 7.
87 Cf. Wolff (1982).
88 Cf. Wolff (1982).
89 Cf. *EN* 1131a10.
90 Cf. *EN* v.5.1133a1.
91 Cf. *to kakōs zētousin* at *EN* v.5.1132b34; cf. Thuc. iii.60–85.
92 For discussion of explanatory power, cf. Chomsky (1965a) and (1965b).
93 Cf. Marx (1969), 33.
94 Cf. Marx (1962), 74.
95 Marx (1962), 61.
96 Marx (1962), 58–59.
97 Marx (1962), 52.
98 "A use value, or good, therefore, has value only because human work in the abstract has been embodied or materialised in it. How, then, is the magnitude of this value measured? By the quantity of the value-creating substance contained in it, the work. The quantity of work itself is measured by its duration, and work time finds its standard of measure in definite divisions of time, as hours, days, etc." [Marx (1962), 53]. Regarding Leontief, cf. note 82.
99 Cf. use of *Maßeinheit* in Marx (1962), 59.
100 For discussion of these issues, cf. Arist. *Met.* vii.8.
101 Marx (1962), vol. 1, Chap. 5, 193.
102 Marx believes that the work in commodities possesses a "conflicted (*zwie-schlächtige*) nature" (56), one of qualitatively different work, the other of simple work. Commodities also are *Zwieschlächtiges*, conflicted things, one nature for use, the other for exchange. With that curious word, Marx says that these two natures, in commodities and in the work contained in them, are incompatible, they do battle (*Schlacht*) with each other. Moore and Aveling in Marx (1967) erroneously render *zwieschlächtige* "two-fold," though with its root Schlacht signifying "battle," "two-battling" or "conflicted" nature are more accurate. The notion of the two-battling natures introduces the analysis of value and recurs throughout *Capital* I. Cf. Marx (1962), 56, 60, 94n31, 351, 358, 675n88. Marx rests much of his analysis on such an antinomy.

9 Reciprocity and reciprocal justice

In the *Nicomachean Ethics* (*EN* v.5) Aristotle says that a city-state (*polis*) holds together through proportionate *antipoieîn*,[1] which means "doing in turn" or "producing in turn."[2] By *antipoieîn*, Aristotle means that members of a community (*koinōnia*), whom he calls "sharers" (*koinōnoí*), relate to each other by producing (*poieîn*) and exchanging goods "in turn." The carpenter produces a house, the shoemaker shoes. The recipients of such actions are affected in turn (*antipascheîn*).[3] The patient is affected by the doctor's treatment, the doctor by the farmer's nourishing food. At the same time, Aristotle also says that the sort of justice that holds together communities of exchange, is proportionate "*to antipeponthos*," which is usually translated as "reciprocity," but its literal meaning is something like "the state of having suffered (or been affected) in turn."[4] Thus the city is held together by proportionate *antipoieîn*, "doing in turn," and proportionate *to antipeponthos*, being affected in turn.[5] Certainly, "reciprocity" sounds nicer and more compact as a phrase, but it glosses over the interactive significance of "doing in turn" and "being affected in turn." With the use of *antipoieîn* and *antipascheîn*, and their roots *poieîn* and *pascheîn*, Aristotle represents a dialectic of doing/producing and being affected that is for him the active substance of a community. One page into *EN* v.5, Aristotle extends the dialectic to the crafts; he explains that

(1) The crafts would have been destroyed, unless as much and in the same way that the producing thing produced (*epoiei to poioûn*), the affected thing was affected (*to paschon epasche*) that much and that way.[6]

In other words, the magnitude and quality of the action of the producer must be exactly received by the recipient. That interesting statement seemed out of place to Reeve, and he omitted it from his translation as "hardly relevant here."[7] But Aristotle's warning to crafts is relevant, first, because it illustrates by analogy the nature of reciprocity, and second, because the producing of each craft affects the citizens, in a way similar to how it affects its own materials, for in the same way that a house builder works raw materials into a livable dwelling so that those components are appropriately affected by change to become a house, so also that house builder produces that house for the shoemaker and that production affects the shoemaker who needs it for his or her household, for if the house builder does not work the raw materials properly and the house is defective, the shoemaker's household suffers.[8] Aristotle discusses such a transaction between a house builder and shoemaker in the text right before the passage Reeve excised.[9] The issue then is whether the producing of a craft is proper or defective, that is, whether its customer receives what is due, or not, and this is a fundamental issue of "reciprocity" that Aristotle raises in the text. Thus when the farmer works the land, the house builder builds a house, and the shoemaker works the leather, the object of each of their activities should be to satisfy the needs of other sharers. In that way, *antipoieîn* as "produce in return" names the activity of different sharers producing different goods and offering them to others, and *antipascheîn* names the consumption of those goods satisfying the needs of those other sharers. "Reciprocity" names both sides of that civic cooperation. Reciprocity is therefore not primarily mathematical but social.[10] It is representable mathematically, but it is not driven by mathematics. Rather, reciprocity is produced not by proportions but by social relations.

If the producing is not proportionate, and the recipients' needs are not met, or they are exploited, then, in such cases, *antipoieîn* as "doing in return" names the return of evil for evil, or retaliation. For immediately after saying that a city-state holds together through proportionate *antipoieîn*, Aristotle explains

(2) For either they seek to return evil, and if they do not, their condition seems to be slavery if they will not retaliate (*antipoieîn*), or they seek to return good, and if not, the giving of a share (*metadosis*) does not occur, but it is due to *metadosis* that they remain together <as a city-state>.[11]

Here we have the use of *antipoieîn* as "retaliate." In communities of exchange (*hai koinōniai hai allaktikai*), if people are exploited in a transaction, Aristotle expects them to "seek to return evil" for the evil they suffered, for otherwise it is as if they were enslaved, not free. As Irwin comments, "Failure to retaliate shows lack of concern (thought to be characteristic of a slave) for one's own status or worth."[12]

Or, if the sharers' needs are satisfied, they seek to return good for good, for the giving of a share of one's produce to another, in Greek *metadosis*, holds the city together. To encourage *metadosis*, the Greeks built a temple of the Graces (*Charites*) in a prominent place (*empodōn*), to encourage "giving in return" (*antapodosis*).[13] Kindness, Aristotle says, should govern exchange.[14] He then moves on to present Proportion A that we discussed in the previous chapter.

Difficulties in the *Nicomachean Ethics*

It is reasonable to ask whether Proportion A meets Aristotle's test of reciprocity. Under (A), are sharers' needs met? Will it produce the necessary reciprocal benefit so that the community remains together? As we saw in Chapter 8, Aristotle proposes as an example of exchange the following:

(3) As farmer is to shoemaker, so the *ergon* of the shoemaker is to that of the
     farmer.[15]

He assigns symbols to the exchangers and their products in saying: "Let a
farmer be α, nourishment γ, a shoemaker β, his *ergon* that is equalized δ," so
that we can restate the proportion with the symbols he assigns:

(A)
$$\frac{\alpha}{\beta} = \frac{\delta}{\gamma}$$

where α and β are the exchanging parties, and γ and δ are their goods (or
money), respectively, and party α is the superior party, that is $\frac{\alpha}{\beta} > 1$. In a
transaction governed by Proportion A, in which the relation between the
sharers is the traditional one of relative status (e.g. relative wealth, birth),
the superior one would appear to receive excess compensation as profit from the
lesser for whatever he provides him, in proportion to the ratio of their respective worth $\frac{\alpha}{\beta}$, for the exchange is not based solely on the worth of the *erga*.[16]
Formula A_{10} derived from Proportion A shows this:

(A_{10})
$$\delta = \frac{\alpha}{\beta} \gamma$$

Formula A_{10} means that party β must hand over an amount of his *ergon* δ that
is greater in value than the *ergon* γ that he receives from party α by the factor
$\frac{\alpha}{\beta}$. As represented in formula A_7 in Chapter 8 the *ergon* of the superior one is
overpriced relative to that of the weaker party. Under Proportion A, party α
receives a profit, party β suffers a loss.

   The defining treatment of profit and loss in Aristotle's writings appears in
the *Nicomachean Ethics* v.4, which opens his discussion of corrective justice.
The chapter states the reasons behind his formulation in the previous chapter
why justice in a mean between the more (profit) and the less (loss) with respect
to two persons and two objects of interest (*pragmata*).[17] Profit (*kerdos*) and loss,
he explains, occur when one party receives an excess (*to pleon*) beyond half
the value of "the good" (*to agathon*) subject to the transaction.[18] A contemporary example is the case represented by Wolff and discussed in Chapter 8 in
which consumers receive less than the value that they pay in retail transactions.
Aristotle represents the situation with a line segment that has been unequally
divided between the two parties; the imbalance must be corrected.[19] Aristotle
concludes:

(4) These names, both loss and gain, have come from voluntary exchange;
     for to have more than one's own is called gaining, and to have less than
     one's original share is called losing, e.g. in buying and selling and in all
     other matters in which the law has left people free to make their own

terms; but when they get neither more nor less but just what belongs to themselves, they say that they have their own and that they neither lose nor gain. Therefore, the just is intermediate between a sort of gain and a sort of loss.[20]

This passage makes it clear that, for Aristotle, reciprocal justice, which he says pertains to "communities of exchange," is a species of corrective justice, for after Aristotle discusses distributive justice, he says that corrective justice is the only "remaining" type of justice and then discusses corrective and reciprocal justice.[21] Moreover, the principal example he gives of injustices requiring correction are those that arise as a result of voluntary exchange.[22] Thus reciprocal justice is part of corrective justice.[23] Just how this affects Aristotle's treatment of exchange, we investigate below.

In the transactions described with Proportion A in *EN* v.5, there is no correction to the profit received by party α. Nor is any other good received by the weaker party to offset the material gain that the superior one receives through the transaction.[24] Making use of his position to make money off the lesser, the one superior in social status makes a profit and the lesser party suffers a loss. There is no reciprocity in that. There is no complementary *antipoieîn* and *antipaschein*. Since Aristotle, like Plato, regards merchants and markets as essential parts of a city, he would allow the merchant to clear enough income to support his household. What we are talking about here is a profit, over and above income to pay necessary expenses.[25] We can understand the effect of Proportion A here by comparing it to Proportion B applied in distribution of common assets (cf. Chapter 8). The use of the ratio $\frac{\alpha}{\beta}$ in (B) guarantees that disbursements do not change the relative position of the wealth of the two parties: What each receives (γ, δ) is in direct proportion to the magnitude of their deposits (α, β), so that afterwards Proportion B' holds true. Their relative position vis-à-vis wealth possessed does not change. Under Proportion A, however, what each receives is the other party's *ergon*, that is α receives δ and β, γ. The proportion $\frac{\delta}{\gamma}$, which Aristotle calls "inverse," regulates exchanges so as to augment the material superiority of party α, so that party β declines in wealth or position.[26] That would seem to be the situation that Aristotle describes, in which the inferior party's circumstances "seem to be slavery,"[27] for this situation differs from that of the distribution of common assets, for there, party α receives only in proportion to what he had already paid into the fund. As Soudek writes in a slightly different context: "If . . . the purchaser is in dire need . . . or if the seller holds a monopolistic position, then what appears on the surface as a 'voluntary' transaction is distorted in spirit and perverted into factual 'extortion'."[28] Aristotle condemns profit making earlier in *EN* v when he says that "If someone makes a profit, we can refer it to no other vice than injustice."[29] Other types of injustice can be referred to some other vice: someone throws away his shield through cowardice; another speaks harshly though irascibility; a third refuses to help another financially through lack of generosity.[30] Not so, says Aristotle, with *pleonexia*, the gaining of some advantage for oneself by taking what belongs to another, or by denying another her due. That can be referred only to injustice. One who commits adultery out of appetite is intemperate, but one who commits adultery for profit is unjust, not intemperate.[31] Thus Aristotle lists "profit," that is love of gain, as the deficiency of justice in his table in the *Eudemian Ethics*.[32] We may disagree with Aristotle here and propose that love of gain is a sort of intemperance. His view, however, is clear, and coheres with his condemnation of the accumulation of wealth through commerce (*chrēmatistikē*) in *Pol.* i.9.

Accordingly, under Proportion A the superior party would certainly "make a profit,"[33] and thus would commit injustice. The exchange is disproportionate since it is not based on proportions of worth of function and worth of *erga*, but on the higher "status" of the superior party. Thus the superior party extracts a profit from the weaker. It seems that transactions representable by Proportion A would not be able to bring about the reciprocity that Aristotle seeks to define in *EN* v.5. The needs of the lesser would not be satisfied in proportion to the goods that the lesser hands over to the superior party. It is consistent with Aristotle's theory of justice that we conclude that under Proportion A, the superior one exploits the lesser, violates the *philia* that constitutes the basis of community, and commits injustice. All this suggests a rejection of Proportion A as a proportion that could govern the exchange of goods in Aristotle's view of reciprocal justice. Thus there seems to be a serious problem internal to *EN* v.5.

The case in which the relation between the sharers is the relative worth of their functions in the community (discussed in Chapter 8) would seem to be different, however. What the superior party receives when his *ergon* is priced at full value[34] would be earned in respect of function, and would represent use value, for example the doctor really did save my daughter's life when she had her first asthma attack, and the large payment I made (through my insurance company) was proportionate to worth. But even here there would seem to be the seed of a social problem, for weaker sharers (who lack such resources) would have to pay large percentages of their income for necessary goods and services provided by sharers whose function was highly valued. Such exchanges would perpetuate or even deepen their relative weakness, and the situation would again "seem to be slavery," though, in this instance, to those of higher function than to those of higher status. Whether $\frac{\alpha}{\beta}$ represents worth as 'status' or worth of function, transactions governed by Proportion A could lay the basis for social discord and the dissolution of a polis, as occurred in Corcyra during the Peloponnesian Wars. That problem might not arise, however, in exchanges where the party with the more highly valued function benefits the lesser by taking a smaller payment in exchange for his work,[35] but there a different problem arises, for party α would not be compensated in accordance with worth, and *that* would appear to be unjust. Does Aristotle propose any solution to such difficulties?

Diagonal pairing: Definition

In concluding his introduction to *EN* v.5, Aristotle says

(5) And that which brings about giving in return (*antidosis*) which is proportional is diagonal pairing (*hē kata diametron suzeuxis*).[36]

Since "diagonal pairing" brings about proportional exchange, it may be a way to define terms of exchange so that the sharers benefit each other and solve the problems that we discuss in the previous section. Aristotle does not explain the meaning of diagonal pairing in *EN* v.5. Thomas d'Aquino believed that Proportion A itself represented diagonal pairing, for he believed that the terms of Proportion A refer to the corners of a square.[37] Though Thomas' hypothesis has been put aside, some modern scholars have followed his lead in assuming Proportion A an instance of diagonal pairing, while others reject his view.[38] Scholars have therefore failed to reach agreement on what the phrase signifies. One has said that diagonal pairing "remains a mystery."[39] If something so crucial to understanding *EN* v.5 is a "mystery" to scholars, we must solve that puzzle in order to make progress. I searched the Aristotelian corpus for any other occurrence of "diagonal pairing" (*hē kata diametron suzeuxis*) in the hope that Aristotle would define the term in some text. I found one other place in the Aristotelian corpus where "diagonal pairing" appears: *Eudemian Ethics* 1242b2– 21, a text on friendship between unequal parties. It is possible that the discussion of diagonal pairing in the *Eudemian Ethics* can help us reach a definition of the term used in *EN* v.5. The *Eudemian Ethics* passage discusses exchanges in which one partner is "superior" (*huperechōn*) to the other,[40] such as in the sort of civic friendship based on usefulness between sharers in a community.[41] As Aristotle says in the same chapter of the *Eudemian Ethics*, "Civic friendship has been established mainly in accordance with usefulness, for men seem to have come together because each is not sufficient for himself."[42] Exchanges between unequal parties are the sort of transactions that are discussed in *Nicomachean Ethics* v.5, where Aristotle says that he is concerned with exchanges between "those who are different and not equal." One party is "superior" to the other. The Eudemian text discusses Proportion A and another, derived proportion, in discussing disputes over the terms of exchange between people who are involved in friendships in which the parties are, as in *EN* v.5, "not equal." Diagonal pairing is an operation performed upon Proportion A to define more favourable terms of exchange for the more needy party.

There are two ways to use *EE* 1242b2–21 in solving the puzzles of *EN* v.5.

1) Use that text only insofar as it provides a definition of "diagonal pairing."
2) Use that text as a source for Aristotle's theory of what is just in exchange.

I call the first the "narrow" application of *EE* 1242b2–21 to *EN* v.5, and the second the "broad." We seem compelled to accept at least the narrow use of *EE* 1242b2–21, for in order to come to some understanding of the use of "diagonal pairing" in *EN* v.5, we need to examine other instances of Aristotle's use of that term, and *EE* 1242b2–21 is the only other text that I have found that uses it. But some might question the applicability of material in texts on friendship to *EN* v.5, and others might challenge the relevance of what is said in any text from the *Eudemian Ethics* to a text in the *Nicomachean Ethics*. Those, however, are objections to a broad use of the Eudemian passage. Here I restrict myself to a narrow use of the passage. But since some will nonetheless insist on raising such objections, even to a narrow use, I briefly rebut them. First, many would agree with Kenny that some version of *EN* v was part of the *Eudemian Ethics*.[43] It therefore seems reasonable to examine a Eudemian text for help in understanding a Nicomachean text. Moreover, regarding the objection against citing texts on friendship in connection with texts on justice, Aristotle himself calls relationships of exchange, such as those examined in *EN* v.5, instances of "civic friendship."[44] He says:

(6)   In all friendships between dissimilars it is, as we have said, proportion that equalizes and preserves the friendship; e.g. in civic friendship (*en têi politikêi*) the return for the shoemaker in exchange for his shoes is in proportion to worth (*kat' axian*), and likewise for the weaver and all other craftsmen.[45]

Aristotle here says that the shoemaker's return is proportional to worth, as in Proportion A from *EN* v.5. Passage (6) is prima facie evidence from the *Nicomachean Ethics* itself that texts on friendship should aide us in understanding *EN* v.5. In addition to *EE* 1242b2–21, we shall refer to one other such text on civic friendship, *Nicomachean Ethics* Book viii, Chapter 14 (*EN* viii.14), which includes a qualitative discussion of the same issues as *EE* 1242b2–21. Though *EN* viii.14 does not discuss diagonal pairing or any proportions, its treatment of civic friendship and of exchange complements those in *EE* 1242b2–21 and *EN* v.5.

Aristotle begins his discussion in *EE* 1242b2–21 by saying that the parties in relationships of unequals often dispute over the proportion in which they are to share in their goods.[46] "Each party expects proportionality, but not in the same way."[47] The party who is superior deems himself worthy of the following kind of proportion, which Aristotle calls "inverse":[48]

(7)   As he is to the lesser, so that which comes into being from the lesser (*to para tou elattonos ginomenon*) [i.e. the product (*ergon*)] is to that which comes into being from him, because he is in a position as ruler to ruled.[49]

The awkward phrase, "that which comes into being from the lesser," reflects Aristotle's view that every skill (*technē*) is practised "so that some thing, of those things that can both be and not be, comes into being, and of those the origin is in the one working, and not in the thing being worked."[50] Passage

(7) describes a proportion identical to Proportion A in *EN* v.5.[51] As Aristotle explains in a parallel passage in *EN* viii.14, "the better supposes that it is fitting for him to have more (*pleon echein*)."[52] Thus "the better" inverts the $\frac{\gamma}{\delta}$ quotient in Proportion B (cf. Chapter 8) to produce Proportion A. In that way, *social relations affect exchange formulae*, as was said in Chapter 8. With the use of the phrase *pleon echein* Aristotle flags the proposed transaction as unjust, for the superior party "derives" Proportion A from (B) through an act of *pleonexia*, which for Aristotle is unjust. As above, by the value of $\frac{\alpha}{\beta}$, the superior one would thus receive a profit.[53] Aristotle then says that if the superior cannot assert his superiority in the transaction, he expects at least to receive from the exchange the same value as the weaker party.[54] Though perhaps most pleasing to our egalitarian sentiments, that situation is not of interest to Aristotle, either in the Nicomachean or the Eudemian text, for in both he is interested in exchange between parties that are "not equal."[55] Aristotle's insistence that inequality must figure in an exchange is disturbing, for it would seem to lead to exploitation of the weak by the strong. But Aristotle answers that dilemma further in the text. First, he says:

(8) But the one who is outdone (*huperechomenos*) reverses (*tounantion strephei*) the proportion [A] and pairs the terms diagonally (*kata diametron suzeugnusin*).[56]

Passage (8) contains the only occurrence of the phrase "diagonal pairing" in the Aristotelian corpus, besides that in *EN* v.5, and the passage and its environs is the only text that *defines* "diagonal pairing." The text shows that diagonal pairing is a procedure for transforming one proportion (A) to produce another. Aristotle's comment following passage (8) makes unambiguous what he means by "diagonal pairing." He says that "the superior one would seem to suffer a loss" from that operation.[57] The superior "suffers a loss" if we "reverse" ratio $\frac{\delta}{\gamma}$ in Proportion A so that we produce a new proportion, $\frac{\alpha}{\beta} = \frac{\gamma}{\delta}$. In Proportion A each *ergon* is diagonally opposed to its producer/sharer. Now, in the new proportion, each *ergon* is paired with its producer/sharer, α with γ, β with δ.[58] So, *EE* 1242b2–21 defines "diagonal pairing" as an operation performed in *reversing* a proportion: the terms that were diagonally opposed to each other in Proportion A are paired as antecedents and consequents. We have already encountered this proportion, put to different use, as Proportion B in the previous chapter. Exchange, however, is unlike distribution, and here the result of applying Proportion B is different: the two parties do not remain in the same relative material positions as before, but the position of the weaker is improved at the expense of the superior. For whenever $\frac{\alpha}{\beta} > 1$ in exchanges governed by Proportion B, the one who draws the most from the transaction is the one who receives γ, and that is party β, for party α gives his *ergon* (γ) to him in exchange for δ, for now the converse of A_6 (cf. previous chapter) is operative, namely,

(B$_1$)
$$N'_\gamma = (\frac{\alpha}{\beta})\, N'_\delta\,,$$

and party α hands over more of his *ergon* than the *ergon* of party β is worth, so that

(B$_2$)
$$\frac{P'_\delta}{P'_\gamma} > \frac{V_\delta}{V_\gamma}$$

where the primes are used to distinguish the N_i and P_i of B$_1$ and B$_2$ from those of A$_3$ (cf. previous chapter), which differ because the ratio $\frac{\alpha}{\beta}$ is applied differently in the two cases. In this exchange, party β receives γ in accordance with his need.[59] The lesser party receives from the superior in proportion to the latter's superiority, that is, to settle the transaction, he hands over much less of his own product in exchange for the goods of the superior one. Thus, diagonal pairing is a transformation applicable to proportions describing exchange relations of all sorts. As applied in *EE* 1242b2–21, diagonal pairing results in a formula that sets terms of exchange more favorable to the lesser of two parties.

We can now define diagonal pairing, as we set out to do early in this section:

> DEF: *Diagonal pairing* is an operation that transforms a formula of the form $\frac{\alpha}{\beta} = \frac{\delta}{\gamma}$ into one of the form $\frac{\alpha}{\beta} = \frac{\gamma}{\delta}$.

As applied to exchange relations in *EE* 1242b2–21, diagonal pairing results in a formula that sets terms of exchange more favorable to the lesser of two parties.

In concluding this section, we can now understand the reference to diagonal pairing in passage (5) from *EN* v.5: Proportional giving-in-return requires the transformation of Proportion A into Proportion B: The result is that the superior party materially benefits the weaker in the exchange.

Diagonal pairing and proportional exchange

Use of diagonal pairing would seem to prevent the superior party from exploiting the weaker in an exchange. But now Aristotle says that under diagonal pairing the superior one suffers a loss, and the friendship and community becomes for him a burdensome office (*leitourgia*).[60] That loss means that the exchange is not proportional, and violates the principle of *EN* v.5 that exchange be proportional. Now the problem that we discussed earlier is simply reversed: Now the lesser party would be exploiting the superior one, and on the very grounds that he is superior.[61] The lesser party participates in giving-of-a-share *only* in handing over goods of less value. There is no reciprocal equality in that. The Eudemian text addresses these problems. It answers:

(9) So, then, some other thing must equalize the friendship and make it proportional. And this is honour (*timē*), the very thing by nature fitting for the
ruler and the god in relation to the ruled. The profit (*kerdos*) [of the lesser
party] must be equalized (*isasthēnai*) in relation to honour.[62]

In other words, an exchange represented by Proportion B is disproportionate.
Such a transaction does not by itself "equalize the friendship and make it proportional" as required in passage (9). Aristotle summarizes the problem in the
parallel text of *EN* viii.14. After stating the demands of each party, surprisingly,
he says, "It seems that each correctly deems himself worthy of having more, and
more should be distributed to each." But, we ask, how is that possible? Aristotle
answers, "but not the same thing, but to the superior one honour and to the
needy one gain."[63] I propose that "not the same thing" refers to the fact that in
Aristotle's view, in the ethical writings, wealth is only one of the goods shared
by members of a community, who also share in security and honour.[64] Aristotle
proposes to make the exchange just by allocating to the superior party honour
as compensation, as a reward for handing over his product to the lesser party
under the terms of exchange of material goods determined by Proportion B.
For Aristotle, an exchange between unequals is made proportional, by making it an exchange of both material and non-material goods. Aristotle reaches
outside the realm of the material to social goods to complete the transaction.
As noted, honour is among the goods apportioned by sharers in a community
in *Nicomachean Ethics* Book v.[65] Apportioning honour to the superior sharer
equalizes the relationship precisely because that confirms that the friendship is
of unequals, and that *he*, not the one who gained materially in the transaction,
is the superior one. That reward of honour is what equalizes the relationship
and makes it proportional, for the superior one, who has no, or less, need of
material goods, can be satisfied through the reward of honour, for it increases
his influence in the community and may protect him from punitive taxation or
court judgments upon his wealth, for by accepting Proportion B he shows that
he is generous and merits *charis*.[66] In that way, in accordance with the demands
of passage (1) in the previous chapter, "those who are different and not equal"
are "made equal" (*isasthēnai*).[67] *Such is the nature of "reciprocal equality":*[68] *Citizens
who are "unequal," are "equalized" by satisfying each party in different ways.* If we
were to assign a monetary value T to the honour given the superior party it
would be equal to the sum of his loss (Z_α) under Proportion B plus the gain
(K_α) that he lost because Proportion A did not govern the transaction, the
point being to reward him for giving up all that value.[69]

Thus "what is equalized in fair exchanges of food, shoes and houses" are
the parties involved, that is, as Aristotle states in passage (9), their "friendship."[70] Scholars have been locked in difficulties over *EN* v.5, because they
have assumed, in accordance with modern convention, that transactions must
be settled solely in material terms. But even in our modern world certain
members of our communities who are not compensated materially in accordance with worth of function (e.g. fire fighters, teachers) are often accorded a

greater share of personal honour (e.g. the emergency personnel who responded on September 11, 2001). With diagonal pairing and the apportionment of honour, Aristotle thus solves two problems: 1) how to structure transactions between unequal parties so that the weak receive what they need, and 2) how to compensate the party superior in status or function for participating in a transaction in which he or she loses material wealth. In this way, Aristotle advances the social democratic thinking of his Greek contemporaries, which scholars have found expressed in the policies of Archytas of Tarentum, who used "reciprocal proportionality" to propose that "the poor receive from the powerful, and the rich give to those in need, both in confidence that through it they will have that which is fair and equal."[71]

But does the use of honour to make "proportional" a transaction determined by diagonal pairing accord with the *Nicomachean Ethics*? Is there any mention of the use of honour in that way in that text? *EN* viii.14 discusses the bestowal of honour upon an individual for having "benefited [others] in goods" in the very sort of exchanges discussed in the Eudemian text.[72] In the *Nicomachean Ethics* too, then, honour is discussed as a means of payment for settling a transaction, that is to make equal "those who are different and not equal." Moreover, in *EN* v.6 Aristotle speaks of rewarding with honour "someone who rules . . . as the guardian of what is just":

(10) He derives no advantage, if indeed he is just, for he does not allot himself more of what is generally good, unless it is proportional to him (*pros auton analogon*). That is the reason he toils for another: and because of that it is said that justice is another's good, as was said also earlier. Some payment or reward (*misthos*) ought to be given to him, and that is honour, that is, a privilege (*geras*).[73]

In this passage praising office holders who, contrary to the norm, do not use their official position to aggrandize themselves or their friends and relatives, we have several important concepts found in the *Eudemian Ethics* and *Nicomachean Ethics* chapters on political economy:

1) that someone can be recompensed with honour for benefiting others,[74]
2) that that payment is "proportional [i.e., "fitting"] to him," that is as Thomson and Tredennick render, "to his merits,"[75]
3) that he is just because he exerts himself for another without material reward (like "the one doing service" in *EN* viii.14),[76] and
4) that he performs such benefit through his virtue.[77]

As passage (10) shows, the use of honour as a means of payment to someone who has benefited another is discussed in *Nicomachean Ethics* Book v. Why, however, is there no mention of the use of honour to balance the transactions discussed in *EN* v.5 as in *EE*1242b2–21? *The reason is that it is simply not necessary*. In *EN* v.5 Aristotle is not presenting a definition and explication of the procedure of diagonal pairing and its implications. Rather, he is referring to a procedure that he has defined elsewhere in his ethical discourses as a means to "bring about *antidosis* (a giving in return)." The reference is similar to his reference to *charis* (grace) in the previous sentence.[78] After so referring to the way things ought to be, he commences his analysis of the problems inherent in exchange relations. Aristotle was leaning against convention in proposing diagonal pairing. For traditionally one's wealth or birth determined one's position in society, and not one's function, as Aristotle proposes. It was common practice for the wealthy or "noble" to have the upper hand over the needy. For it is always the case, in Aristotle's view, and as noted above, Soudek independently warns, that the stronger will be more able than the weak to determine the terms of exchange, for the weak really need that apartment and, despite everything, they succumb to the rent-demand of the landlord. When that fact over-determines exchange, for Aristotle, it is time to reverse the quotient of *erga*. By invoking diagonal pairing Aristotle distinguishes between what is just and what is conventionally practiced. Aristotle's sensitivity to this problem is illustrated in his frequent use of the doctor as an example of a function in a community. For Aristotle's father was a doctor, but in Athens doctors were regarded as simple craftsmen.[79]

One final objection: Now that we know what diagonal pairing is, would it not be simpler to regard Proportion A as the result of applying diagonal pairing to the proportion for distribution that Aristotle presents earlier in *EN* v?[80] Were we to accept that suggestion, however, we would also have to accept the idea that Aristotle has two theories of reciprocal justice, one presented both in the *Eudemian Ethics* and in *EN* viii.14, which regards just exchange as one that materially benefits the weak, and another in *EN* v.5, which regards it just for the strong to exploit the weak, and that only the theory in the *Eudemian Ethics* and in *EN* viii.14 is consistent with his principle in *EN* v.1 that justice is "another person's good . . . for it does what benefits another"[81] – not the theory that he enunciates shortly afterwards in *EN* v.5. Following that suggestion introduces not simplicity, but manifold complications and contradictions. Therefore, in addition to all the other reasons given here, economy of interpretation supports the understanding of Aristotle's theory of reciprocal justice given in this book.

To sum up our discussion: In *Nicomachean Ethics* Book v, Chapter 5, we found a problem with Proportion A in that it permits superior sharers to exploit weaker members of a community. We considered Aristotle's comment that "diagonal pairing" brings about a "giving in return" (*antidosis*) which is proportional, and found that Aristotle's definition of that term shows 1) that diagonal pairing is an operation that transforms a formula so that the terms that were diagonally opposed to each other are paired as antecedents and consequents, and 2) that diagonal pairing produces terms of exchange of the material goods that are more favorable for the lesser party in a transaction between parties who are unequal. But since the lesser party would receive a gain and the superior a loss, such a diagonal transaction would not be proportional. Aristotle proposes to make it proportional by apportioning honour to the superior party as a reward, for honour increases his influence in the community and may protect him from punitive taxation or court judgments upon his wealth. Therefore, we conclude that in just proportional exchange under Aristotle's theory of reciprocal justice, superior sharers in a community materially assist the needy, and receive honour as a reward.[82] This analysis confirms two additional points. First, that reciprocal justice is part of corrective justice, for reciprocal justice is designed to correct the results of past exploitation of the weak by the strong. Second, that reciprocal justice accomplishes re-distribution of the goods of the *polis* to those in need.[83] With diagonal pairing, Aristotle turns exchange into a mechanism of redistribution and invents a new form of the practice of reciprocity that, though not noticed by Polanyi, more or less falls within his account of "Reciprocity as a form of integration . . . employing both redistribution and exchange as subordinate methods."[84]

Aristotle's two "realities"

In *Nicomachean Ethics* Book v, Chapter 5, Aristotle asserts two conflicting "realities." On the one hand, he says:

(1) In reality(*tēi alētheiai*) it is impossible for sharers and their *erga* [the terms of Proportion A] to be commensurable.[85]

On the other hand, he also says:

(2) Everything must be measured by someone thing . . . and that in reality (*tēi alētheiai*) is need.[86]

Theses (1) and (2) prompt questions: On the one hand, if need measures all things, on what grounds does Aristotle say at the same time that the terms of Proportion A are incommensurable? On the other hand, if they are truly incommensurable, how could need serve as a common measure for them? I see answers to those questions in Aristotle's theory of the formation of communities and city-states. Aristotle's reasoning seems to be:

1) The sharers are different,[87] "unequal" and incommensurable.
2) These different, unequal individuals cannot satisfy all their needs by themselves, but must satisfy some of them from other individuals.
3) For that reason, they join in various associations (first households, then villages, finally the polis).[88]

That is, because Aristotle's sharers differ, not only do they have something to offer each other, but they also must come together to satisfy their own needs which they cannot individually satisfy by themselves, but can satisfy only by entering into relations of civic friendship with each other and sharing in each other's *erga*. For that reason, everything exchanged must somehow be made comparable,[89] for insofar as an *ergon* of one sharer satisfies the need of another, whose *ergon* satisfies the need of a third and so on, *erga* and sharers become sufficiently comparable, so that people who are "different and not equal . . . [are] made equal."[90] To represent that comparability, Aristotle continues, currency came along, and became an intermediate, for it measures everything.[91] Currency became by convention the "exchange-token" of need.[92] It serves as a security for us to be able to meet our needs in the future.[93] By making everything commensurable, it equalizes them.[94] But, like everything else, even it has a price that fluctuates.[95] Aristotle emphasizes the conventional nature of currency by proposing an etymology from *nomos*, for "it is not by nature, but by convention, and it is in our power to alter it and make it useless."[96] The point here is that – though currency is the conventional means for treating goods as commensurable in transactions – it is need that establishes commensurability in fact and by nature, for need is what brings the members of the community together to exchange *erga*. "Because people need many things, and because one person calls on a second out of one need and on a third out a different need, many people gather in a single place to live together as partners and helpers. And such a settlement is called a city," says Socrates in the *Republic*.[97] Need underlies the conventional commensurability of currency, because the use of currency as an exchange-token of need is not by nature but by convention.[98] Therefore, to ensure that the arbitrariness of convention does not leave the need of the weaker unsatisfied, Aristotle introduces diagonal pairing, so that that need is satisfied, and the weaker does not come to regard his condition as slavery,[99] and seek to return evil for evil.[100] For the community was formed for the purpose of satisfying the needs of its members – not as a retail sales market. For that reason, need measures, and, as it were, trumps everything, for it refers back to the foundation of the community. Need determines transactions through diagonal pairing, which invokes need to reconstruct an exchange so that it satisfies such need.[101]

The community meets such need through its "superior" members, who benefit the more needy ones, and that relationship characterizes for Aristotle a special sort of civic friendship, whose aim is to maintain the existence, the being of the lesser party (*hē tou eînai proairesis*).[102] Thus, friendship subsumes justice,[103] for the source of just behaviour in the community is the various relations of civic and other friendship that exist between its sharers. Perhaps that is why Aristotle treats friendship in the two penultimate books of the *Ethics* as a treatment of the more universal virtue later, for, as he says, we are introduced to the virtue of friendship from birth, and through that learn just behaviour.[104]

Thus it is a function of "superior" members of the community to support the existence of weaker ones.[105] In this way, such a superior sharer uses wealth the best,[106] and in doing so, he fulfills a communal function, for wealth is one of the qualities of the community,[107] and its use consists in spending and giving.[108] The beneficiaries give honour back in turn, says Aristotle. It seems reasonable to conclude, then, that in Aristotle's view sufficient commensurability with respect to need is a good solution to the problem of incommensurability of exchangers and *erga*. For, if there somehow were strict commensurability, as is often assumed in economic theory, the parties would exchange their products under terms abstracted from their needs and their association in community. Though the resulting transaction might fit modern notions of fairness, it would not, for Aristotle, be just, since it would not benefit the lesser party to the exchange. As he says, justice is "another person's good, for it is related to another; for it does what benefits another,"[109] and such is the result of diagonal pairing, for not only is the lesser party benefited, but also the superior with the reward of honour that the superior receives, "the very thing by nature fitting for the ruler and god in relation to the ruled."[110] It is therefore wrong to say that Aristotle's solution of sufficient commensurability is an "admission of failure" for an effort to establish strict commensurability, for in outlining the incommensurability of sharers and *erga*, Aristotle identifies a difficulty, which he solves with his concept of *sufficient* commensurability.[111] Strict commensurability is not desirable.

Aristotle's theory has come under criticism from contemporary advocates of fairness.[112] Such criticism defends popular contemporary belief that justice is fairness.[113] The argument runs as follows: although "it is not *unjust* . . . to benefit someone else more than they deserve," such actions "fail to be just" because they do not properly reward and recognize "personal desert."[114] The transaction between the superior party and the lesser outlined in *EE* 1242b2–21 is the sort of act that fails to be "just," according to the claim. Because the superior materially benefits the lesser beyond his "personal desert," the transaction is not "fair," for it is formulated based on difference between the parties to the transaction; it does not treat them as equals. I dwell on the claim that such acts "could be just but are not."[115] How could we adjust the transaction to make it "just," that is "fair," according to this argument? I propose that the transaction would begin to satisfy such a standard of fairness, were the ratio $\frac{\alpha}{\beta}$ in Aristotle's proportions to equal 1. But, under Aristotle's theory, such a transaction would no longer be just, because it is no longer structured to aid the weaker party, for it does not take into account the relative circumstances of the two parties, but rather treats them as equals, when they are not. I argue that the phrase "personal desert" in "rewarding and recognizing personal desert," a key phrase in the "fairness" argument, is homonymous, and that the criticism of Aristotle fallaciously rests on that homonymy.[116] Under a modern "work ethic" sort of account, the shoemaker deserves to receive a house from the house builder because he is a hard-working artisan, with professional standards for his product: the receipt of the house rewards him insofar as his shoemaking has been the means for him to accumulate the wealth with which to pay for the house. But under Aristotle's account of reciprocity in a community, the shoemaker deserves to receive the house because he is a member of such and such a community in which it is his function to practise the *techne* of shoemaking, just as it is the house builder's function to practice that of house building. To deny his need of a house, the community would have to deny its own need for his function. It can no more do that than it can get along with a two-legged stool. The fairness critique of Aristotle is based on the first reading of what "personal desert" signifies, while Aristotle's theory makes use of the second. Thus, for Aristotle, it is not fair to set $\frac{\alpha}{\beta} = 1$, because doing so ignores the fact that the two sharers are different, that they have different functions, different identities within the community, and that the community relies on each of them in relying on their differences. Aristotle builds such difference into his theory when he says that "it is impossible for things that differ so much to be commensurable."[117] For Aristotle, *need* should determine the allocation of material goods, not what is fair or just in the abstract. For under the principle of need, we focus on who needs what, and what is fitting to whom, and construct the transaction on that basis. What is just in exchange is determined by the relationship between the parties, rather than some imagined, "intrinsic" value of their goods, apart from human need. For Aristotle, reciprocity is established through meeting the needs of all parties: of the lesser for goods, of the superior for honour.[118] The result is his own, peculiar form of the proposition: From each according to his ability, to each according to his need.[119] Rejecting conventional Greek signifiers of worth,[120] Aristotle adopts function (*ergon*) as his signifier, for function expresses identity within a community. Function is thus the basis of justice. The best flute player gets the best flute, not the buyer willing to pay the most money. The rich man unskilled in flutes or shoemaking cannot succeed as a flute player or a shoemaker. He just does not have the skills. In so basing his theory of reciprocal justice upon an incommensurability and incomparability of sharers, Aristotle seems to express a thought of the unconditional worth of every human being.[121]

Aristotle's theory of reciprocal justice arises from his view that we each live in two complementary "realities": On the one hand, we are "different and not equal," and so stand apart from others. Yet on the other hand, because of difference, we each have something to contribute to others, something that they need. Further, since we are "different," we are not able to provide for ourselves everything that we need, and so must associate with others to satisfy our own needs. Thus, the human becomes civilized, not because it wants to, though it may want to, but because it must. Aristotle's theory of reciprocal justice suggests that civilization is the constant interchange among the "different and not equal." The result is rather different from modern notions of justice and right. We moderns have sought protection for ourselves as individuals under the principle of the equality of all. That is often interpreted to be based on a sameness of the nature of all. But in Aristotle's system, it is not an equality derived from an assumed sameness that protects the weak, but the recognition of one's difference that protects the individual from marginalization, or elimination, and grants one rights within the community. For the community needs each incommensurable other in order to function and survive. Therefore, the community acts collectively to satisfy the needs of each sharer, whatever one's condition may be. For honour is bestowed as a collective act of the community,[122] for the weak sharer cannot accomplish that alone. Through the allocation of honour, the community balances the weakness of its lesser members with the strength of its superior ones, so that the weak receive what they need, and, hence, the opportunity to pursue the good life themselves.[123] Thus, surprisingly, it is through inequality that the rights of the individual are protected. Thus justice for the individual lies not in equality, but in difference, in, as it were, "inequality."

Notes

1 *tôi antipoieîn gar analogon summenei hē polis* at *EN* v.5.1132b33–34.
2 Liddell and Scott (1897) provide "do in return" as a first meaning for *antipoieîn*, which they construct from the first meaning of *poieîn*, "to do." I construct *antipoieîn*, "to produce in return," from the second meaning of *poieîn*, "to make, produce, create." Other translations of *antipoieîn* include "retaliate" (Liddell and Scott, 1897), "requital" (Ross' translation in Aristotle, 1984), and "reciprocity" (Irwin's translation in Aristotle, 1999, and Reeve's in Aristotle, 2014). I note on those translations the following: Aristotle uses a different phrase ordinarily translated as "reciprocity," namely, *to antipeponthos*, the perfect participle of the verb *antipaschō*, which is the contrary of *antipoieîn*. "Retaliation" is a negative, vengeful action, but *antipoieîn* can be either positive or negative, while "requital" means a discrete act of repaying or returning something, such as money, whereas *antipoieîn* carries with it the sense of constant social cooperation. I translate *antipoieîn* as "doing in return" and "producing in return," which are the two literal translations of *antipoieîn*, constructed from *poieîn*, which means either "to do" or "to produce, make, create."
3 *Antipascheîn* appears in *EN* v.5 in its perfect participle *antipeponthos* and perfect infinitive *antipeponthenai*.
4 Cf. *EN* v.5.1132b31–33. Burnet (1900), 223 translates *to antipeponthos allōi* (1132b23) as "that which has had done to it the opposite of something else." Gauthier and Jolif (2002), 373 render *to antipeponthos* as: *le fait de subir en retour ce que l'on a fait subir*, that is "the act of undergoing in return what you have made someone else undergo."
5 Cf. *EN* v.5.1132b31–34.
6 Cf. *EN* v.5.1133a14–16.
7 Cf. his note in Aristotle (2014), 264n365. Ross in Aristotle (1984) and Irwin in Aristotle (1999) both include the clause, and Gauthier and Jolif (2002), 379 reject the arguments of Ramsauer and Stewart that the passage is an interpolation.
8 Burnet (1900), 226 says that *to poioûn* and *to paschon* must refer to α and β in Proportion A (cf. Chapter 8) and compares use of them to "the case . . . of the doctor who provides health and his 'patient.'" Gauthier and Jolif (2002), 379 agree that "*poioûn* and *paschon* refer to the two parties who engage in exchange."
9 Cf. *EN* v.5.1133a7–14.
10 Gauthier and Jolif (2002), 372 (and many others) fall into the trap that reciprocity is a mathematical concept only. To support this view they cite Euclid's treatment of reciprocals in the *Elements*, but Euclid wrote that text after Aristotle's passing.
11 Cf. *EN* v.5.1132b34–33a2.
12 Cf. Aristotle (1999), 232.
13 Cf. *EN* v.5.1133a3–4.
14 Cf. *EN* v.5.1133a4–5. I choose "has shown kindness" out of the translations proposed in Liddell and Scott (1897) for *charisamenos*, because, I argue, "has shown

kindness" is closest to what Aristotle signifies by the term in *EN* v.5: that under the affect of *charis*, one individual, whom I name "A," renders concrete assistance to another, "B." For *charizomai* as "show kindness," cf. Liddell and Scott (1897), *charizomai* I.1; for *charis* as "kindness" or "gratitude" cf. *charis* II.1, 2. That is preferable to Irwin's "has been gracious" in Aristotle (1999).

15 Cf. *EN* v.5.1133a32–33.
16 On Proportion A, cf. Chapter 8. Birth plays a role in transactions between the free and the enslaved.
17 Cf. *EN* 1131a10–18.
18 Cf. *EN* 1132a14–19.
19 Cf. *EN* v.4.1132a24–29.
20 *EN* 1132b11–19; Ross' translation from Aristotle 1908b.
21 Cf. *EN* 1131b25.
22 Cf. *EN* 1132b11.
23 Danzig (2000) also argues this.
24 One candidate for such a good is security (cf. *EN* v.2.1130b2).
25 Cf. *Pol.* vi.8.
26 On "inverse," cf. *EE* 1242b7.
27 Cf. *EN* v.5.1133a1.
28 Cf. Soudek (1952), 64.
29 Cf. *EN* v.2.1130a32.
30 Cf. *EN* v.2.1130a14–24.
31 Cf. *EN* v.2.1130a 24–27.
32 Cf. *EE* 1221a4.
33 That profit K_α in money is

$$K_\alpha = (N_\delta V_\delta) - (N_\gamma V_\gamma) = N_\gamma [(\frac{\alpha}{\beta}) V_\delta - V_\gamma] \qquad (A_{12})$$

which is > 0, because α's *ergon* is overpriced relative to β's (cf. A_6 and A_7; N, V defined as above in A_1 and A_7).
34 Represented by formula A_8 in Chapter 8.
35 Represented by formula A_9 in Chapter 8.
36 Cf. *EN* v.5.1133a5–7. I translate the Greek as "diagonal pairing" since that signifies the algebraic operation that Aristotle names with the phrase, in contrast to Jackson's "cross-conjunction" (cf. Jackson, 1879, 94–5), which he coined to name a geometric construction that first appeared in Thomas Aquinas' commentary on the *Nicomachean Ethics* (cf. Thomas, 1964, 421, 427). For *suzeugnūmi*, "pair together," cf. Liddell and Scott (1897).
37 Thomas' use of a square neither expresses nor represents anything about Proportion A, but has only distracted scholars from a genuine appreciation of Aristotle's theory of proportional exchange. Cf. previous and following notes.
38 H. Jackson (1879) and Soudek (1952), 59 agree with Thomas. Burnet (1900) and Joachim in Aristotle (1951) put aside his hypothesis. Soudek (1952), 64–68 documents how Thomas' reading of *EN* v.5 has been reproduced down through centuries of scholarship.
39 Meikle (1997), 60, a remark that calls into question his claim to understand the chapter.
40 Cf. *EE* 1242b7.
41 Cf. *chrēsimon*, *EE* 1242b2.
42 *EE* 1242a6–7; translation revised from Aristotle (1984).
43 Cf. Kenny (1978) and Barnes (2004).

44 Cf. Cooper (1990).
45 *EN* ix.1.1163b32–35.
46 Cf. *EE* 1242b5.
47 *EE* 1242b6.
48 Cf. *EE* 1242b7.
49 Cf. *EE* 1242b8–10.
50 EN vi.4.1140a10–14.
51 Strangely, Jackson (1879), 95–96, interprets the passage as if the Greek read: *hōs autos pros ton ellatō, houtō to par' autou ginomenon pros to para tou ellatonos* rather than the Greek he quotes: *hōs autos pros ton ellatō, houtō to para tou ellatonos ginomenon pros to par' autou.*
52 Cf. *EN* viii.14.1163a26–27.
53 Cf. formula A_{12} (note 33).
54 Cf. *EE* 1242b10–11.
55 It is surprising that after Aristotle goes to some length to emphasize that he is interested in examining exchange relations only between "those who are different and not equal," that Heath, Meikle and Judson all deny that, and assert that Aristotle is only interested in the case where the parties are treated as equals; cf. references cited in note 5, Chapter 8.
56 Cf. *EE* 1242b15–16.
57 Cf. *EE* 1242b16–17.
58 It is unclear in Solomon's translation of passage (8) (cf. Aristotle, 1984a) whether "proportion" refers to Aristotle's Proportion A or rather to a proportion for determining payments out of a common fund based on prior contributions to that fund (discussed also in *EN* v.3), which is algebraically the same as proportion B, so that a reversal would result in our Proportion A. There are two problems with such a reading: 1) It does not correspond with the Greek, for each of the two *men . . . de* clauses discussing distribution (1242b12–13, 13–15) are closed, and the *de* of 1242b15–16 (passage (8)) replies to the *men* of 1242b6. 2) Solomon's reading would have the superior one suffer a loss through Proportion A rather than the gain he actually secures.
59 Thus, contrary to Scaltsas (1995), 259, the transaction is determined by the lesser party's individual need for the *erga* of the superior one, not by some generalized need for them "in society."
60 Cf. *EE* 1242b16–18, cf. *EN* viii.14.1163a29. That loss under Proportion B:

$$Z_\alpha = (N'_\gamma V_\gamma) - (N'_\delta V_\delta) \approx N'_\gamma (V_\gamma - \frac{\beta}{\alpha} V_\delta) \tag{B_3}$$

for, in contrast to A_{10}, here $N'_\gamma V_\gamma > N'_\delta V_\delta$ since $\gamma > \delta$ as $\frac{\alpha}{\beta} > 1$.

61 For as the lesser argues in elsewhere in the *Nicomachean Ethics*, "what is the use in being a friend to an excellent or ruling person if one is not going to benefit from it?" (cf. *EN* viii.14.1163a34–35).
62 Cf. *EE* 1242b18–21.
63 Cf. *EN* 1163b1–3.
64 Cf. *EN* v.2.1130b30–32.
65 Cf. *EN* v.2.1130b30–32.
66 Cf. Ober (1989), 240–242 on the threat of punitive judgments against the wealthy, and 226–230 and 231–233 on how generous liturgies protected the wealthy.
67 Meikle (1997), 25–26 claims that Aristotle's denial of strict commensurability between exchangers and their *erga* (cf. passage (4) in Chapter 8) "is tantamount to an admission that he does not know what is equalized in fair exchanges of food,

shoes and houses." Meikle's critiques of *EN* v.5 make no mention of passage 9, above. Until Meikle comments on that passage, we are compelled to put aside his objection. In addition, Meikle (1991), 194 objects to Aristotle's view that an inequality of exchangers must figure in an exchange. He assumes that a case where $\frac{\alpha}{\beta} > 1$ could only lead to exploitation.

68 Cf. *Pol.* ii.2.
69 So, $T = Z_\alpha + K_\alpha$, where Z_α is defined in formula B_3, and K_α in formula A_{12}.
70 That answers Meikle's criticism, noted at the outset of this chapter; cf. Meikle (1997), 25–6. Cf. also *EN* viii.14.1163b11–12.
71 Translation of Fragment 47B3 in Diels and Kranz (1956) from E. Minar (1942), 91, revised by Soudek (1952), 57. Pack (2010), 42 says: "Aristotle is in favor of promoting the middle class partly by executing socioeconomic policies that to some extent take from the rich and give to the poor, taking from those with an excess and giving to those with a deficiency." Randall (1960), 255 comments: "Aristotle thus stands for the omnicompetence of the state. There is nothing that political government must refrain from doing, if it makes for human welfare. Aristotle thus quite literally is stating the theory of the 'welfare state.'"
72 Cf. *EN* viii.14.1163b3–4, 12–14.
73 *EN* v.6.1134b2–7.
74 Cf. passage (10) and *EN* viii.14.1163b3–4, 12–14.
75 Cf. passage (10) and *EN* viii.14.1163b11–12. Cf. Thomson and Tredennick's translation in Aristotle (1955).
76 At 1163b18.
77 Cf. *EN* viii.14.1163b3–4, and Thomson and Tredennick in Aristotle (1955).
78 Cf. *EN* v.5.1133a3–5.
79 De Ste. Croix (1981), 271 writes: "Doctors, in the earlier periods of Greek history, were also placed in much the same category as other 'craftsmen': in Homer the doctor is grouped among *dēmioērgoi*, with the seer, the carpenter and the minstrel (*Od.* xvii.382–5); and in Plato he is put on the same level as the shipwright (*Gorg.* 455b)."
80 As Soudek (1952), 59.
81 Cf. *EN* v.1.1130a3–4.
82 Therefore, D. McKerlie (2001), 135 misses the mark when he says that Aristotle's "conception of the common good does not lead him to give special priority to helping the badly off."
83 As Polanyi (1968a), 152 also says: "Reciprocity as a form of integration gains greatly in power through its capacity of employing both redistribution and exchange as subordinate methods."
84 Polanyi (1957b), 153.
85 Cf. passage (4a), Chapter 8.
86 Cf. passage (3), Chapter 8.
87 In *eîdos*; cf. passage (1), Chapter 6.
88 Cf. *Pol.* i.2.1252b12–16, 27–30.
89 Cf. passage (1), Chapter 8.
90 Cf. passage (1) in Chapter 8.
91 Cf. *EN* v.5.1133a19–21. This passage follows directly after the text quoted in passage (1) in Chapter 8.
92 Cf. *EN* v.5. 1133a29.
93 Cf. *EN* v.5.1133b10–13.
94 Cf. *EN* v.5.1133b16–17.
95 Cf. *EN* v.5.1133b13–14.
96 Cf. *EN* v.5.1133a30–31.

97 Cf. *Rep.* ii.369c.
98 Cf. *EN* v.5.1133a30–31. On the one hand, in exchanges governed by Proportions A or B, the terms are *treated* as commensurable, and may be *represented* in units of currency. Despite that, on the other hand, it is the relative need of the parties that determines the transaction, not "price" or currency.
99 Cf. *EN* v.5.1133a1.
100 Cf. *EN* v.5.1132b34.
101 Judson (1997), 168–169 proposes that "need measures all things" means, for Aristotle, that the value of *erga* are measured by how much exchangers need them. That proposal leads to a "problem," reasons Judson, "that just prices will be lower for the rich than the poor," since the rich are already "well provided" with goods, and hence need the goods of others less (171). Diagonal pairing resolves the social problem that Judson envisions. Judson's own solution – to make "just prices relatively resilient to variations in how given exchangers are actually situated" (171) – would eliminate from Aristotle's theory a determining role for need in transactions.
102 Cf. *EE* 1244a24, 27–28.
103 Cf. *EN* viii.9.
104 Cf. *EE* 1242a40, *EN* viii.12. Does this then mean that friendship is "complete virtue" rather than justice, contrary to *EN* v.1.1129b31–30a1, 3–5? Cf. Chapter 7.
105 Booth (1993), 60 notes: "Finley argues that the practice of liturgies as a way of seeing to the city's various needs, but above all as a manner of transferring wealth from the well-off to the poor, had its origins in an age "when the aristocratic households performed essential public services ... by expending labour and materials at their private disposal" [Finley 1973, 151]. This aristocratic ethos of the duty of assistance to the city and its poor is evident in Isocrates' statement that in former times those who possessed wealth came to the aid of the poor and delivered them from want, and on a more abstract level, in Aristotle's discussion of honourable expenditures (gifts) on services to the gods and the city."
106 Cf. *EN* 1120a6–7.
107 Cf. *Pol.* iv.12.1296b18.
108 Cf. *EN* iv.1.1120a8.
109 Cf. *EN* v.1.1130a4, cf. also v.6.1134b5–6.
110 *EE* 1242b18–20. Moreover, strict commensurability would eliminate an opportunity for the superior one to practice the virtues.
111 Meikle (1997), 35. Or, as Marx (1967), 65 puts it, "only a make-shift for practical purposes."
112 E.g. Hunt (1975), 237.
113 As argued by Rawls, who, however, has not criticized Aristotle in this way, for his system is more complicated. Cf. Rawls (1958), 164–194; Rawls (1999).
114 Hunt (1975), 242, 237.
115 Hunt (1975), 237.
116 For discussion of homonymy and Aristotle's theory of it, cf. Shields (1999).
117 Cf. *EN* 1133b18–20.
118 Cf. *EN* viii.14.
119 This well-known phrase, from Marx's *Critique of the Gotha Programme*, is believed to be a paraphrase of *Acts* 4:32–35.
120 Cf. *EN* v.3.1131a25.
121 Thus I disagree with the claim of Cordner (1994), 294 that that thought "has no place at all in Aristotle's ethics."
122 Cf. *EN* viii.14.1163b7–8.
123 Thus Aristotle himself solves the problem raised in Nussbaum (1988a), of how to improve artisans and farmers so that they can participate more fully in civic affairs.

10 Grace in Aristotle's theory of exchange

I have deferred treatment of the role that Aristotle assigns "grace" (*charis*) in his critique of political economy up to this point, so as to first present clearly the concepts and formulae discussed until now. It is now time however to take up that role and that controversy.

Only Polanyi and Finley embrace Aristotle's unusual remarks in the *Nicomachean Ethics* proposing that grace (*charis*) play a role in exchange.[1] Polanyi says of Aristotle's proposal, "Nothing, I feel, could show better the meaning of reciprocity." He refers here to Aristotle's call for the exercise of "kindness" in two-party exchange transactions. He contrasts Aristotle's remarks with "the marketing view that invested barter with the qualities which are the very reverse of the generosity and grace that accompanied the idea of reciprocity."[2] Other commentators from Thomas d'Aquino to Miller and Meikle reject or ignore the Philosopher's suggestion that *charis* govern exchange.[3] Meikle has gone so far as to say that to the principal issues of *EN* v.5 "*koinônia* and the spirit of the Graces and of gift and counter-gift, have no application."[4] That assertion reflects a difficulty in our thinking, in our understanding of Aristotle's views, for Aristotle says that grace and the Graces *do* play or at least *should* play a role. Moreover, the language of "gift and counter-gift" is prominent in the chapter (cf.: *metadosis, antapodosis, antidosis, anthupēretêsai*).[5] I propose that scholarly failure to understand Aristotle's claim of a role for grace in exchange is one reason for our poor understanding of *EN* v.5. As Aristotle says, preliminary to any investigation, it is necessary for us to go through the things that are puzzling.[6] In my view, our efforts to understand Aristotle's thought will fail until we comprehend the role he assigns grace in exchange. I claim that it is not helpful to brush aside Aristotle's remarks on grace, if we are to arrive at an adequate understanding of his views. It is the task of this chapter to confront and resolve that issue. To do so, I will draw from and discuss passages from the *Nicomachean Ethics*, the *Eudemian Ethics*, the *Politics* and the *Rhetoric*.

Aristotle says that the Greeks established sanctuaries to the Graces to encourage reciprocal giving (*antapodosis*) among the citizens in communities of exchange.[7] He explains that under the affect of grace we reciprocate kindness shown us and then take the lead in showing kindness ourselves in the future.[8] Aristotle argues in the *Rhetoric* that exercising graciousness means serving someone in need, often by giving them material assistance.[9] For example, under proportional giving-of-a-share, a superior party accepts terms beneficial to a weaker one, even if she would thereby lose wealth (cf. Chapter 9).[10] That is just, because, as Aristotle says,

(1) Justice is the only virtue that seems to be another person's good, for it is related to another, for it does what benefits another.[11]

Such gracious conduct is part of the reciprocity which Aristotle says is necessary to preserve city-states because they are "composed of people who differ in kind".[12] Such remarks are at odds with some contemporary theories of justice and with some readings of Aristotle's ethical works.[13] Therefore, an effort to clarify Aristotle's peculiar idea of the exercise of grace in exchange promises to be illuminating. Here, I am interested in understanding the relationship that Aristotle is drawing between grace and relations of exchange among citizens who differ in kind, for he says that citizens must differ to compose a city-state, as we saw in Chapter 6.[14]

Charis, in brief

Aristotle's remarks about grace appear near the outset of his discussion of reciprocal justice in the *Nicomachean Ethics*. Aristotle says that in communities of exchange if the citizens do not benefit each other, then

(2) Giving-of-a-share (*metadosis*) does not occur, but it is by giving-of-a-share that they remain together. That is the reason (*dio*) they established a sanctuary of the Graces (*Charitēs*), so that there would be giving-back-in-turn (*antapodosis*).[15]

In the passage, Aristotle asserts that the Greeks built sanctuaries to the Graces in order to prompt their citizens to give each other a share of their *erga*, of what they produce, or of a service they provide, capable of satisfying human need, so that they would thereby remain together, for to share and meet each other's needs was the original reason why they came together.[16] Aristotle's use of the conjunction *dio* links the establishment of the sanctuary to *metadosis*, giving-of-a-share, the reciprocal exchange, that he says is vital to the community. There is no one English word that translates *metadosis*. We can only approximate it with a hyphenated phrase "giving-of-a-share". I argue that *metadosis* means that we must not only share with each other, but, in accordance with Aristotle's definition of justice, reproduced in passage (1), we must benefit each other. I must give the other what she needs, not just what I can argue is monetarily equivalent to her goods. If I do not, the giving-of-a-share does not occur, but it is by the giving-of-a-share that we remain together.[17] *Antapodosis*, like *metadosis*, can also only be translated with a hyphenated phrase, giving-back-in-turn.

Aristotle tells us what sort of behaviour is characteristic of grace immediately after passage 2, and so describes the behaviour that would produce *antapodosis*. He guides us towards understanding how, in his opinion, grace can play a role in exchange. He says:

(3) It is peculiar to grace (*charis*) that we must serve-in-turn (*anthupēretêsai*) the one who has shown kindness (*charisamenos*) to us, and take the lead in showing kindness (*charizomenos*) in the future ourselves.[18]

In this passage Aristotle means that under the affect of *charis*, one individual, whom I name "A," renders concrete assistance to another, "B." Below I will introduce texts from elsewhere in Aristotle's works that support that reading. *Rhetoric* B.7 says that *charis* accompanies giving or service. It cites the following as an instance of *charis*: "for example, the one who gave the mat in the Lyceum."[19] That text also says that such a *charisamenos* serves (*hupereteō*) someone.[20] Moreover, it states that the recipient of help is in a state of *need* (*deēsis, chreia*).[21] Thus the kindness is not gratuitous, but meets a need. The *charisamenos* is not just exhibiting a *manner* of graciousness, as when we hold a door open for someone, but rather does something concrete to assist a needy person, for example gives them a mat, or supports them in exile.[22] The *charisamenos* is also equipped with the means to render such assistance, for example she has a mat to spare or the means to obtain one.[23] Passage (3) calls for a two-fold response to such kindness: 1) that we be kind in turn to the one who shows kindness to us, and 2) that we be kind in the future, that is that B, after A has shown kindness, i) reciprocate in some way, for example show gratitude (*charis*) to A, and ii) take the initiative in showing kindness (*charizomenos*) to A or others in the future.[24] Aristotle would have us compete in being kind and grateful, rather than in taking advantage of each other. A similar practice of reciprocal kindness is described by Plato's Socrates in the *Gorgias*:

(4) [T]his alone of good deeds (*euergesiaí*) makes the one experiencing kindness (*eû pathonta*) desire to do kindness in turn (*ant' eû poieîn*), so that it seems to be a good sign that if someone who has done kindness with respect to this good deed, he will experience kindness in turn (*anti' eû peisetaí*).[25]

Here Plato, as does Aristotle in passage (3), describes someone doing kindness which is experienced by another, who then is moved to be kind in turn.

The relationship of *charis* is usually *asymmetric*. If B is needy and has nothing to sleep on, and A gives B a mat, how can B reciprocate? Perhaps, only by expressing thanks in some way, because he is without means. Thus we find in Aristotle the traditional asymmetric understanding of relationships of *charis* (*gratia*) that is known from Roman patron–client relations: The patron protects the client or provides material support, in gratitude for which the client supports the patron's election campaign or renders honour to the patron. In summary, in *EN* v.5, under the affect of *charis*, a person of means renders concrete assistance to someone in need, who, in turn, also under the affect of *charis*, reciprocates in some way. In this way, *charis* produces *metadosis* and *antapodosis* in the community, as in passage (2).

Those who established the sanctuaries to the Graces acted, claims Aristotle, to encourage citizens to behave graciously towards each other. Such gracious conduct is grounded in the reciprocity that Aristotle argues is necessary to preserve a community composed of people who differ in kind.[26] For sharers fulfill differing functions in a community (cf. Chapter 8). If sharers did not differ, they would have nothing to offer each other, and, moreover, they would not necessarily need each other, for they could quite possibly fulfill all their needs by themselves. But people who differ are not each able to easily provide for all of their needs. Some of their needs are more difficult or nearly impossible for them to meet as meeting those needs involves capacities that they lack. Thus the citizens need each other, because they each need access the capacities of others, because, at the very least, they need the different goods that others are capable of producing. My difference in kind from others puts me in need of those others. I move towards the other out of my difference. In their nature, inasmuch as they differ from each other, sharers need each other. Consequently, they need to share with each other. Thus, they need be gracious towards each other. The need for graciousness therefore arises from the fact that citizens differ in kind (*eîdos*). In the ethical writings, Aristotle builds such exhortation to behave graciously, towards the other, into his theory of political economy and represents it mathematically, placing terms representing the key dimensions of variability into proportion with each other. His formulae express: 1) that we are other in *eîdos*, and 2) how we must benefit those who are other than we in *eîdos*.[27] I will not repeat discussion of those topics here, for they are presented in Chapters 8 and 9. Here I only relate that material to *charis*.

In exchange transactions as understood by Aristotle, the application of the ratio $\frac{\alpha}{\beta}$ in Proportion A (cf. Chapter 8) guarantees that party β could never improve himself, for the relative quantities that they receive of each other's goods are determined by the ratio $\frac{\alpha}{\beta}$, which represents their relative economic, social or political position in the community. In accordance with Proportion A, the superior one always receives the lion's share of the good subject to a transaction. The result is that the weaker is fixed in his inferior position. No matter how good his *erga* may be, he cannot improve his position by any transaction. His constant experience is loss, the acceptance of which could become for him a disposition of character, for he must accept subservience (*areskeia*), or seek retaliation,[28] and neither course is conducive to achieving the good life (*eû zēn*) towards which Aristotle advises us all to strive, for vices such as subservience or vengeance are obstacles to the development of virtue. As a result of such exploitation, the weaker party has no reason to "serve in turn," or "show kindness" to the superior one; he is not a *charizomenos* (cf. passage (3)). By contrast, a superior party, who insists on application of proportion A in an exchange, seeks "gain" (*kerdos*) rather than justice in his dealings with others.[29]

He is overreaching (*pleonektei*).[30] As "the better, [he] supposes that it is fitting for him to have more (*pleon echein*)."[31] With the use of the phrase *pleon echein* Aristotle flags such transactions as unjust, for *pleon echein* means to have more than one's share. The superior party insists on Proportion A through an act of *pleonexia*, greed. So, the superior one is not a *charisamenos* (cf. passage (3)). A transaction governed by proportion A is a deviation from, or corruption (*parekbasis*) of civic friendship. To Aristotle, it expresses the corruption of communal exchange by commerce (*hē kapēlikē*).[32] Both parties are reduced to ungraciousness.

That would seem to be a terrible result, by the standards of graciousness and kindness that we have reviewed. But Aristotle has a solution: To bring about gracious conduct in exchange, that is, to bring about giving-back-in-turn and giving-of-a-share, Aristotle proposes right after passage (3) and right before he begins his discussion of exchange, the following:

(5) And that which brings about giving in return (*antidosis*) which is proportional is diagonal pairing (*hē kata diametron suzeuxis*).[33]

Since giving-in-return (*antidosis*) and giving-back-in-turn (*antapodosis*) – which is the result of the inspiration of the Graces (cf. passage (2)) – are equivalent expressions, grace and "diagonal pairing" each seem to play roles in bringing about equivalent states. Thus it is likely that there is some relation between them. Chapter 9 presents a derivation of the meaning of "diagonal pairing" and of the way it transforms Proportion A into another proportion through which the lesser party benefits in, rather than loses from a transaction. Aristotle compensates the superior party for the loss of wealth through such a transaction by the award of honour, that is social influence and protection from punitive lawsuits against his or her wealth. With diagonal pairing and the apportionment of honour, Aristotle constructs a transaction which meets the needs of both parties: the weak receive the material goods they need, and the superior party the social good that is more valuable to her or him than the material wealth she surrenders. That is the economic impact of grace in social relations.

At this juncture, the transaction may cease to be bilateral, for the weaker has not the capacity to properly honour the superior, a task that only the larger community can actualize, for in bodies of citizens, "what is common is given to the one who does good service to what is common, and honour is common (*koinon*)."[34] Even if the weaker party were to testify in court to the *charis* of the superior, even then he relies on the community, as the jury, to "honour" the superior one with a favorable judgment. Therefore, the transaction is not one of bilateral exchange relations, as we ordinarily conceive such: Through the allocation of honour, the community balances the weakness of its lesser members with the strength of its superior ones, so that the weak receive what they need, and, hence, the opportunity to pursue the good life themselves.[35]

As is characteristic of exchanges governed by grace, the transaction is asymmetric. Through grace the superior party accepts from the weaker party material goods less in value than those he provides the weaker. In just proportional exchange in Aristotle's economic thought, superior sharers in a community materially assist the needy, and receive honour in compensation.[36] For Aristotle, that is simply common decency. For the decent person is superior to the merely just,[37] because he is not, as Irwin translates, "an exact stickler for justice" (*ho mē akribodikaios epi to cheîron*).[38] Rather, he is inclined to take less, and does not insist on his full rights (*elattōtikos*), even if he has the law on his side (*kaiper echōn ton nomon boēthon*).[39] Aristotle's proposal that the superior party in transactions be kind to the lesser and give him something beyond what he pays for, calls into question the claim that "In the *Nicomachean Ethics* we find no mention of kindness [or] charity."[40] Certainly, passage (1) makes that claim doubtful, for a practice of justice that must benefit someone else contradicts the modern notion that justice is only a matter of settling accounts fairly under a contract,[41] and seems to involve kindness or charity in some way.

The ontology of grace

The relationship through which superior members of a community benefit the more needy ones characterizes for Aristotle a special sort of civic friendship, the aim of which is to maintain the existence, the being, of the lesser party.[42] "For the superior one who benefits another wishes, by his own *ergon*, that the other exist, and that other must give back in turn (*antapodidonai*) to the one who has given existence (*to donti to eînai*)."[43] Here again we see *antapodosis* at work. It is a function of "superior" members of the community to support the existence, the being, of weaker ones. In this way, such a superior sharer uses wealth the best,[44] and in doing so, he fulfills a communal function, for wealth is one of the qualities of the community,[45] and its use consists in spending and giving.[46] The beneficiaries give honour back in turn.

Aristotle's proposal encourages superior parties to practise the virtue of generosity, which *for them* is essential to the good life as a life of virtue, for the superior ones too have needs requisite to the good life, such as opportunities for practising the virtues towards other sharers. Moreover, the superior party's practice of grace inspires the practice of grace in his beneficiaries (cf. passage (3)), for, as Aristotle says, we are moved to serve in turn the one who has been kind to us, and in the future to take the initiative in acting kindly ourselves. The person who experiences kindness (*charis*), expresses gratitude (*charis*) and is moved to be kind (*charizomenos*) in the future.[47] Thus the grateful person becomes the kind person. By giving a material benefit to the lesser, the superior gives the lesser the material sufficiency (*autarkia*) for practising the good life, for the good life requires a level of material sufficiency.[48] Due to the beneficence of the superior party, the weaker would obtain respite from the material want that interferes with experiencing the good life,[49] and thus for expressing the virtue of generosity towards others. In this way, the lesser is enabled to rise from passivity, as a receiver, to activity, as a giver, for "all things desire and love existence" and "we exist in activity, since we exist by living and doing."[50] Thus, "the giver has more being than the receiver";[51] the superior one supports not just the mere existence of the lesser, but also his existence as a virtuous individual.

The superior party is honoured, not for his possession of wealth, but for his practice of grace in his disposition of his wealth, not because he *is* a ruler (*archōn*), but because of the *way* that he rules. In the final analysis, it is not out of fairness that we promote the ability of each and all to experience the good life, but for the stability of the polis, for citizens who are able to experience the culture that the community offers are thereby bound more closely to the community, and become less likely to separate themselves off as a faction, or resort to violence.[52] As Ober notes, Aristotle was one who "expressed deep concerns that the resentment of class inequality among the poor would lead to social upheavals."[53] His proposal may be his way to reduce friction between the wealthy and the poor and reverse polarization between classes – certainly a problem in America today where income inequality has become extreme.[54]

Aristotle encourages us to act graciously, kindly and generously in our dealings with others. One grounding for his recommendation proves to be ontological. Members of a community have to differ in *eîdos* if they are to be able to be of any meaningful use to each other, beyond just being "another hand." For they come together to satisfy each other's needs, for individually they are not able satisfy all of their needs and, consequently, need others. For in differing in function and in *eîdos* they exhibit different capacities and those differing capacities enable some to satisfy some needs, and others to satisfy other needs. Thus, the human reaches out to the other, and enters into civic friendship with the other, not just insofar as they are the same, but also insofar as they differ. Friendship, then, has an origin in the nature of things, for I must associate with others in order to meet my needs, but insofar as those others fulfill different functions in the community than I fulfill and thus satisfy needs that I cannot satisfy or satisfy as well, I esteem those others as valuable, as worthy of the goods that we produce together and of the life that we try to build together, regardless of how differently placed on the social status scale we may be, for our social bonds arise from our very being. For we need the other in order to enjoy a complete existence, for the stronger must exercise the virtue of generosity, and her beneficiaries that of gratitude. When we are so benefited, we must, in turn, take the first opportunity to benefit others, and so exhibit grace both as benefactor and beneficiary. In so aiding his weaker other, the superior one cares for himself, for he acknowledges that he is as dependent on the community as his weaker partner, for each differs in function, and each needs the other and the *erga* of the other. Thus, for Aristotle, by caring for others I care for myself. In this way, Aristotle would overcome the alienation that paralyzes the contemporary world.

Notes

1 Cf. Polanyi (1957a), and Finley (1977).
2 Polanyi (1957a), pp. 110–111.
3 Cf. Meikle (1997), 154; Judson (1997); Miller (1998). The Western tradition that neglects grace in connection with *EN* v.5 stretches back to Thomas d'Aquino's *Commentary on Aristotle's Nicomachean Ethics*. Thomas passed over the issue of grace in Aristotle's economic thought as though it had no significance (cf. Thomas, 1993).
4 Meikle (1997), 154.
5 In contrast to the critics, Polanyi (1957a) and McCarthy (1990) grant that both issues are important to understanding the text.
6 Cf. *Met.* 995a24–25.
7 Cf. *EN* v.5.1133a2–4. I leave whether and where such sanctuaries may have been established to archaeologists and historians. Cf. Pausanias (1918), 9.35.1: "at Athens, before the entrance to the Akropolis, the Kharites are three in number." Burnet (1900), 225 notes that Pausanias also reports sanctuaries to the Charites in the *agora* at Sparta, Orchomenos and Olympia.
8 Cf. *EN* v.5.1133a4–5.
9 Cf. *Rh.* B.7. 1385a21–33.
10 Cf. *EE* 1242b15–21, *EN* 1133a5–7.
11 *EN* v.1.1130a3–4.
12 *Pol.* 1261a 23–4.
13 For example Cordner (1994), 293 claims that in the *Nicomachean Ethics* there is no mention of kindness or of the virtue of charity. Cordner's claim is discussed below.
14 *Pol.* 1261a22–31.
15 *EN* v.5.1133a2–4.
16 Cf. *Pol.* i.2.
17 Cf. *EN* v.5.1132b33–33a2.
18 Cf. *EN* v.5.1133a4–5. I choose "has shown kindness" out of the translations proposed in Liddell and Scott for *charisamenos*, because, I argue, "has shown kindness" is closest to what Aristotle signifies by *charis* in *EN* v.5. For *charizomai* as "show kindness," cf. Liddell and Scott (1897), *charizomai* I.1; for *charis* as "kindness" or "gratitude" cf. *charis* II.1, 2. That is preferable to Irwin's "has been gracious" in Aristotle (1999).
19 *Rh.* B.7.1385a27–28.
20 Cf. *Rh.* B.7.1385a32, 33. Liddell and Scott on *hupereteō*: "in the best Greek, simply *to be a servant, do service, serve.*"
21 *deēsis* at *Rh.* B.7.1385a21, 26, 32; *chreia* at 33.
22 Cf. *Rh.* B.7.1385a25–26.
23 Cf. *Rh.* B.7.1385a27–28.
24 In his commentary on the *Rhetoric*, Konstan has shown that "gratitude" is the best translation of *charis* (in the phrase *charin echein*) when it refers to the affect produced in the recipient of assistance. Cf. Konstan (2006), Chap. 7. Liddell and Scott *charis* II.2 agrees.
25 *Gorg.* 520e. Gauthier and Jolif (2002), 372 cite this passage, but not for this purpose.
26 *Pol.* ii.2.1261a22–31.
27 Cf. Gallagher (2012) and (2014a).
28 Cf. *EN* v.5.1132b34.
29 Cf. *EE* 1221a4.
30 Cf. *EN* ix.8.1168b19.
31 Cf. *EN* viii.14.1163a26–27.

32 Cf. *Pol.* i.9.1257a18.
33 Cf. *EN* v.5.1133a5–7. I translate the Greek as "diagonal pairing" since that signifies the algebraic operation that Aristotle names with the phrase, in contrast to Jackson's "cross-conjunction," which he coined to name a geometric construction that first appeared in Thomas Aquinas' commentary on the *Ethics* (cf. Chapter 9). For *suzeugnūmi*, "pair together," cf. Liddell and Scott (1897); cf. Jackson (1879), 94–95; Thomas (1964), 421, 427.
34 *EN* viii.14.1163b6–8.
35 Thus Aristotle himself solves the problem raised in Nussbaum (1988a) of how to improve artisans and farmers so that they can participate more fully in civic affairs.
36 Aristotle's proposal in *EE* 1242b2–21 coheres with his proposals for public assistance for the poor in *Pol.* vii.10, where he recommends: 1) That the poor be exempt from having to contribute for the common meals of the city; 2) That the state provide block grants to the poor for the establishment of homesteads; 3) That the wealthy pay for the attendance of the poor at obligatory meetings of the assembly so that they can take off work. Aristotle's proposals exhibit a concern that the community assist the needy in a way that has not received due attention. It is as if Aristotle believes that out of the loins of the poor may come the next general, and therefore the community must join together to help the poor man raise and provide for his family and involve them in public affairs.
37 *EN* v.10.1137b11.
38 Irwin's translation in Aristotle (1999) is quoted.
39 *EN* v.10.1138a1–2.
40 Cordner (1994), 293. McKerlie (2001), 135 also misses the mark when he says that Aristotle's "conception of the common good does not lead him to give special priority to helping the badly off."
41 Cf. Hunt (1975), 237. Here I do not refer to Rawls, whose view of fairness requires the well off to spend in such a way that they benefit the least advantaged. Such a view is closer to Aristotle's; cf. Rawls (1999).
42 Cf. *EE* 1244a24, 27–28.
43 Cf. *EE* 1244a28–30. Rackham in Aristotle (1981) renders: "For the superior friend and benefactor wishes existence to belong to his own work—and to him who gave one existence it is one's duty to give existence in return." But 1) to call another human being one's "work" seems a departure from Aristotle's use of *ergon* elsewhere in the ethical writings (cf. the section on Incommensurability in Chapter 8), and 2) to expect a symmetric relationship between unequals seems contrary to Aristotle's treatment of such friendships, for the weaker party cannot be expected to render existence to the stronger and the Greek does not support such a reading.
44 Cf. *EN* 1120a6–7.
45 Cf. *Pol.* 1296b18.
46 Cf. *EN* 1120a8.
47 This study thus confirms that Konstan (2006) is right to say that the primary affect associated with charis is gratitude.
48 Cf. *Pol.* 1253b25.
49 Cf. the useful discussion in Meikle (1997), 44–45.
50 Cf. *EN* ix.7.
51 Cf. Hunt (1975), 243.
52 Cf. *EN* 1132b33–33a2.
53 Cf. Ober (1989), 197.
54 Cf. Ober (1989), 241; cf. Piketty and Saez (2014), and Chapter 14.

Part III

Contemporary application

Social welfare analysis: theory

Introductory note

Part III of *Aristotle's Critique of Political Economy* applies Aristotle's theory to a problem in contemporary political economy, namely, social welfare analysis. Chapter 11 discusses issues and problems with contemporary theories of social welfare. Chapter 12 reviews Aristotle's theory of exchange, presents case studies on the role of inequality in contemporary economy, and derives an Aristotelian Social Welfare Function.

11 The state of social welfare analysis

Most contemporary measures of social welfare are based on estimations of the presumed welfare of individuals. Those values are aggregated to advance a measure of social welfare for a society. But societies are not mere aggregates of individuals, for then societies would be like heaps of sand, rather than communities of interdependent, cooperating persons, and as Aristotle argues, if a city-state, or any other composite, were a mere "heap," it could not constitute a unity,[1] for it is the nature of an organic unity that it cannot be composed of things that are like one another (such as grains of sand or other identical individuals); moreover, a composite unity is more than its elements.[2]

That contemporary approaches to social welfare are individualistic, rather than social, is clear from what their proponents say. In the case of the capability approach, Sen explains: "Capabilities . . . are notions of freedom, in the positive sense: what real opportunities you have regarding the life you may lead . . . [T]he value of the living standard is given by the capability to live various types of life."[3] In Sen's remark, "freedom," of course, refers to the freedom of the individual to choose the life she leads. Likewise, Nussbaum describes the capability question as follows: "[T]he real question one must ask is, What are people actually able to do and to be? What real opportunities for activity and choice has society given them?"[4] Again, the focus here is on capabilities available to individuals. Nussbaum elaborates the capability approach by advancing a list of multiple, specific capabilities for the individual: to live, to have good health, to move freely from place to place and so on.[5] Fleurbaey and other advocates of primary goods also evaluate social welfare by reference to individuals' living standards as defined recently by Fleurbaey with a combination of income, capabilities and satisfaction.[6] Utilitarian approaches are also individualistic, for they are based on "a particular philosophical thesis of the subject matter of morality, namely, the thesis that the only fundamental moral facts are facts about individual well-being."[7] Of a different sort is the measure of Gross Domestic Product (GDP) per capita. The presumption of that measure is that if the GDP per capita is increasing then average well-being is increasing, a notion that is refuted below.

In defense of all these measures, one could argue that if individuals in a society have those capabilities, or those primary goods, or that GDP per capita, surely that would mean social welfare is at a certain optimum level, right? I answer, "Not necessarily." Methods of aggregating the presumed welfare of individuals *cannot* represent *social* welfare. GDP per capita is said to tell us what an "average individual" enjoys as income, but in any case, it tells us nothing about anyone's social relation to others. The approaches of Nussbaum and the followers of Rawls assemble components of a minimum human living standard chosen by them, for which the aim and the result is individualistic, that is do individuals have these "opportunities" or "goods." I call all such approaches "aggregate."

In my view, a shortcoming of the capabilities approach is that it focuses on how well the individual is, without addressing how well the society as a whole is, that is how well it functions. Nussbaum's work on indices continues to measure social health as an aggregate of individual well-being. It is more interesting than GDP per capita, but remains of the same sort, that is an aggregate measure of how well individuals are in relation to a list of criteria chosen by experts. In contemporary approaches, the assumption – unsubstantiated – is that if the individual is doing well enough, then therefore the society is healthy. This can lead right back to the supposition that if individuals *on average* are doing well, then society is well. That is a result presently achieved in GDP per capita data as the rich are doing fabulously well in material terms and, in GDP data, their high income is averaged over the whole society to give the impression that everyone is doing well. But social welfare cannot be a mere aggregate, for insofar as the welfare with which we are concerned is *social*, it can only be expressed in terms of active relationships of all individuals, all to each other. Concepts like capabilities, primary goods, standard of living, GDP per capita, are all abstractions from the real social process that makes them possible.

Individuals' lives, living standards and capabilities, are largely determined by the specific nature of the society of which they are a part. The individual assesses what s/he is capable of doing, or being, in reference to the labour market, that is society's determination of what s/he is worth, and that unfortunately determines in many instances what s/he thinks, as attested by Sen's concept of adaptive preferences. The reason why contemporary Western theoreticians draw up models of social welfare that revolve around the individual is because they are reflecting the values of societies that present the individual with a market basket of commodities that s/he must acquire to be socially accepted. Accordingly, individualistic approaches to social welfare end up being subjective and culturally specific. I believe that Sen rejects Nussbaum's proposal to draw up a list of specific capabilities, because every such list will reflect the society and culture of those who draw it up.[8]

Attempts to specify an optimum individual standard of living (qua capabilities or primary goods) are undermined by philosophical argument on the diversity and incommensurability of second-order ends. Alkire argues:

The capability approach conceives of poverty reduction as multidimensional. That is, it recognizes that more than one human end . . . has intrinsic value in a society, and that the set of valued ends and their relative weights will vary with the diversity of individuals and cultures. But if human ends are diverse in kind and cannot be adequately represented by a common measure such as income or utility, this creates a problem. It becomes impossible to choose 'rationally' between options that pursue different sets of ends . . .[9]

As Rawls (following Kant), would say, we do not agree on ends. If that is true, we cannot agree on an approach that is based on assigning value to ends. Crespo argues, "ends are heterogeneous, and cannot always be substituted for each other."[10] Therefore, there cannot be agreement on a list of capabilities (qua Nussbaum), nor on coherent social policy to actualize such a list, since there must be multiple such lists, rendering public policy either incoherent or subject to the power of a minority. There is no solution to this problem inside a philosophical framework in which the freedom of the individual is a fundamental value.[11]

In contrast to the theories reviewed above, Aristotle is concerned, not with how well-off individuals are, but with how well people cooperate with each other. He calls that *reciprocity (to antipeponthos)*. He says in *Politics* ii.2 and in *Nicomachean Ethics* v.5 that reciprocity is what preserves states. Suppose ζ is something that preserves societies, then social welfare would be dependent on ζ. For Aristotle, ζ is reciprocity. By contrast, contemporary approaches focus on how adequately my basic needs and expectations are met or how much freedom I have: interesting but different questions from how well citizens are cooperating with each other. The first is a question the answer to which can quickly veer into listing desired commodities, from homes to mobile phones, for if "being able to have attachments to things and persons outside ourselves"[12] is necessary, then I need a mobile phone and a pair of skis.[13]

The only contemporary estimates of social welfare that begin to represent social relations are the Gini index and "rich-to-poor" inequality ratios, for insofar as they compare the income of members of a society to each other, and since that income is derived from social activity and social relationships, Gini and inequality ratios say something about the relationship of society to itself, for I have income insofar as I possess or have produced or will produce something of value to others; moreover, my income represents my capacity to call upon others to meet my needs and satisfy my fancy. Thus Gini and inequality ratios, as measures of *relative* income, indicate something about the relationship of society to itself. One problem with them, however, is that neither is formulated as a maximizing function, that is, were either maximized, it would be *inequality* that would increase, not social welfare. Moreover, Gini and inequality ratios yield values nearly identical for countries differing widely in development and social structure. Table 11.1 shows that inequality ratios and the Gini index fail to capture aspects of social welfare that distinguish the

Table 11.1 Gini index and inequality ratios for several countries. Data from UNDP (2009).

$\frac{R}{P}$ (ratio of income share of top decile of the population to that of lowest)

Denmark	8.1
Togo	8.3
Russian Federation	11
Iran	11.6

Gini index

Togo	34.4
Spain	34.7

countries paired (Russia and Iran, Denmark and Togo, Spain and Togo). A more dynamic representation is called for.

I argue in subsequent chapters that social welfare is best understood in relation to reciprocity, which signifies the relationship of a society to itself. Since we are not isolated, self-sufficient individuals living alone in deserted milieu, our representation of social welfare must represent our nature as social beings, in the words of Aristotle, as "political animals." A meaningful metric of social welfare will capture that reciprocal relationship. In contrast, conceptions of social welfare that focus on the individual, fail to express that reciprocal relation of a society to itself. In the following chapters, I present a proposal for quantifying that relationship.

Notes

1 Cf. *Met.* Z.17.1041b12. ἐπεὶ δὲ τὸ ἔκ τινος σύνθετον οὕτως ὥστε ἓν εἶναι τὸ πᾶν, [ἂν] μὴ ὡς σωρὸς ἀλλ᾽ ὡς ἡ συλλαβή – ἡ δὲ συλλαβὴ οὐκ ἔστι τὰ στοιχεῖα, translated by Ross: "Since that which is compounded out of something so that the whole is one is not like a heap but like a syllable – and the syllable is not its elements," and for another 20 lines of text Aristotle shows why a composite is more than its elements (cf. Aristotle, 1924).
2 Cf. previous note, and *EN* v.5, *Pol.* ii.2.
3 Sen (1986), 48–49.
4 Nussbaum (2011), 59.
5 Nussbaum (2006), 58. Though Nussbaum has questioned Sen's emphasis on freedom (cf. Nussbaum, 2006, 61ff.), her approach remains oriented to providing capabilities to the individual. She writes, "Some freedoms limit others. The freedom of rich people to make large donations to political campaigns limits the equal worth of the right to vote" (2006, 61). Accordingly, Nussbaum would rather defend the worth of the individual vote over the freedom to influence a candidate through large contributions.
6 Cf. Fleurbaey (2015).
7 Cf. Scanlon (1982), 108.

8 Sen, one of the originators of the capabilities approach, opposes the formulation of a "canonical list of capabilities, chosen by theorists without any general social discussion or public reasoning," on the grounds that people should be allowed to settle these matters on their own (cf. Sen, 2004b; Nussbaum, 2006, 61ff and note 15), that is that theorists violate democratic deliberation in imposing a list of capabilities upon those in need. In other words, many in traditional or collectivist societies might reject some of the items on Nussbaum's list of capabilities, as specifically "Western".

9 Alkire (2002), 85–86, cited in Crespo (2014), 92. Alkire adds, "*if* one means by rational what is meant by 'rational choice theory', namely, the identification and choice of a maximally efficient or productive option, the one (or one of the set) in which the total benefits minus the total costs is the highest possible."

10 Crespo (2014), 95.

11 A solution is possible, however, within a communalistic framework, but discussion of that is outside the scope of this book.

12 Capability #5 in Nussbaum (1990), 225.

13 Nonetheless, Sen and Nussbaum's work on capabilities has been very important in shifting attention in contemporary economic discourse away from desires and utilities and towards needs.

12 Derivation of an Aristotelian Social Welfare Function

Aristotle says that states are preserved by the practice of reciprocity in exchanges among their citizens.[1] Aristotle emphasizes that what is just in exchange is proportional, for the *polis* stays together through proportional reciprocal action.[2] Communities lacking reciprocity are unstable, for citizens who are exploited due to the absence of reciprocity, "return evil for evil."[3] In ancient Athens, reciprocity included redistribution as a subordinate method of social integration.[4]

For Aristotle, reciprocity appears in the role of relative social status or power in a transaction. Aristotle represents how relative social status or power affects an exchange with a proportion, as follows:

(1) The party who is superior deems himself worthy of the following inverse proportion: As he is to the lesser, so that which the lesser produces is to that which he produces, because he is in a position as ruler to ruled.[5]

Or, as expressed in a formula:

(A)
$$\frac{\alpha}{\beta} = \frac{\delta}{\gamma}$$

for which the superior party is α, his product γ, the lesser party β, and his product δ. As Aristotle explains in a parallel passage in the *Nicomachean Ethics*, "the better supposes that it is fitting for him to have more (*pleon echein*)."[6] The terms α, β represent the social status of the exchangers, or, as Aristotle puts it, their "worth," for example, in an oligarchy, the amount of wealth possessed.[7]

Aristotle is interested in the extent to which citizens exploit or benefit each other in relation to their relative social status. His social criticism of the Greece of his time, following the discussions in Plato's *Republic*, is that the strong exploit the weak. He represents that by including the ratio $\frac{\alpha}{\beta}$ in his formula of exchange (formula A, above). As we shall see below, to correct social injustice Aristotle proposes that the strong benefit the weak in proportion to the very ratio $\frac{\alpha}{\beta}$ under which the weak are ordinarily exploited. For Aristotle, if reciprocity is practised, people's needs are met and the *polis* stays together.[8] Moreover, if the weak receive what they need, they have the opportunity to pursue the good life. In this way, Aristotle himself solves the problem raised by Nussbaum, of how to improve artisans and farmers so that they can participate more fully in civic affairs.[9] The ratio $\frac{\alpha}{\beta}$ is, in contemporary parlance, an inequality ratio. Aristotle was the first to apply such a ratio to social welfare analysis. In accordance with the use of that inequality ratio in exchange formulae, Aristotle holds that all relationships of exchange are asymmetrical.

Formula A is unusual. Conventional theories of value, such as those of Smith, Marx, Mill or Jevons, consider only commodities in the exchange ratios.[10] But Aristotle also includes the exchangers. Here I defend the usefulness of inequality ratios as measures of social welfare that today still serve the purposes for which Aristotle advanced them in the *Nicomachean* and the *Eudemian Ethics*, to represent the degree of *reciprocity* practised in a society.

The result of an exchange governed by formula A is that the party with higher status or more power exploits the one with less. A simple transformation of formula A illustrates this. Consider

(A₁) $$\delta = \frac{\alpha}{\beta}\gamma$$

which states that the value of product δ that party β has to hand over to party α will be a multiple of the value of product γ that party α hands over to β, by the factor $\frac{\alpha}{\beta}$.[11] That means that exchange value is a function not only of the value of the goods exchanged, but also of the social status of the exchangers. Joining Nussbaum in rejecting the assumption of the social contract tradition that "contracting parties are rough equals,"[12] we achieve at least a psychic liberation from the exploitation that that assumption conceals. The ratio $\frac{\alpha}{\beta}$ measures the relative social status or power of the parties to the exchange, which amounts to the potential rate of exploitation of one party by the other. The two following case studies show that such exploitation continues today.

Contemporary case study A: purchase of a US tractor by a Brazilian farmer

Let the United States be party α and a Brazilian farmer party β, who purchases an agricultural tractor from a US company. The US government adds a 15% export duty on top of the list price for tractors being exported to Brazil.[13] In this case, $\frac{\delta}{\gamma} = 1.15$ and $\frac{\alpha}{\beta} \geq 1.15$.[14] This example reveals the United States using its greater power to exploit Brazil. That rate of exploitation is at least 15 per cent. (I say "at least," and indicate that with $\geq$, because here I neglect factors such as currency exchange rates and debt service on invested capital.)

In effect, in this example, the value of Brazilian agricultural goods produced with tractors and exported to the United States are devalued by 15 per cent. Such exploitation may force a country to devalue its currency. Thousands of similar cases exist in international trade.

Contemporary case study B: housing

The international housing crisis suggests that there has been exploitation of home buyers by financial institutions. One aspect of this exploitation is illustrated by the gap between what I hypothetically call the "real value" of a home and an inflated or speculative market value. Such a gap is revealed, I claim, in the collapse of housing prices in OECD countries. Home prices were driven up through speculation in financial instruments, the value of which began to collapse in 2007. We consider mortgaged sales, in which a bank, as holder of the mortgage, becomes the seller (party α), because the buyer (party β) must pay the holder of the mortgage in order to secure a free and clear title.

Example: Housing prices have fallen 37 per cent in Spain from 2007 to 2013.[15] The average price in 2007 was 59 per cent higher than the price in 2013. Assume that the price in 2013 is closer to the real value of the house, title to which is held by the mortgage holder. Then, $\frac{\delta}{\gamma} = 1.59$ and $\frac{\alpha}{\beta} \geq 1.59$.[16] This case suggests that financial institutions have been using their power to exploit home buyers, for after the market collapse homebuyers were still required to pay off the face value of loans. That rate of exploitation is at least $\frac{\alpha}{\beta} = 1.59$. In effect, the buyer's resources are devalued by 37 per cent.

The use of social status in contemporary theory

Moreover, John Rawls builds social status and worth into his difference principle, which elaborates the second of his two principles of justice in *A Theory of Justice*. In Rawls' model of the difference principle, the higher status and wealth of party x_1 determines that x_1 benefits more from a distribution/transaction than the less advantaged party x_2. Rawls argues that any curve that represents transactions between two unequal parties, x_1, x_2, labelled OP by Rawls in Figure 3.1, Chapter 3, "is always below the 45° line, since x_1 is always better off,"[17] that is something like Aristotle's Proportion A is always followed under Rawls' scheme (cf. Chapters 3 and 8). Thus Rawls recognizes, and incorporates into his theory inequality within a society.

To begin to work out a numerical example relating Aristotle's and Rawls' models, note that in Aristotle's discourse, the more advantaged party x_1 would be assigned a higher worth than the less advantaged party x_2, that is, $\frac{\alpha}{\beta} > 1$. Thus Rawls' model can be represented in the terms of Aristotle's and vis-versa (cf. Chapter 3). Since Aristotle's theory of the role of social status in exchange was formulated, circulated and debated throughout the philosophical world for two millennia prior to Rawls' formulation of the difference principle, it is reasonable to conclude that Aristotle's theory influenced Rawls.[18]

In Rawls' theory, the difference principle is chosen "behind the veil of ignorance" because, Rawls imagines, when we are hypothetically "veiled" from knowing whatever social position we will hold in life, we would want to make sure that our needs are satisfied no matter where we end up in the social hierarchy, that is whether we are party α or party β in Aristotle's model. The difference principle is both Aristotelian and Kantian. The Kantian adopts it under the doctrine that each human is an end in him- or herself.[19] Aristotle adopts his own version because he is not blind to the effect of inequality in exchange. Rawls recognizes that imbalances, inequalities, will come to be, and with the difference principle attempts to prevent them from becoming overwhelming for the weak. Aristotle likewise was concerned that inequality would lead to exploitation, social injustice and civil strife.[20] Unlike Rawls, however, Aristotle does not accept the view that the more advantaged x_1 must always benefit more from a distribution or transaction than the less advantaged party x_2. In contrast to Rawls, Aristotle would dramatically alter inequality by requiring that whoever in a transaction is of higher social status *benefit*, not exploit, his weaker partner, by the proportion of their respective social status, by agreeing to terms of exchange more favourable to the weaker party.[21] (That is a principle that Rawls rejects in his determination of a fair wage.[22])

In conclusion, two case studies, and Rawl's theory of justice, all support the view that relative social status or power continues today to determine terms of exchange, both in international trade and within a society. The case studies show that that is exploitative to the lesser parties in such transactions. Aristotle, however, would use that relative social status as an instrument for benefiting those same lesser parties. I now turn to formulate an Aristotelian Social Welfare Function based on the principles examined so far.

Derivation of an Aristotelian Social Welfare Function

The ratio $\frac{\alpha}{\beta}$ expresses the relative social status of parties to an exchange, that is, the degree to which one party may exploit the other. Clearly, if α exploits β in the ways illustrated in the case studies, then reciprocity, in Aristotle's sense, would seem to be lacking in the transaction, for Aristotle says that if exchangers do not benefit each other, then "Giving-of-a-share (*metadosis*) [of each other's goods] does not occur, but it is by giving-of-a-share that they [the members of the community] remain together," for certainly if one party exploits the other, the first party is not benefiting the second.[23]

I propose that if social welfare in a country improves, then the average value of $\frac{\alpha}{\beta}$ in exchanges would decline towards 1, or, expressing that as a positive function, the average value of $\frac{\beta}{\alpha}$ would increase.[24] That is, the following quantity would increase:

(C₁)
$$\mathbf{W_A} = \frac{1}{n}\sum_{i=1}^{n}\varepsilon_i$$

where $\varepsilon = \frac{\beta}{\alpha}$, n being the number of transactions. If the average value of $\frac{\beta}{\alpha}$ increases, then W_A would increase. I investigate W_A as a candidate for a Social Welfare Function. I call W_A *reciprocity,* or *reciprocal social welfare. I propose that this quantity measures reciprocity in a society as the degree to which redistribution is practised,*[25] *the degree to which members of a society cooperate to benefit each other.*

We are also interested in how W_A changes, that is whether social welfare in a community is improving or worsening. We formulate the time rate of change of reciprocal social welfare as:

(C₂)
$$\mathbf{R_W} = \frac{\mathbf{W_{A.t+1}} - \mathbf{W_{A.t}}}{\mathbf{W_{A.t}}},$$

where t is a time index. Chapter 14 presents results in estimating W_A for entire societies. R_W is indicated by the slope of the curves in the figures.

Notes

1 Cf. *Pol.* ii.2.1261b30; EN v.5.
2 *EN* v.5.1132b34–5, cf. 1132b31–33, 1133a6.
3 Cf. *EN* v.5.1132b33f.
4 Cf. Polanyi (1957a), and (2001), 157–158.
5 *EE* 1242b8–10.
6 *EN* viii.14.1163a26–27.
7 Cf. *EN* v.3.
8 Cf. *EN* 1133ᵃ1–5.
9 Cf. Nussbaum (1988).
10 Cf. Chapter 8, endnote 84.
11 This is true regardless of the value of $\frac{\alpha}{\beta}$, i.e., if $\frac{\alpha}{\beta} < 0$, then β exploits α. The long form of this analysis appears in Chapter 8, section on "Quantifying Aristotle's incommensurables."
12 Cf. Nussbaum (2006), 69, 71.
13 Cf. WTO (2013) for rates of export tariffs on tractors and other goods.
14 The farmer pays $104,000 for a Case IH Maxxum 120 tractor at the time the tractor leaves a US port. Thus $\delta = \$104,000$, since δ is what party β hands over to party α to obtain the tractor. Approximately $14,000 of that price is an export tax that the Brazilian must pay the US government because of a 15.4 per cent US duty on exports of tractors to Brazil. We can deduct that $14,000 from δ to arrive at something closer to the real value of the tractor, that is, a list price, which is closer than $104,000 to the value of the work (*ergon*) of party α, which we signify with the term γ. Then, $\gamma = \$90,000$. Then $\frac{\delta}{\gamma} = 1.15$ Then, by formula (A), $\frac{\alpha}{\beta} \geq 1.15$. (Cf. <http://caseih.ironbuilder.com/viewSummary.aspx> for prices of Case IH tractors prior to export.)

15 From first quarter 2007 to fourth quarter 2013, according to data published by Instituto Nacional de Estadística (www.ine.es). Cf. also casas.facilisimo.com/preciometro/.

16 In this example, $P_{2013} = 0.63 * P_{2007}$, or $P_{2007} = 1.59 * P_{2013}$, where P_i indicates the market value of a home in year i. A buyer in 2007 has surrendered, for a house, a sum of cash and notes of indebtedness totaling $1.59 * P_{2013} = \delta$. Assume that P_{2013} is closer to the real value of the house, title to which is held by the mortgage holder. Then, $P_{2013} \approx \gamma$, and $\dfrac{\delta}{\gamma} = 1.59$. According to formula (A), then $\dfrac{\alpha}{\beta} \geq 1.59$.

17 Rawls (1999), 66.

18 I am indebted to Leo Michelis for this suggestion. Nonetheless, despite Rawls' use of relative material worth or social status in the difference principle, Rawls (1999), §48 nominally rejects Aristotle's social criticism that the "worth" a community assigns an individual is invariably a factor in determining exchanges that she makes with others.

19 Cf. *Grounding for the Metaphysics of Morals*, Indianapolis, 1993, section 2.

20 Cf. *EN* v.5.1132b33–33a2.

21 Cf. *EE* 1242b2–21, esp. b15–16, Gallagher (2012), and Chapter 9 for Aristotle's revision of Proportion A.

22 Cf. Rawls (1999), 268, 271, where he rejects the notion "to each according to his needs."

23 *EN* 1133ᵃ1–2; cf. ᵃ3–5; *EE* 1242b2–21, esp. 1242b15–21.

24 I draw this suggestion from Aristotle's *Eudemian Ethics*. Cf. Gallagher (2012) for complete discussion.

25 This does not include measure of the reciprocal compensation to the "superior" party in the form of "honour," that is, social influence and protection from law suits, as discussed in Gallagher (2014b) and in Chapters 9 and 10.

Part IV

Contemporary application

Social welfare analysis: results

Introductory note

Part IV of *Aristotle's Critique of Political Economy* develops a method of estimating values of the Aristotelian Social Welfare Function presented in Chapter 12 and presents values for a number of countries. Chapter 13 presents the estimating technique, and Chapter 14 presents the results of numerical studies of several countries and discusses those results.

13 Estimating values of an Aristotelian Social Welfare Function

A direct determination of W_A (cf. Chapter 12) would measure – and average – the inequality ratio $\varepsilon = \frac{\beta}{\alpha}$ in effect in each exchange in a society – a rather formidable task in data collection and computation. Instead, we *estimate* W_A for a whole society: We approximate W_A for any given year with the ratio of the income shares of lower quintiles of a population to the income shares of higher quintiles. Our assumption is that the movement of such ratios would follow that of W_A, that is

$$(D) \qquad\qquad \mathbf{W_A} \approx \frac{Q_j}{Q_i}$$

where i, j are indices for one or more income quintiles. We justify D as follows:

1) Since in C_1 (cf. Chapter 12), W_A is the average value of $\frac{\beta}{\alpha}$ in transactions throughout an economy, namely, the average relative social status in effect in transactions, then if social status correlates with income, relative income represents relative social status,[1] that is $\frac{\beta}{\alpha}$.

2) In using ratios of income quintiles to estimate W_A, we implicitly assume that everyone in an economy carries out transactions with everyone else, at least indirectly, which assumption is valid insofar as the market mediates all transactions.

Therefore, in accordance with (1) and (2), it is reasonable to estimate W_A by ratios of quintiles of the income shares of the less well-off to those better off. Piketty also recommends study of income shares.[2] Moreover, it is correct to say that income represents power or social status, for our income is what enables us to make demands upon others. As Marx wrote: "The individual carries his social power in his pocket."[3] Since we here study relative income and rates of change of relative income, we escape from the Easterlin paradox and other problems associated with using data on absolute values of income.

Below, we study:

(D$_1$)
$$\mathbf{W_A} \approx \frac{Q_5}{Q_1}.$$

The ratio $\frac{Q_5}{Q_1}$ represents the relationship between the poorest quintile of the population and the richest.

In addition, in order to investigate the validity of $\frac{Q_5}{Q_1}$ as a measure of social welfare, we also study:

(E)
$$\frac{Q_5 + Q_4 + Q_3 + Q_2}{Q_1},$$

which is the ratio of all four lower quintiles to the top quintile. The ratio $\frac{Q_5 + Q_4 + Q_3 + Q_2}{Q_1}$ represents the relationship between the lower four quintiles of the population and the most advantaged top quintile. Comparing graphs of E with those of $\frac{Q_5}{Q_1}$ may help us verify whether $\frac{Q_5}{Q_1}$ is a good measure of social welfare for all, for if the shape of curves of E follows those of $\frac{Q_5}{Q_1}$ then we have evidence that $\frac{Q_5}{Q_1}$ represents the social welfare interests of all. E, however, is not an estimate of the two party exchanges that we have studied to this point. E simply represents the relative income shares of the lower four quintiles in relation to the highest. We can also use $\frac{Q_5 + Q_4 + Q_3 + Q_2}{Q_1}$ to investigate Piketty and Saez's conclusion that "More than 15 percent of US national income was shifted from the bottom 90 percent to the top 10 percent in the United States" from 1976 to 2007.[4] In other words, we can use this ratio to study the effect of contemporary, accelerating income inequality upon all.

Because $\sum_{i=1}^{5} Q_i = 1$, we can simplify $\frac{Q_5 + Q_4 + Q_3 + Q_2}{Q_1}$ to

(E)
$$\frac{Q_5 + Q_4 + Q_3 + Q_2}{Q_1} = \frac{1 - Q_1}{Q_1} = \frac{1}{Q_1} - 1$$

Some discussion is in order. First, all ratios $\frac{Q_j}{Q_i}$, including E, are *dimensionless quantities*. It is claimed that a process modeled with dimensionless quantities *"becomes more transparent"*[5] (more on that below). Many dimensionless quantities are ratios, such as D, D_1 and E.[6] This unusual property that inequality ratios are dimensionless, contrasts with other proposed measures of social welfare.

Second, the argument that inequality ratios are a better measure of social welfare than those based on primary goods, or capabilities, is supported by recent research showing that higher inequality retards economic growth, while "equality seems to drive higher and more sustainable growth."[7] If that is true, a Social Welfare Function that maximizes that driver for growth, for example W_A, represents an economy's capacity for growth, and hence, the ability of people to improve their welfare. In support of the view that inequality retards economic growth, Atkinson, Piketty and Saez have shown that "the surge in top incomes [i.e. the rise in inequality] over the last thirty years has a dramatic [negative] impact on measured economic growth,"[8] and Piketty and Saez argue that rising top incomes, that is growing inequality, was a contributing cause to the Great Recession.[9] Economic growth is the train by which many escape poverty and improve their welfare. That mechanism is not represented in the individualistic approaches to social welfare discussed in Chapter 11.

Third, the quantitative estimate of W_A investigated here is an *inverse* inequality ratio. As the inverse, it is subject to *maximization* (unlike $\frac{P}{R}$ or the Gini index).[10] Its rate of change R_W provides a dynamic representation of the evolution of inequality (cf. figures in Chapter 14), and proves far more instructive than the static values of $\frac{P}{R}$ or the Gini index.

Under Aristotle's theory of reciprocity and its measure presented here, it may well be that "an egalitarian hunting and fishing society" would have more reciprocity than, say, contemporary America, though the average American may have more goods and services at her disposal. There is nothing strange in that conclusion, since it is probably the case that there was more social cooperation in earlier societies, for example mediaeval Europe, than there is today. If some readers disagree with Aristotle on the importance of reciprocity, that does not mean *ipso facto* that Aristotle is wrong (or if they prefer, that I am wrong), but only that they are following contemporary beliefs about social welfare while Aristotle (and I) obviously are not. Maybe we could arrive at other, even better ways of understanding how well people are cooperating, but the focus on reciprocity and relative social status is Aristotle's approach, as Chapters 8 and 9 show.

The reader may object that our quantitative estimates of the Aristotelian Social Welfare Function are also a function of the instrumental good, income, like GDP per capita. But these estimates – unlike GDP per capita or the original Rawlsian formulation of social welfare as that of the least advantaged – are a function, *not* of the absolute value of an individual's income or of average income, but rather of *relative* income, that is the ratio of income shares of quintiles of the population to each other as an estimate of the average value of $\frac{\beta}{\alpha}$ effective throughout the economy. As such, it signifies *reciprocity*, which I claim is an intrinsic good, for, as Aristotle says, reciprocity preserves societies.[11]

Notes

1 Recent work showing that relative income correlates with perceived well-being, would seem to support that hypothesis. Cf. Clark et al. (2008).
2 Cf. Piketty (2013), 269.
3 Marx (1972), 156, 157.
4 Piketty and Saez (2013), 458.
5 Says Vlček in foreword to Kuneš (2012), which is a good source on dimensionless quantities from Avogadro's number on. Emphasis added.
6 E.g. Boyle's number.

7 Ostry et al. (2014), 17, 4.
8 Cf. Atkinson et. al. (2011), 8; cf. also Alvaredo et. al. (2013); and Tyson (2014). Tyson is former chair of the US President's Council of Economic Advisors.
9 Piketty and Saez (2013), 473.
10 Up to $\frac{Q_5}{Q_1} = 1$, the unlikely state where both quintiles receive the same income share.
11 *Pol.* ii.2.1261b30.

14 Quantitative studies in an Aristotelian Social Welfare Function

Reciprocal social welfare as measure of prosperity

This chapter presents figures showing $\frac{Q_5}{Q_1}$ and $\frac{1}{Q_1}-1$ for several nations over recent decades.[1] The average rate of change of $W_A \approx \frac{Q_5}{Q_1}$ is represented by the average slope of the graphs. If $\frac{Q_5}{Q_1}$ correlates with W_A, and the graph of $\frac{Q_5}{Q_1}$ has a *positive* slope, then in the represented society, reciprocal social welfare − and, I argue, for those in lower quintiles, the economy − is improving. This appears to have been the case in Ukraine from 1995 to 2011, in Ecuador from 1999 to 2014, in Thailand from 1981 to 2011, and in Iran from 1986 to 2005 (cf. Figures 14.1 through 14.4). Other countries whose $\frac{Q_5}{Q_1}$ data exhibit a positive slope include Cambodia and Mali.

Figure 14.1 Ratio of income and consumption share of the lowest quintile of the population to the highest in percentages $(\frac{Q_5}{Q_1})$, for Ukraine, 1988–2013. Source for raw data: World Bank.

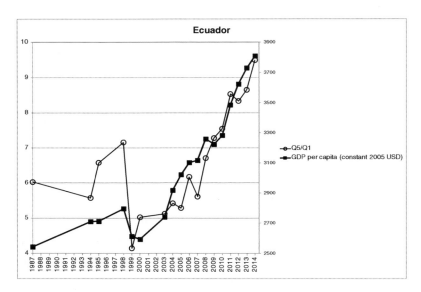

Figure 14.2 Plot of circles shows ratio of income and consumption share of the lowest quintile of the population to the highest in percentages ($\frac{Q_5}{Q_1}$), for Ecuador, 1994–2012, with scale on left abscissa. Plot of squares shows GDP per capita in constant 2005 dollars, for Ecuador, 1994–2012, with scale on right abscissa. Source for raw data: World Bank.

If $\frac{Q_5}{Q_1}$ correlates with W_A, and the graph of $\frac{Q_5}{Q_1}$ has a *negative* slope, then social welfare is declining and at least for the lower quintiles the economy is in recession, for the wealthiest benefit from transactions proportionately more than those less well off. The data shows that this is the case dramatically in the USA but also in Germany (cf. Figures 14.5 and 14.6). Russia and Ukraine show a precipitous drop in social welfare from 1988 to 1995 and then recover to different degrees. Other East European countries show such a sudden fall in social welfare, but do not recover.[2]

The reader may question whether a fall in $\frac{Q_5}{Q_1}$ really indicates that an economy is in recession at least for lower quintiles of the population, or whether a rise in that ratio signifies that the economy is growing. I direct attention to Figures 14.7, 14.8 and 14.9, which show E, that is $\frac{1}{Q_1}-1$, the ratio of the sum of the income shares of the lower four quintiles to that of the highest, for Ukraine, the USA, and Germany in the same periods as represented in Figures 14.1, 14.5 and 14.6. For the periods represented, a comparison of Figures 14.7, 14.8 and 14.9 with Figures 14.1, 14.5 and 14.6, respectively, shows that $\frac{1}{Q_1}-1$ (our measure of social welfare for the lower four quintiles) fell when $\frac{Q_5}{Q_1}$ fell, and for Ukraine, rose when $\frac{Q_5}{Q_1}$ rose. Figure 14.1 is one of the more complicated of the seven graphs of $\frac{Q_5}{Q_1}$. Nonetheless, Figure 14.7, the graph of $\frac{1}{Q_1}-1$

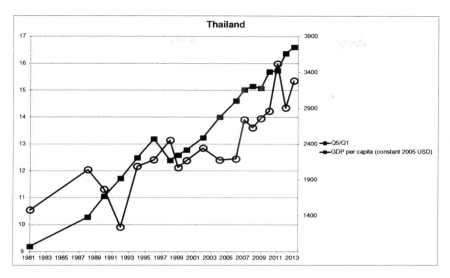

Figure 14.3 Plot of circles shows ratio of income and consumption share of the lowest quintile of the population to the highest in percentages $(\frac{Q_5}{Q_1})$, for Thailand, 1981–2013, with scale on left abscissa. Plot of squares shows GDP per capita in constant 2005 dollars, for Thailand, 1981–2013, with scale on right abscissa. Source for raw data: World Bank.

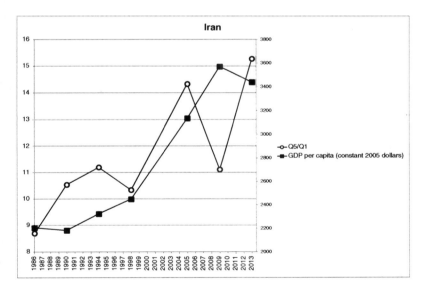

Figure 14.4 Plot of circles shows ratio of income and consumption share of the lowest quintile of the population to the highest in percentages $(\frac{Q_5}{Q_1})$, for Iran, 1986–2013, with scale on left abscissa. Plot of squares shows GDP per capita in constant 2005 dollars, for Iran, 1986–2013, with scale on right abscissa. Source for raw data: World Bank.

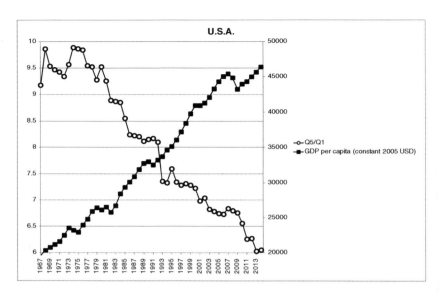

Figure 14.5 Descending plot (circles) shows ratio of income and consumption share of the lowest quintile of the population to the highest in percentages $(\frac{Q_5}{Q_1})$, for the USA, 1967–2014, with scale on left abscissa. Ascending plot (squares) shows GDP per capita in constant 2005 dollars (World Bank data), for the USA, 1967–2014, with scale on right abscissa. Sources for quintile data: US Census Bureau.

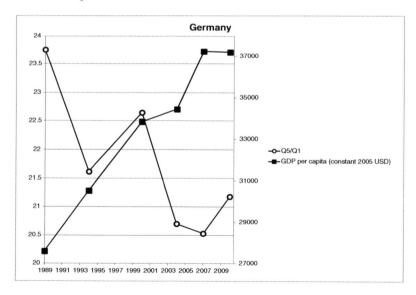

Figure 14.6 Descending plot (circles) shows ratio of income and consumption share of the lowest quintile of the population to the highest in percentages $(\frac{Q_5}{Q_1})$, for Germany, 1989–2010, with scale on left abscissa. Ascending plot (squares) shows GDP per capita in constant 2005 dollars with scale on right abscissa, for Germany, 1989–2010. Source for raw data: World Bank.

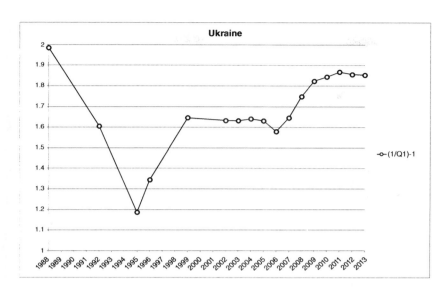

Figure 14.7 Ratio of the income and consumption share of the four lower quintiles of the population to the highest quintile in percentages ($\frac{1}{Q_1}-1$, cf. text), for Ukraine, 1988–2013, with scale on abscissa. Source for raw data: World Bank.

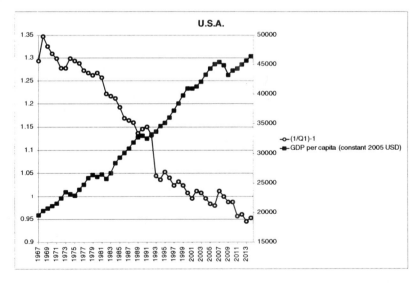

Figures 14.8 Descending plot (circles) shows ratio of income and consumption share of the four lower quintiles of the population to the highest quintile in percentages ($\frac{1}{Q_1}-1$, cf. text), for the USA, 1967–2014, with scale on left abscissa. Ascending plot (squares) shows GDP per capita in constant 2005 dollars, for the USA, 1967–2014, with scale on right abscissa. Sources for raw data: U.S. Census Bureau, World Bank.

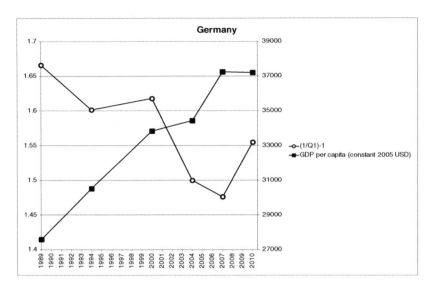

Figures 14.9 Descending plot (circles) shows ratio of income and consumption share of the four lower quintiles of the population to the highest quintile in percentages ($\frac{1}{Q_1}-1$, cf. text), for Germany, 1989–2010, with scale on left abscissa. Ascending plot (squares) shows GDP per capita in constant 2005 dollars, for Germany, 1989–2010, with scale on right abscissa. Sources for raw data: World Bank.

for Ukraine, follows the shape of Figure 14.1 closely. Similarly, Figure 14.8 (U.S.A.) is similar to Figure 14.5 and Figure 14.9 (Germany) to Figure 14.6. Upon reflection, this is not surprising, for Piketty and Saez have shown that it is the upper echelons of income that determine the level of inequality in an economy. The income share of the upper quintile represents the "denominator" of social injustice and determines the shape of the curves in all the figures. Piketty and Saez have shown that periods of high inequality are periods of economic stagnation, as is ours.[3]

In accordance with Figures 14.5 and 14.8 and the argument interpreting them, the US economy has been in recession since the mid-1970s. That is hardly a surprising conclusion to anyone who has followed the devolution of US basic industry since that time, a decline that has thrown skilled steel, machine tool and auto workers out of work in their industries and into low-paying jobs at MacDonald's and Burger King, if that.

In conclusion, if the graph of $\frac{Q_5}{Q_1}$ has a *negative* slope, then social welfare is declining and the economy is in recession for the middle and lower classes. Since $\frac{1}{Q_1}-1$ represents how well the majority of a population, that the lower four quintiles, are doing relative to the richest, I propose it as an additional measure of social welfare.

GDP per capita and social welfare

Figures 14.5, 14.6, 14.8 and 14.9 show how problematic is Gross Domestic Product (GDP) per capita as a measure of social welfare, at least in advanced sector countries such as the USA and Germany. In recent decades, increase in GDP per capita correlates with decrease in social welfare, as measured by either $\frac{Q_5}{Q_1}$ or $\frac{1}{Q_1}-1$. (Table 14.1 shows the correlation coefficients for the USA and Germany for GDP per capita and $\frac{Q_5}{Q_1}$ and for GDP per capita and $\frac{1}{Q_1}-1$. The negative correlation in the U.S. case is almost perfect [-0.97].[4]) Figures 14.5, 14.6, 14.8 and 14.9 are consistent with the supposition that there is now a negative correlation between GDP per capita and social welfare, as measured by either $\frac{Q_5}{Q_1}$ or $\frac{1}{Q_1}-1$. It appears that if $\frac{Q_5}{Q_1}$ and $\frac{1}{Q_1}-1$ do not decline, GDP per capita cannot rise; or for GDP per capita to increase, $\frac{Q_5}{Q_1}$ and $\frac{1}{Q_1}-1$ must decline. In recent years, for the U.S. or Germany to grow in terms of GDP per capita, the economy must contract for the lower four quintiles (as indicated by the fall in $\frac{1}{Q_1}-1$). This suggests, alarmingly, that for advanced sector economies, such as the U.S. and Germany, GDP per capita does not measure growth, but rather contraction of the economy.[5] Our data on the dimensionless quantities $\frac{Q_5}{Q_1}$ and $\frac{1}{Q_1}-1$ make "transparent" the evolution of contemporary economies by exposing the hoax of a "growth" while the majority of a population suffers.[6]

But Figures 14.2, 14.3 and 14.4 show that an economy can grow in social welfare and in GDP per capita at the same time. Figure 14.2 shows that $\frac{Q_5}{Q_1}$ in Ecuador grew in parallel with GDP per capita over a period of 15 years from 1999 to 2014. (The positive correlation between GDP per capita and $\frac{Q_5}{Q_1}$ is an impressive 0.9.) Likewise, Figure 14.3 shows that in Thailand, growth in both $\frac{Q_5}{Q_1}$ and GDP per capita follow each other over a period of 32 years (with a correlation coefficient of 0.85). Iran's curve for GDP per capita in Figure 14.4 also follows the growth of its curve for $\frac{Q_5}{Q_1}$ over a significant period of 20 years

Table 14.1 Correlation coefficients between $\frac{Q_5}{Q_1}$ and GDP per capita, and between $\frac{1}{Q_1}-1$ and GDP per capita for several countries

Country	Correlation coefficient between $\frac{Q_5}{Q_1}$ and GDP per capita	Correlation coefficient between $\frac{1}{Q_1}-1$ and GDP per capita
USA	−0.97	−0.97
Germany	−0.48	−0.8
Ecuador	0.9	
Thailand	0.85	
Iran	0.7	
Mali	0.92	
Cambodia	0.93	

from 1986 to 2005 (correlation coefficient = 0.7).[7] Even though Iran's $\frac{Q_5}{Q_1}$ suffers a sharp drop after the imposition of sanctions in 2006, it rebounds by 2013 to again parallel Iran's curve of GDP per capita. Growth in $\frac{Q_5}{Q_1}$ also closely correlates with GDP per capita in Mali from 1994 to 2009 (correlation coefficient = 0.93) and in Cambodia from 2004 to 2012 (correlation coefficient = 0.92). These figures demonstrate that GDP per capita and $\frac{Q_5}{Q_1}$ increase in tandem in four different regions of the world: South America, East Asia, the Middle East and Africa. Thus it is not a general law of economy that social welfare must fall with increasing GDP per capita, it seems to be so only in some developed capitalist economies. It seems in those countries that an increase in GDP per capita largely reflects what Aristotle calls *chrēmatistikē,* money making for its own sake through commercial and financial transactions rather than investment in mining, manufacturing, construction and energy that benefits the majority and draws other parts of the work force into some complimentary, supporting activity. *The issue is whether the increase in GDP reflects an increase in industrial activity* that benefits all. If so, then GDP per capita and $\frac{Q_5}{Q_1}$ can increase in tandem, as they do in in Ecuador, Thailand, Cambodia, Mali and Iran in the periods discussed above. That, unfortunately, is not the case overall in the USA and Germany. Moreover, the fact that GDP per capita does not correlate with social equity in advanced sector countries but does in select developing nations means that the inclusion of GDP per capita in the UNDP Human Development Index distorts its values, since it reflects qualitatively different phenomena in different countries; in some countries it reflects mainly "financials," in others "productive" economic activity in mining, manufacturing, construction and energy.[8] The data reported here on Ecuador, Thailand, Iran, Cambodia and Mali suggest that we have a new indicator of economic growth in the ratio $\frac{Q_5}{Q_1} \cdot \frac{Q_5}{Q_1}$, the ratio estimating the Aristotelian Social Welfare Function, is an indicator of economic growth that is ethical, for in order that $\frac{Q_5}{Q_1}$ grow, the economy has to grow for the lowest quintile, the lowest quintile must become better off, for under moral economic growth the condition of the poorest quintile must improve. Our study of $\frac{1}{Q_1} - 1$ shows that if the poorest quintile improves, the economy will grow for at least the lower four quintiles. This does not mean that the absolute value of the income of the top quintile must decline, but it does mean, justly, that its share of national income must decline. Unethical growth, where the share of national income of the top quintile increases and that of the lowest quintile declines, as has occurred in the USA since 1970s, should be made illegal.

Contrast between Europe and the United States

Figures 14.5 and 14.8 indicate that social welfare and, I argue, the economy have been steadily on the decline in the United States since at least 1976.

Figure 14.8 supports the conclusion of Piketty and Saez that significant national wealth has been transferred from the bottom 90 per cent to the uppermost 10 per cent.[9] For from 1976 to 2013 the total share of the lower *four* quintiles fell from 128 per cent of the share of the single highest quintile to 95 per cent of that share. In 1968, those lower four quintiles received 135 per cent of the income of the highest quintile; since 2009 the four have received in total just under what the upper quintile itself enjoys by itself. It is not surprising then that recent work shows that social mobility has been low in the United States in recent decades, making it difficult for offspring to escape the deterioration in living conditions represented by Figures 14.5 and 14.8.[10]

Figure 14.6 shows that also in Germany $\frac{Q_5}{Q_1}$ has fallen as GDP per capita has increased, but Germany has not produced the gross inequities that have developed in the USA. In 2010 reciprocal social welfare in the United States, as measured by $\frac{Q_5}{Q_1}$, was 6.5 per cent, while in Germany in the same year it was over 21 per cent, more than three times the US value. In 2009, France's value was over 23 per cent, Italy's almost 19 per cent, Spain's 16.5 per cent, and Greece's 17.5 per cent.[11] The same pattern follows for values of $\frac{1}{Q_1}-1$. In 2010 reciprocal social welfare as measured by $\frac{1}{Q_1}-1$ in the United States was just less than 1 (0.988), that is the top quintile enjoyed more income and consumption than the lower four quintiles taken together (cf. Figure 14.8). But in Germany in the same year, $\frac{1}{Q_1}-1$ was greater than 1.5, more than 50 per cent higher than the US value (cf. Figure 14.9).[12] The pattern in Germany continues in the rest of Europe: France's value for $\frac{1}{Q_1}-1$ is also 1.5, Greece, Italy and Spain have values of approximately 1.4.[13] The down-up alternation of Germany's curves for $\frac{Q_5}{Q_1}$ and $\frac{1}{Q_1}-1$ shows that the results of social policy there are not always negative, as they seem, alarmingly so, in the United States, where the decline of $\frac{Q_5}{Q_1}$ and $\frac{1}{Q_1}-1$ is nearly continuous. The negative correlation between GDP per capita and $\frac{Q_5}{Q_1}$ is much weaker in the case of Germany (-0.48) than in the United States. The higher values for social welfare in Germany can be attributed to its "social market" capitalism: "The German system of political economy attempts to balance social concerns and market efficiency," explains Gilpin, for the German state and private sector provide "a highly developed system of social welfare."[14] Such social welfare policies are not unique to Germany, which is simply "representative of the 'corporativist' or 'welfare state' capitalism of continental Europe, in which capital, organized labour and government cooperate in the management of the economy," explains Gilpin.

This study confirms that Europeans defend the social welfare of their peoples better than Americans. Europeans enjoy values of reciprocal social welfare (as measured by $\frac{Q_5}{Q_1}$) 2½ to 3½ times greater than Americans. All that indicates that there is a stronger community bond in at least continental European countries. This difference in social welfare between Europe and America may have its roots in the circumstance that American capitalism "did not develop on the foundation of a feudal system, but developed rather from itself . . . not as the result of a centuries-old movement, but rather as the starting-point of a new movement."[15] As a result, the mediaeval traditions of community and of feudal ties among individuals and classes do not exist in America.

Developing countries with growth in social welfare

In contrast to advanced sector nations, reciprocal social welfare in some developing nations increased over recent periods. In Ecuador, reciprocal social welfare, as measured by $\frac{Q_5}{Q_1}$, more than doubled from 1999 to 2014, for an increase of 129 per cent, for an average annual increase of +8.6 per cent (= $R_w > 0$, cf. p. 170). In Thailand, reciprocal social welfare increased 61 per cent from 1992 to 2011, an average annual increase of +3.2 per cent. In Iran, reciprocal social welfare increased 63 per cent from the mid-1980s to 2005, an average annual increase of +3 per cent.[16] By contrast, social welfare in the United States *decreased* −18 per cent from the mid-1980s to 2005, an average annual decline of −0.9 per cent ($R_w < 0$). The absolute value of reciprocal social welfare in Ecuador was 9.49 in 2014, 56 per cent higher than the United States for the same year. In Thailand in 2011 reciprocal social welfare was 16, more than double the US value, higher by 155 per cent. In Iran in 2013 reciprocal social welfare was 15.2, more than twice the US value, more than 150 per cent greater. These figures seem strange in contrast to the wealth and luxury enjoyed by some in the United States, but that's the point. That wealth is not shared in US society. There is extremist inequality.

Another impressive story is that of Ukraine. With the break-up of the Soviet Union and Comecon, social welfare, as measured by $\frac{Q_5}{Q_1}$, plummeted in Eastern Europe from the 25–31 per cent levels enjoyed in the late 1980s down to 8 per cent in Russia in 1993, 17 per cent in Poland in 1993 and 13 per cent in Ukraine in 1995. Russia has climbed back up only to the range of 12–14 per cent (cf. Figure 14.10), Poland to about 19 per cent, but Ukraine recovered by 1999 to 23 per cent and by 2011 had climbed to over 29.3 per cent, close to its value of 31 per cent in 1988 (cf. Figure 14.1). In this connection, reciprocal social welfare also serves to evaluate recent "regime changes" hailed as beneficial. It is disheartening that the lower class in Poland is worse off now after change wrought by *Solidarność*. The situation for the middle classes in Poland is not any better: The ratio of the income shares of the lower four quintiles to the top quintile ($\frac{1}{Q_1} - 1$) fell from 1.85 in 1985 to 1.43 in 1996, only to decline further to 1.4 and remain there through 2010, a decline in toto of 27 per cent. Hungary's value for $\frac{1}{Q_1} - 1$ fell from 2.1 in 1987 to 1.63 in 1993 − a decline of 30 per cent − and has flucuated around that value since. Lithuania fell from 2.04 in 1988 to 1.38 in 1993 and has stayed near that value since, a fall of 47 per cent. It would appear based on Piketty and Saez's analysis of what has occurred in the United States,[17] that there has been a significant shift of national income in these countries from the lower quintiles to the highest. This all indicates that the living standards of wage-earning

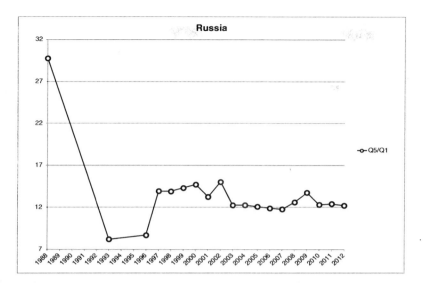

Figure 14.10 Ratio of income and consumption share of the lowest quintile of the population to the highest in percentages ($\frac{Q_5}{Q_1}$), for the Russian Federation, 1988–2012. Source for raw data: World Bank.

households in Eastern Europe were higher under the Soviet system than they are today. Nonetheless, all these former Comecon nations still boast values of reciprocal social welfare significantly higher than the United States.

Power of dynamic graphs

Dynamic graphs of $\frac{Q_5}{Q_1}$ enable us to distinguish social welfare for two countries with nearly identical $\frac{R}{P}$ values, for example, Russia and Iran. From the figures in Table 11.1 (cf. Chapter 11), it would appear that social welfare in Russia and Iran is roughly the same and that the societies are polarized to the same degree. But Figure 14.4 shows that social welfare in Iran increased from 1986 to 2005. Russia, on the other hand, as shown in Figure 14.10, has fluctuated around the value of 13 per cent from 1999 to 2012 as it continues to struggle with the aftereffects of abandoning socialism. Nonetheless, social welfare in Russia is much higher than in the United States, 96 per cent higher in 2012. Social welfare in Russia has been largely stable and has not systematically declined as has social welfare in the United States.

Conclusion

Parts III and IV of *Aristotle's Critique of Political Economy* have presented a derivation of an Aristotelian Social Welfare Function and report data estimating values of that function for a number of countries over recent decades. Following Aristotle's *Ethics* and *Politics*, the function represents social welfare in the relationship of a society to itself, that is the degree of reciprocity practised. Analysis of data estimating values of the function shows that the Aristotelian Social Welfare Function is a new indicator of economic growth, indeed, of ethical economic growth. This study has shown, however, that GDP per capita is not a universal measure of economic growth valid everywhere, for in some "advanced" capitalist countries growth in GDP per capita correlates with economic decline for the vast majority of the population.

The Aristotelian Social Welfare Function proves to be more relevant than contemporary measures of social welfare that focus on the condition of the individual rather than the society. Analysis of data on the new Social Welfare Function confirms that one significance for inequality data is that they reveal a transfer of national income to an increasingly wealthy minority from a majority that is becoming less well off.[18] The new Social Welfare Function promises to be useful to developing and emerging nations in justifying socio-economic policies that promote reciprocity, for now that the polices of the United States are shown to lead to the sort of maldistribution of benefits that we see in the case of Figure 14.5, institutions under the sway of the United States are not in a strong position to demand that other nations, for example Ukraine, tear down their social systems or impose austerity in order to meet the requirements of policies that lead to the results represented in that figure.

Moreover, with the results so far determined and to be elaborated, Brazil and other countries[19] that suffer under US export policies are provided with grounds for requesting that the World Trade Organization pressure the United States to roll back exorbitant export tariff rates, in order to encourage reciprocity in international trade. Studies in the Social Welfare Function may also provide home buyer associations with additional grounds for arguing that existing mortgage loan balances be scaled back to reflect reality.

Finally, Roddie argues that because families care for the well-being of their children, they exhibit an aversion to inequality as follows: If social mobility is low, as Chetty et al. argue for the United States, then – Roddie argues – an aversion to inequality is focused on the wealthy. That is so, I argue, because those better off are more able to ensure that their offspring are successful.[20] As $\frac{1}{Q_1} - 1$ has declined over recent decades, many have seen their "American Dream" end in a rude awakening of foreclosures and bankruptcy. Parents see or at least envisage their children living worse off than themselves. Where could this lead? Following historical precedent, I note that the 1929 height in the concentration of national income in the United States was followed by a sustained recession that gave rise to considerable social agitation. Perhaps something of that sort is around the corner. It is possible that the United States, and perhaps other OECD countries, are set for another equalization of income shares as Piketty and Saez document occurred no later than 1942 and was sustained until 1974.

Notes

1 The choice of the specific countries presented here was determined in part by the availability of data and in part by interest in the results of those countries. The United States and Russia were therefore chosen out of interest in how they would stand in regards to social welfare; Germany was chosen out of Europe because more data was available there; and Ukraine, Ecuador, Thailand and Iran were chosen because they all exhibit positive slopes in their curves of $\frac{Q_5}{Q_1}$ over significant periods of time, and they represent diverse regions of the world.

2 $\frac{Q_5}{Q_1}$ in Poland dropped from 28 per cent in 1985 to 17 per cent in 1993 and fluctuated between 17 per cent and 19 per cent up to 2011; Hungary's value has fallen from 35 per cent in 1987 down to 21 per cent in 2007; Latvia fell from 32 per cent in 1988 to 15 per cent in 2003 and fluctuated between 15 per cent and 16 per cent through to 2009; Lithuania fell from 32 per cent in 1988 to 15 per cent in 2008 (calculations of $\frac{Q_5}{Q_1}$ from World Bank data).

3 Cf. Piketty and Saez (2010).

4 I calculated the correlation coefficients using the Excel 2016 CORREL and Pearson functions. The values are identical. The weaker correlation between GDP per capita and $\frac{Q_5}{Q_1}$ in the case of Germany is discussed in the text.

5 Note: The data on Germany for 1989 do not include East Germany, but for 1994 and subsequent years they do (cf. World Bank, 2016). Given that social welfare in East Germany in 1988, following the East Bloc pattern, was probably in the range of 28–30 per cent, it is not clear how unification affected the combined data.

6 On dimensionless quantities cf. Kuneš (2012).

7 Although only a few data points are plotted in Figure 14.4 for GDP per capita (because of restrictions to the plotting method used for a two curve graph), a graph of GDP annual data follows the same average slope as Figure 14.4 for the period from 1999 to 2011.

8 GNI per capita – used in the Human Development Index – includes GDP per capita. Cf. UNDP (n.d).

9 Cf. Piketty and Saez (2013), 458, 473.

10 Cf. Chetty et al. (2014).

11 Calculations of $\frac{Q_5}{Q_1}$ from OECD data

12 In comparing absolute values of $\frac{1}{Q_1}-1$ for different countries, note that absolute equality, where each quintile enjoys 20 per cent of national income, would require that $\frac{1}{Q_1}-1 = 4$.

13 Based on World Bank data.

14 Cf. Gilpin (2001), 168–169.

15 Marx (1972), 884. Cf. also Marx (1997), 463.

16 This pattern is not followed in all emerging and developing nations. For example, in China, reciprocal social welfare fell from 25 in 1985 to 9.9 in 2010 (calculations based on World Bank data).

17 Cf. Piketty and Saez (2013), 458, 473.

18 On that, also cf. Piketty and Saez (2013).

19 E.g. Thailand, which endures an 11.4 per cent export tariff on tractors imported from the United States. Cf. WTO (2013).

20 Roddie (2015) supposes the aversion stems from "an individual's concern for the competition faced by his descendants" from the more numerous offspring of the better-off. In an age of low fertility among the well-off, success of offspring may be a better means of comparison.

Conclusion

This book has presented some disturbing socio-economic concepts from antiquity. First, while giving us a bright and optimistic picture of what "living well" (*eû zên*) was in practice for Athenians and what Aristotle in particular means by that phrase, the book has made it clear that *eû zên* is impossible for today's peoples to achieve without a radical change in national economies and international relations. For the core of *eû zên* is that a people be self-sufficient and able to deliberate on its future, and to in fact deliberate on that future, while having almost all the principal factors that determine its future under its control (cf. Chapter 7). That is impossible for all peoples in the civilized world today since in every case parties and forces outside their control, and concerning which they are thus unable to deliberate, determine the outcome of any matter about which they attempt to deliberate. For Aristotle says that we cannot deliberate over matters that are out of our control.[1] *Eû zên* has become lost culture. Should we then discard the ancient notion of *eû zên* as some irrelevant cultural anachronism and forget about achieving it? I suggest that future work on this problem examine two types of states:

1) Those that have achieved continuous or near-continuous progress in the degree of reciprocity practiced in their societies (e.g. Ecuador) and those that have achieved a stable high degree of reciprocity in the past (e.g. Hungary and other east European states prior to 1989).
2) Those that have attempted to achieve a degree of "near total self-sufficiency" (*autarkeia*)[2] in the modern world.

Of course, the latter such states are considered "backward" from the standpoint of contemporary international trade policies, but investigating how they achieve whatever degree of *autarkeia* that they enjoy, and its consequences for their social life, may yield some insight as to how to move towards achieving the self-sufficiency necessary to enjoy *eû zên* in today's world.

Part of Aristotle's doctrine of *eû zên* is that there are limits to wealth acquisition and to self-sufficiency through it, for he says in the *Politics* that the self-sufficiency achievable through wealth acquisition, useful for the good life, is limited (cf. Chapter 7). His point is that for a Greek citizen, further wealth accumulation beyond what is needed to support the household and its political and cultural praxis is only possible by involvement in mercantile trade and such, and that makes one dependent on markets when before one was independent of them. For Aristotle, wealth accumulation has a natural limit, beyond which further accumulation is a perversion of the function of economic activity, which is to sustain *eû zên*. The pursuit of "unconstrained wealth acquisition" is incompatible with the pursuit of *eû zên*. This doctrine clearly offers an indictment of our contemporary society, in which wealth acquisition, not *eû zên,* is the goal of almost everyone's activity.

Finally, to live well is to engage in moral praxis, especially the practice of justice. But the practice of justice in Aristotle's sense immediately puts today's denizen at odds with modern society, for, as emphasized in this book, Aristotle's little noticed definition of justice is to do "what benefits another," to serve "another person's good."[3] Justice for Aristotle does not wear blindfolds and does not enforce contracts, for the just person benefits his partner in need (cf. Chapter 9). To practise justice in Aristotle's sense requires swimming upstream against the torrent of contemporary culture: hardly easy.

We have identified three reasons why most people in today's world cannot experience *eû zên* or must struggle to do so. First, their societies are not self-sufficient. Second, most people pursue unlimited wealth acquisition. Third, to achieve *eû zên* means to practise justice in a way contrary to contemporary mores.

Another disturbing matter presented in this book is Plato and Aristotle's unusual doctrine that the people who make up a state must differ, "in nature," says Plato, and equivalently, "in kind," says Aristotle, for otherwise, they argue, the association (*koinōnia*) will fail, for people must differ at least in their talents if they are going to have anything to exchange with each other (cf. Chapter 6). Aristotle goes so far as to say that people in a community who differ in function must be incommensurable, and that their difference must be represented in any exchange proportion. From this comes the fundamental theorem of Aristotle's theory of value: That the value of any product is proportional to the function of its producer in the community of the *polis*. Aristotle realistically extends that theorem to another which states: That the exchange value of your good (product or labour or money) is proportional to your social status. One point of that representation is that people who are more powerful exploit those who are weaker, which is confirmed by contemporary research on exchange (cf. Wolff 1982 and Chapter 12 here).

The theorem of Plato and Aristotle that people differ in nature contradicts the Enlightenment doctrine that all are the same in nature and equal, a doctrine upon which modern social thought rests. Since it is possible that Plato and Aristotle are right (and Chapter 6 presents compelling argument for their position), it would behoove us to reconsider social theory from their standpoint. Doing so might enable us to solve some problems in the contemporary world, for Aristotle's view is that people should be helped out of any condition of inequality, for despite public Enlightenment philosophy and social thought, people are treated as though they are different anyway.

This study has advanced a new measure of economic growth in the rate of increase of reciprocal social welfare (cf. Chapters 13 and 14). That metric is ethical: For an economy to grow, it must grow for all people who participate in it or are subject to it. In addition, the book has presented us with a new evaluation of the use of GDP per capita as a metric of economic growth: In some advanced sector economies GDP per capita negatively correlates with social welfare (as measured by our ratios $\frac{Q_5}{Q_1}$ and $\frac{1}{Q_1}-1$). In other words, in those economies, for GDP per capita to rise, the condition of the lower four quintiles of a population must worsen: Rising GDP per capita corresponds to economic decline. This is a disturbing finding. But in some developing economies (e.g. Ecuador) GDP per capita closely correlates with $\frac{Q_5}{Q_1}$. I propose that investigation of the whys for both these phenomena merits attention and may be an avenue of escape from present day economic problems.

To review some more basic conclusions: Part I of this book has shown that Aristotle's critique of political economy has considerable influence on the theories of political economy of Karl Marx, Karl Polanyi, John Rawls, Amartya Sen and Martha Nussbaum. That fact argues that Aristotle articulated a theory of political economy, contrary to modern naysayers. That Part has also shown that a careful reading of Rawls' work reveals extensive influence from Aristotle, not only in his formulation of his "Aristotelian Principle," but also in his development of his "difference principle" (cf. Chapter 3). Moreover, although Sen and Nussbaum are positively influenced by Aristotle, this study has shown that their notion of "functionings" has nothing to do with Aristotle's rigorous concept of the "human function" (cf. Chapter 5). This study has also shown that the capabilities approach does not measure social welfare but rather the welfare of the individual (cf. Chapter 11).

Part II has systematically presented Aristotle's theory of value and his theory of exchange – starting from the metaphysical conceptions upon which they are based and culminating in the development of a system of equations that represent his theories. That is a direct argument that Aristotle articulated a theory of political economy, and refutes the contention of Marx and his followers that Aristotle did not articulate a theory of value. Chapter 8 refutes Marx's argument for the strict commensurability of goods, and laments the inability of his theory to represent the effect of inequality in exchange. Aristotle's theories have more explanatory power than corresponding modern theories of value and exchange.[4]

Finally, Part III has applied Aristotle's theories to develop an Aristotelian Social Welfare Function (SWF) that estimates reciprocity in a society. Part III has estimated values of that function for several countries, including Ukraine, Ecuador, Thailand, Iran, the United States, Germany and Russia. Results are discussed in Chapter 14.

Notes

1 Cf. *EN* iii.3, vi.9
2 Cf. *Pol.* i.2.1252b27–30 and Chapter 7.
3 Cf. *EN* 1130a1, 3–5.
4 For discussion of explanatory power, cf. Chomsky (1965a) and (1965b).

Bibliography

Works by Aristotle and his contemporaries

Texts in Greek

Aristotle. 1920. *Aristotelis Atheniensium Respublica*. Ed. by F. G. Kenyon. Oxford: Clarendon Press. Referred to as "*Ath. Res.*"

Aristotle. 1963. *Aristotelis De Anima*. Ed. by W. D. Ross. Oxford: Clarendon Press. Referred to as "*An.*"

Aristotle. 1991. *Aristotelis Ethica Eudemia*. Ed. by R. R. Walzer and J. M. Mingay. Oxford: Clarendon Press. Referred to as "*EE*".

Aristotle. 1894. *Aristotelis Ethica Nicomachea*. Ed. by I. Bywater. Oxford: Clarendon Press. Referred to as "*EN*".

Aristotle. 1957. *Aristotelis Metaphysica*. Ed. by W. Jaeger. Oxford: Clarendon Press. Referred to as "*Met.*"

Aristotle. 1937. *Parts of Animals*. Ed. and trans. by A. L. Peck. London: Heinemann. Referred to as "*PA.*"

Aristotle. 1955. *Aristotelis Parva Naturalia*. Ed. and comm. by W. D. Ross. Oxford: Clarendon Press.

Aristotle. 1957. *Aristotelis Politica*. Ed. by W. D. Ross. Oxford: Clarendon Press. Referred to as "*Pol.*"

Homer. 1922. *Odyssiae Libros*. In *Homeri Opera*, vols. 3 and 4. Ed. by T. Allen. Oxford: Clarendon Press. Referred to as "*Od.*"

Pausanias. 1918. *Description of Greece*. Ed. and trans. by W. Jones. London: Heinemann.

Plato. 1903. Gorgias. In *Platonic Opera*, vol. 3. Ed. by J. Burnet. Oxford: Clarendon Press. Referred to as "*Gorg.*"

Plato. 2003. *Rempublicam*. Ed. by S. Slings. Oxford: Clarendon Press. Referred to as "*Rep*".

Thucydides. *Thucydidis Historiae*, vols. 1 and 2. Ed by H. Jones. Oxford: Clarendon Press.

Translations and commentaries

Aristophanes. 1967. *The Congresswomen*. Ann Arbor, MI: University of Michigan Press.

Aristote. 1960. *Politique*. Ed. by J. Aubonnet. Paris: Société d'édition Les Belles Lettres.

Aristotle. 1981. *The Athenian Constitution, the Eudemian Ethics, On Virtues and Vices*. Ed. and trans. by H. Rackham. London: Heinemann.

Aristotle. 1984a. *The Complete Works of Aristotle*, 2 vols. Ed. by J. Barnes. Princeton: Princeton University Press.

Aristotle. 1984b. *The Constitution of Athens*. Trans. by F. G. Kenyon, rev. by J. Barnes. In Aristotle (1984a). Kenyon's original trans. available at http://classics.mit.edu/Aristotle/athenian_const.1.1.html

Aristotle. 2016. *De Anima*. Trans. and comm. by C. Shields. Oxford: Clarendon Press.

Aristotle. 1908a. *Metaphysics*. Trans. by W. D. Ross, Oxford: Clarendon Press. Available at http://classics.mit.edu/Aristotle/metaphysics.html

Aristotle. 1908b. *Nicomachean Ethics*. Trans. by W. D. Ross. Oxford: Clarendon Press. Available at http://classics.mit.edu/Aristotle/nicomachaen.html

Aristotle. 1951. *Nicomachean Ethics*. Ed. and comm. by H. Joachim, Oxford: Clarendon Press.

Aristotle. 1999. *Nicomachean Ethics*. Trans. by T. Irwin. Indianapolis: Hackett Publishing.

Aristotle. 2004. *The Nicomachean Ethics*. Trans. by J. Thomson and H. Tredennick. London: Penguin.

Aristotle. 2014. *Nicomachean Ethics*. Trans. by C. D. C. Reeve. Indianapolis: Hackett Publishing.

Aristotle. 1995. *Politics*. Trans. by E. Barker and R. F. Stalley. Oxford: Oxford University Press.

Aristotle. 1998. *Politics*. Trans. by C. D. C. Reeve. Indianapolis: Hackett Publishing.

Aristotle. 1995. *Politics, Books I and II*. Trans. with comm. by T. Saunders. Oxford: Clarendon Press.

Herodotus. 1987. *The History*. Trans. by David Grene. Chicago: University of Chicago Press.

Homer. 1965. *The Odyssey of Homer*. Trans. by R. Lattimore. Chicago: University of Chicago Press.

Lysias. 1930. *Lysias*. Ed. and trans. by W. R. M. Lamb. Cambridge, MA: Harvard University Press. Referred to as "Lys."

Plato. 1997a. *Gorgias*. In Plato (1997b).

Plato. 1997b. *Complete Works*. Ed. by J. Cooper and D. S. Hutchinson. Indianapolis: Hackett Publishing.

Plato. 1992. *Republic*. Trans. by G. M. A. Grube and C. D. C. Reeve. Indianapolis: Hackett Publishing Co.

Plutarch. 1916. "Life of Pericles." In *The Parallel Lives*. Cambridge, MA: Loeb Library.

Thucydides. 1954. *Peloponnesian Wars*. Trans. by Rex Warner. London: Penguin.

Xenophon. 1897. *Oeconomicus*. In *The Works of Xenophon*. Trans. by H. G. Dakyns. London: Macmillan. Referred to as "Xen. Oecon." Available as Project Gutenberg EBook 2008 at http://www.gutenberg.org/files/1173/1173.txt

Secondary sources

Alkire, S. 2002. *Valuing Freedoms*, Oxford: Oxford University Press.

Alvaredo, F., Atkinson, A., Piketty, T. and Saez, E. 2013. "The top 1% in international and historical perspective." *Journal of Economic Perspectives* 27 (3): 1–21.

Anand, P., Santos, C. and Smith, R. 2009. "The measurement of capabilities," in Basu, K. and Kanbur, R. *Arguments for a Better World: Essays in Honor of Amartya Sen*. New York: Oxford University Press, 283–310.

Atkinson, A., Piketty, T. and Saez, E. 2011. "Top incomes in the long run of history." *Journal of Economic Literature* 49(1): 3–71.

Barnes, J. Ed. 1977. *Articles on Aristotle 2: Ethics and Politics.* London: Duckworth.

Barnes, J. 2004. "Introduction." In Aristotle (2004).

Becker, J. F. 1977. *Marxian Political Economy.* Cambridge: Cambridge University Press.

Blyth, M. 2002. *Great Transformations.* Cambridge: Cambridge University Press.

Booth, W. J. 1993. *Households: On the Moral Architecture of the Economy.* New York: Yale University Press.

Brading, D. A. 1991. *The First America.* Cambridge: Cambridge University Press.

Burnet, J. 1900. *Ethics of Aristotle.* London: Methuen.

Carmichael, D. 2007. Review of Nagle (2006). *Canadian Journal of Political Science* 40: 1061.

Carver, T. 1980. "Marx's two-fold character of labour." *Inquiry* 23: 349–352.

Cary, M. 1933. "The population of Athens." Review of A. W. Gomme, *The Population of Athens in the Fifth and Fourth Centuries B.C.* Oxford: Blackwell, 1933. *The Classical Review* 47(6): 224–225.

Charles, D. 1988. "Perfectionism in Aristotle's political theory: Reply to Martha Nussbaum." *Oxford Studies in Ancient Philosophy,* Suppl. Vol.: 185–206.

Chetty, R., Hendren, N., Kline, P., Saez, E. and Turner, N. 2014. "Is the United States still a land of opportunity? Recent trends in intergenerational mobility." *American Economic Review, Papers and Proceedings,* 104(5): 141–147.

Chomsky, N. 1965a. *Aspects of the Theory of Syntax.* Cambridge, MA: MIT Press.

Chomsky, N. 1965b. *Cartesian Linguistics.* New York: Harper and Row.

Clark, A., Frijters, P. and Shields, M. 2008. "Relative income, happiness, and utility: An explanation for the Easterlin paradox and other puzzles." *Journal of Economic Literature,* 46(1): 95–144.

Cooper, J. 1990. "Political animals and civic friendship." In Patzig (1990).

Cordner, C. 1994. "Aristotelian virtue and its limitations." *Philosophy* 69: 291–316.

Courant, R. 1937. *Differential and Integral Calculus,* 2nd edn, vol. 1. London: Blackie.

Crespo, R. 2013. *A Re-Assessment of Aristotle's Economic Thought.* London: Routledge.

Danzig, R. 2000. "The political character of Aristotelian reciprocity." *Classical Philology* 95: 399–424.

Defourney, M. 1914. *Aristote: Theorie économique et politique sociale.* Louvain: Annales de l'Institut supérieure de philosophie.

Depew, D. 1981. "Aristotle's *De Anima* and Marx's theory of man." *Graduate Faculty Philosophy Journal* 8(1–2): 133–187.

Deslauriers, M. 2013. "Political unity and inequality." In Deslauriers, M. and Destrée, P. *The Cambridge Companion to Aristotle's Politics.* Cambridge: Cambridge University Press.

Diels, H. and Kranz, W. Eds. 1956. *Die fragmente der Vorsokratiker.* Berlin: Weidmann.

Dixon, W. and Kay, G. 1995. "Marx's theories of value: A response to Cartelier and Williams." *Cambridge Journal of Economics* 19(4): 509–522.

Dobbs, M. 1973. *Theories of Value and Distribution since Adam Smith.* Cambridge: Cambridge University Press.

Dodd, W. E. 1919. *The Cotton Kingdom.* New Haven: Yale University Press.

Dowding, K., Martin, V. H., Anand, P., Hunter, G., Carter, I. and Guala, F. 2009. "The development of capability indicators." *Journal of Human Development and Capabilities* 10(1): 125–152.

Driver, J. 2014. "The history of Utilitarianism." *Stanford Encyclopedia of Philosophy.* Available at https://plato.stanford.edu/entries/utilitarianism-history/.

Easterlin, R. 1974. "Does economic growth improve the human lot? Some empirical evidence." In David, P. and Reder, M. 1974. *Nations and Households in Economic Growth.* Burlington: Elsevier, 89–125.

Finley, M. 1953. "Land, debt and the man of property." *Political Science Quarterly* 68: 249–68. Reprinted in Finley (1982).

Finley, M. 1973. *The Ancient Economy*. Berkeley: University of California Press.

Finley, M. 1977. "Aristotle and Economic Analysis." In Barnes (1977), 140–158.

Finley, M. 1982. *Economy and Society in Ancient Greece*. Ed. by B. D. Shaw and R. P. Saller. New York: Viking Press.

Fleurbaey, M. 2015. "Beyond income and wealth." *Review of Income and Wealth* 61(2): 199–219.

Fortenbaugh, W. 1977. "Aristotle on slaves and women." In Barnes (1977).

Galbraith, J. K. 1958. *The Affluent Society*. Boston: Houghton Mifflin.

Gallagher, R. 1998. "Aristotle's use of self-refutation in his treatment of the Republic." *Newsletter of the Society for Ancient Greek Philosophy* 9 (Nov/Dec)(3): 1–14.

Gallagher, R. 2011a. "Aristotle on *eidei diapherontes*." *British Journal for the History of Philosophy* 19(3): 363–384.

Gallagher, R. 2011b. "Aristotle's *peirastic* treatment of the *Republic*." *Archiv für Geschichte der Philosophie* 93(1): 1–23.

Gallagher, R. 2012. "Incommensurability in Aristotle's theory of reciprocal justice." *British Journal for the History of Philosophy*. 20(4): 667–701.

Gallagher, R. 2014a. "In defense of moral economy: Marx's criticisms of Aristotle's theory of value." *Archiv für Rechts- und Sozialphilosophie*, 100(1): 112–129.

Gallagher, R. 2014b. "The role of grace in Aristotle's theory of exchange." *Methexis* 26: 145–162.

Gallagher, R. 2018. "An Aristotelian Social Welfare Function." *Archiv für Rechts- und Sozialphilosophie*, 104(1).

Gauthier, R. A. and Jolif, J. Y. 1970. *L'Éthique à Nicomaque*, 2nd edn. Paris: Beatrice-Nauwelaerts.

Gigon, O. 1965. "Die Sklaverei bei Aristoteles." In Fondation Hardt. *La "Politique" d'Aristote*. Geneva: Fondation Hardt, 245–276.

Gilpin, R. 2001. *Global Political Economy*. Princeton: Princeton University Press.

Goodfield, E. 2014. *Hegel and the Metaphysical Frontiers of Political Theory*. London: Routledge.

Gould, C. 1978. *Marx's Social Ontology*. Cambridge, MA: MIT Press.

Granovetter, M. and Swedberg, R. 2011. *The Sociology of Economic Life*, 3rd edn. Boulder, CO: Westview Press.

Hanke, L. 1935. *The First Social Experiments in America*. Cambridge, MA: Harvard University Press.

Hanke, L. 1949. *The Spanish Struggle for Justice in the Conquest of America*. Philadelphia: University of Pennsylvania Press.

Hanke, L. 1952. *Bartolomé de Las Casas*. The Hague: Springer Netherlands.

Hann, C. and Hart, K. 2012. *Economic Anthropology: History, Ethnography, Critique*. Cambridge: Polity Press.

Heath, T. 1949. *Mathematics in Aristotle*. Oxford: Oxford University Press.

Hegel, G .W. F. 1932. Jenenser Realphilosophie I. In *Sämtliche Werke*, Bd. 19. Ed. by Georg Lasson and J. Hoffmeister. Leipzig: F. Meiner.

Hegel, G .W. F. 1977. *The Phenomenology of Spirit*. Trans. by A.V. Miller. Oxford: Oxford University Press.

Hesse, M. 1965. "Aristotle's Logic of Analogy." *Philosophical Quarterly* 15: 328–340.

Howatson, M. C. 1989. *The Oxford Companion to Classical Literature*. Oxford: Oxford University Press.

Humphreys, S. 1978. *Anthropology and the Greeks*. London: Routledge.

Hunt, L. 1975. "Generosity." *American Philosophical Quarterly* 12: 235–244.

Irwin, T. 1988. *Aristotle's First Principles*. Oxford: Oxford University Press.

Jackson, H. 1879. *The Fifth Book of the Nicomachean Ethics of Aristotle*. Cambridge: Cambridge University Press.

Jackson, M. W. 1985. "Aristotle on Rawls: A critique of quantitative justice." *J. Value Inquiry* 19: 99–110.

Jackson, M. W. 1990. "Justice and The Cave." *Social Philosophy Today* 4: 259–274.

Jenkins, W. S. 1935. *The Pro-slavery Thought in the Old South*. Chapel Hill: University of North Carolina Press.

Jevons, W. S. 1924. *The Theory of Political Economy*. London: Macmillan.

Johnson, V. 1939. "Aristotle's theory of value." *American Journal of Philology* 60: 445–451.

Judson, L. 1997. "Aristotle on Fair Exchange." *Oxford Studies in Ancient Philosophy* 15: 147–175.

Kant, I. 1993. *Grounding for the Metaphysics of Morals*. Indianapolis: Hackett Publishing.

Kenny, A. 1978. *The Aristotelian Ethics*. Oxford: Oxford University Press.

Klein, F. 1945. *Elementary Mathematics From an Advanced Standpoint*. New York: Dover.

Konstan, D. 2006. *The Emotions of the Ancient Greek*. Toronto: University of Toronto Press.

Kontos, P. 2011. *Aristotle's Moral Realism Reconsidered*. New York: Routledge.

Kraut, R. 2013. "Aristotle and Rawls on the common good." In M. Deslauriers and P. Destrée. Eds. *The Cambridge Companion to Aristotle's Politics*. Cambridge: Cambridge University Press.

Kühner, R. 1898. *Aüsführliche Grammatik der Griechischen Sprache*. Hannover: Hahn.

Kuneš, J. 2012. *Dimensionless Physical Quantities in Science and Engineering*. Burlington: Elsevier.

Leontief, W. 1959. "The problem of quality and quantity in economics." *Daedalus* 88(4): 622–632. Reprinted in Leontief, W. 1966. *Essays in Economics: Theories and Theorizing*. Oxford: Oxford University Press.

Leshem, D. 2016. "What did the Ancient Greeks mean by *oikonomia*?" *Journal of Economic Perspectives* 30(1): 225–231.

Levitt, K.P. 2014. "Preface." In Polanyi (2014a).

Liddell, H., and Scott, R. 1897. *A Greek-English Lexicon*, 8th edn. Oxford: Oxford University Press.

McCarthy, G. 1990. *Marx and the Ancients*. Savage, MD: Rowman and Littlefield.

McCloskey, D. N. 2016. *Bourgeois Equality*. Chicago: University of Chicago Press.

McKerlie, D. 2001. "Aristotle's theory of justice." *Southern Journal of Philosophy* 39: 119–141.

McLellan, D. 1973. *Karl Marx*. New York: Macmillan.

McNeil, D. 1990. "Alternative interpretations of Aristotle on reciprocal exchange." *Public Affairs Quarterly* 4: 55–68.

Mannheim, K. 1940. *Man and Society*. New York: Harcourt, Brace.

Marcuse, H. 1941. *Reason and Revolution*. Oxford: Oxford University Press.

Marx, K. 1904. *A Contribution to the Critique of Political Economy*. Chicago: Kerr.

Marx, K. 1962. *Das Kapital. Band I*. In Marx, K., and Engels, F. *Werke*, Band 23, S. 11–802. Berlin, DDR: Dietz Verlag. Available at: http://www.mlwerke.de/me/me23/me23_000.htm.

Marx, K. 1967. *Capital, vol. 1*. Ed. by F. Engels, Trans. by S. Moore and E. Aveling. New York: International Publishers.

Marx, K. 1969. *Die deutsche Ideologie*. In Marx, K., and Engels, F. *Werke*, Band 3, S. 5–530. Berlin, DDR: Dietz Verlag. Available at: http://www.mlwerke.de/me/me03/me03_009.htm

Marx, K. 1973. *Grundrisse*. London: Penguin.

Marx, K. 1976. *Capital, Volume 1*. Trans. by B. Fowkes. London: Penguin.

Marx, K. 1997. *The German Ideology*, Part I. In: Easton, L. and Guddat, K. Trans. and Eds. *Writings of the Young Marx on Philosophy and Society*, Indianapolis: Hackett Publishing, 403–473.

Meikle, S. 1985. *Essentialism in the Thought of Karl Marx*. LaSalle, IL: Open Court.

Meikle, S. 1991a. "Aristotle and exchange value." In Keyt, D. and Miller, F. D. Eds. *A Companion to Aristotle's Politics*. Oxford: Oxford University Press. Reprinted in Meikle, S. Ed. 2002. *Marx*. Aldershot: Ashgate.

Meikle, S. 1991b. "Aristotle on equality and market exchange." *Journal of Hellenic Studies* 11: 193–196.

Meikle, S. 1997. *Aristotle's Economic Thought*. Oxford: Oxford University Press.

Mill, J. S. 1848. *Principles of Political Economy*. London: Parker.

Miller, F. 1998. "Was Aristotle the first economist?' *Apeiron* 31: 387–398.

Mills, C. W. 1959. *The Sociological Imagination*. New York: Oxford University Press.

Minar, E. 1942. *Early Pythagorean Politics in Practice and Theory*. Baltimore: Waverley Press.

Mulgan, R. 2000. "Was Aristotle an 'Aristotelian Social Democrat'?" *Ethics* 111: 79–101.

Munck, R. 2006. "Globalization, Labour and the 'Polanyi Problem'." In Phelan, C. Ed. *The Future of Organized Labour*. Bern: Peter Lang.

Nagel, E. 1961. *The Structure of Science: Problems in the Logic of Explanation*. New York: Harcourt, Brace and World, Inc.

Nagle, D. B. 2006. *The Household as the Foundation of Aristotle's Polis*. New York: Cambridge University Press.

Natali, C. 1990. "Aristote et la chrematistique." In Patzig (1990).

Newman, W. L. 1887. *The Politics of Aristotle*. Oxford: Clarendon Press.

Nussbaum, M. C. 1987/1993. "Non-relative virtues: an Aristotelian approach." In Nussbaum and Sen (1993). Earlier versions appeared as Wider Working Paper #32, 1987, and in *Midwest Studies in Philosophy*, 1988.

Nussbaum, M. C. 1988a. "Nature, function, and capability: Aristotle on political distribution." *Oxford Studies in Ancient Philosophy*, Suppl. Vol.: 145–184.

Nussbaum, M. C. 1988b. "Reply to David Charles." *Oxford Studies in Ancient Philosophy*, Suppl. Vol.: 207–214.

Nussbaum, M. C. 1990a. "Aristotelian Social Democracy." In Douglass, R. B., Mara, G. and Richardson, H. 1990. *Liberalism and the Good*. New York and London: Routledge, 203–252.

Nussbaum, M. C. 1990b. "Aristotle on Human Nature and the foundation of ethics." In Altham, J. E. J. and Harrison, R. Eds. 1990. *World, Mind, and Ethics: Essays on the Ethical Philosophy of Bernard Williams*. Cambridge: Cambridge University Press, 102–110.

Nussbaum, M. C. 2000. *Women and Human Development: The Capabilities Approach*. Cambridge: Cambridge University Press.

Nussbaum, M. C. 2006. "Poverty and Human Functioning: Capabilities as Fundamental Entitlements." In Grusky, D. and Kanbur, R. 2006. *Poverty and Inequality*. Stanford: Stanford University Press.

Nussbaum, M. C. 2011. *Creating Capabilities*. Cambridge, MA: Bellknap Press.

Nussbaum, M. C. and Sen, A., eds. 1993. *The Quality of Life*. Oxford: Clarendon Press. Page references are to the WIDER edition.

Ober, J. 1989. *Mass and Elite*. Princeton: Princeton University Press.

OECD. n.d. OECD.StatExtracts, "Income distribution and poverty." <http://stats.oecd.org/Index.aspx?DataSetCode=IDD>

Olshewsky, T. 1968. "Aristotle's use of analogia." *Apeiron* 2: 1–10.

Orum, A. and Dale, J. 2009. *Political Sociology*. Oxford: Oxford University Press.

Ostry, J. D., Berg, A. and Tsangarides, C. G. 2014. "Redistribution, inequality, and growth." IMF Staff Discussion Note SDN/14/02, Feb.

Pack, S. 2010. *Aristotle, Adam Smith and Karl Marx*, Cheltenham: Edward Elgar.

Paley, F. A. 1921. Notes to *Demosthenes, Against Phormio*. Cambridge: Cambridge University Press. Available at http://www.perseus.tufts.edu/hopper/text?doc=Per seus:text:1999.01.0076:speech=34:section=37andhighlight=grain%2Cdistribution. Accessed 10 January 2017.

Patzig, G. Ed. 1990. *Aristoteles Politik*: Akten Des XI. Symposium Aristotelicum Friedrichshafen/Bodensee 25 August – 3 September 1987. Göttingen: Vandenhoeck & Ruprecht.

Pecirca, J. 1967. "A note on Aristotle's conception of citizenship and the role of foreigners in fourth century Athens." *Eirene* 6: 23–26.

Piketty, T. 2013. *Le capital au XXI siècle*. Paris: Éditions du Seuil. Published in English translation as *Capital in the 21st Century*. Cambridge, MA: Harvard University Press, 2014.

Piketty, T. and Saez, E. 2003. "Income inequality in the United States, 1913–1998." *Quarterly Journal of Economics* 118(1): 1–39.

Piketty, T. and Saez, E. 2013. "Top incomes and the Great Recession." IMF Economic Review 61(1): 456–478.

Piketty, T. and Saez, E. 2014. "Inequality in the long run." *Science* 344 (6,186): 838–844.

Piketty, T. and Zucman, G. 2014. "Capital is back: Wealth-income ratios in rich countries 1700–2010." *Quarterly Journal of Economics* 129(3): 1,155–1,210.

Polanyi, K. 1944. *The Great Transformation*. New York: Farrar & Rinehart. Reprinted Boston: Beacon Press, 1957.

Polanyi, K. 1957a. "Aristotle discovers the economy." In Polanyi, Arensberg and Pearson (1957), 64–94.

Polanyi, K. 1957b. "The Economy as Instituted Process." In Polanyi, Arensberg and Pearson (1957), 243–270.

Polanyi, K. 1959. "Aristotle and Galbraith on Affluence." Sent to me by Kari Polanyi Levitt from the Karl Polanyi archive, Concordia University, Montréal, Canada. Hungarian translation published as "Polányi Károly: Arisztotelész és Galbraith a jólétről" in *Szociológiai Szemle* 13(1) (2003), 137–142.

Polanyi, K. 1968a. *Primitive, Archaic, and Modern Economies*. Ed. by G. Dalton. Garden City, NY: Anchor Books.

Polanyi, K. 1968b. "Appendix." In Polanyi (1968a), 120–138.

Polanyi, K. 2014a. *For a New West*. Cambridge: Polity Press, 2014.

Polanyi, K. 2014b. "Market Elements and Economic Planning in Antiquity." In Polanyi (2014a).

Polanyi, K., Arensberg, C. and Pearson, H. Eds. 1957. *Trade and Market in the Early Empires*. Glencoe IL: The Free Press.

Price, A.W. 1990. *Love and Friendship in Plato and Aristotle.* Oxford: Oxford University Press.

Pritchard, D. M. 2015. *Public Spending and Democracy in Classical Athens.* Austin: University of Texas Press.

Randall, J. H. 1960. *Aristotle.* New York: Columbia University Press.

Rawls, J. 1958. "Justice as fairness." *Philosophical Review* 67: 164–194.

Rawls, J. 1975. "A Kantian Concept of Equality." *Cambridge Review* (February): 94–99.

Rawls, J. 1999. *A Theory of Justice,* 2nd edn. Cambridge, MA: Harvard University Press.

Rawls, J. 2001. *Justice as Fairness: A Restatement.* Cambridge, MA: Harvard University Press.

Rieger, E. and Liebfried, S. 2003. *Limit to Globalization.* Cambridge: Polity Press.

Robinson, J. 1947. *An Essay on Marxian Economics.* London: Macmillan.

Roddie, C. 2015. "Demographic competition and inequality aversion." Cambridge University, working paper. Available at https://economics.nd.edu/assets/159868/

Ste. Croix, G. E. M. de. 1981. *The Class Struggle in the Ancient Greek World.* Ithaca: Cornell University Press.

Samuelson, P. 1948. *Economics, An Introductory Analysis.* New York: McGraw-Hill.

Scaltsas, T. 1995. "Reciprocal justice in Aristotle's *Nicomachean Ethics.*" *Archiv für Geschichte der Philosophie* 77: 248–262.

Scanlon, T. M. 1982. "Contractualism and Utilitarianism." In Sen, A., and Williams, B. Eds. *Utilitarianism and Beyond.* New York: Cambridge University Press.

Schofield, M. 1990. "Ideology and Philosophy in Aristotle's Theory of Slavery." In Patzig (1990).

Schumpeter, J. 1954. *History of Economic Analysis.* London: Allen and Unwin. Republished: 2006. Routledge, Taylor and Francis e-library.

Scruton, R. 2010. "Music and morality." *American Spectator* 43(1): 42–45.

Sen, A. 1973/1997. *On Economic Inequality,* 2nd edn. Oxford: Clarendon Press.

Sen, A. 1979, "Utiliarianism and Welfarism." *The Journal of Philosophy* 76: 463–489.

Sen, A. 1980. "Equality of What?" In S. McMurrin, ed., *Tanner Lectures on Human Values* I. Cambridge: Cambridge University Press. Available at https://economics.nd.edu/assets/159868/ Reprinted in Rawls, J., et al. 1987. *Liberty, Equality and Law.* Cambridge: Cambridge University Press.

Sen, A. 1984. *Resources, Values and Development.* Cambridge MA: Harvard University Press.

Sen, A. 1985. "Well-being, agency and freedom: The Dewey Lectures 1984." *Journal of Philosophy* 82 (April).

Sen, A. 1986. "The Standard of Living." In S. McMurrin, ed., *Tanner Lectures on Human Values* VII. Cambridge: Cambridge University Press.

Sen, A. 1987. *On Ethics and Economics.* Oxford: Basil Blackwell.

Sen, A. 1992. *Inequality reexamined.* Cambridge, MA: Harvard University Press.

Sen, A. 1993. "Capability and Well-Being." In Nussbaum and Sen (1993), 30–53.

Sen, A. 2004a. "Elements of a Theory of Human Rights." *Philosophy & Public Affairs* 32(4): 315–356.

Sen, A. 2004b. "Capabilities, Lists and Public Reasons: Continuing the Conversation." *Feminist Economics* 10(3): 77–80.

Sen, A. 2005. "Human Rights and Capabilities." *Journal of Human Development* 6(2): 151–166.

Shields, C. 1999. *Order in Multiplicity.* Oxford: Oxford University Press.

Shields, C. 1990. "The First Functionalist." In Smith, J.-C., ed. 1990. *Essays on the Historical Foundations of Cognitive Science.* Dordrecht: Kluwer, 19–33.

Simpson, P. 1998. *A Philosophical Commentary on the Politics of Aristotle.* Chapel Hill: University of North Carolina Press.

Skinner, A. S. and Wilson, T. Eds. 1975. *Essays on Adam Smith.* Oxford: Clarendon Press.

Smith, A. 1904. *An Inquiry into the Nature and Causes of the Wealth of Nations*, 5th edn. Ed. by Edwin Cannan. London: Methuen and Co. Available at http://www.econlib.org/library/Smith/smWN1.html#I.4.13

Smith, A. 1790. *The Theory of Moral Sentiments.* Reprinted 1975. Oxford: Clarendon Press.

Soudek, J. 1952. "Aristotle's theory of exchange." *Proceedings of the American Philosophical Society* 96: 45–75.

Stigler, G. J. 1975. "Smith's travel on the ship of the state." In Skinner and Wilson (1975).

Thomas d'Aquino [Aquinas]. 1964. *Commentary on Aristotle's Nicomachean Ethics*, vol. 1. Trans. by C. I. Litzinger. Chicago: Regnery.

Tocqueville, A. de. 1988. "Etat social et politique de la France avant et après 1789." In Tocqueville, A. de. 1988. *L'ancien régime et la révolution.* Paris: Flammarion.

Tyson, L. 2014. "The rising costs of U.S. income inequality." *Project Syndicate*, 30 Nov.

United Nations Development Program (UNDP). 2009. *Human Development Report.* New York: United Nations Organization.

United Nations Development Program (UNDP). 2016. *Human Development Reports: Human Development Index* (HDI). New York: United Nations Organization. Available at http://hdr.undp.org/en/content/human-development-index-hdi

US Census Bureau. 2016. "Selected measures of household income dispersion: 1967–2014." Washington DC: US Census Bureau. Available at <http://www.census.gov/hhes/www/income/data/historical/inequality/Table%20IE-1.pdf>. Income quintile data downloaded 3 April 2016.

van Riel, R. and van Gulick, R. 2014. "Scientific Reduction." *Stanford Encyclopedia of Philosophy.* Available at https://plato.stanford.edu/entries/scientific-reduction/

Wallach, J. R. 1992. "Contemporary Aristotelianism." *Political Theory* 20: 613–641.

Wartofsky, M. 1983. "Karl Marx and the Outcome of Classical Marxism, or: Is Marx's Labor Theory of Value Excess Metaphysical Baggage?" Presented at Eightieth Annual Meeting of the American Philosophical Association, Eastern Division. *Journal of Philosophy* 80 (11): 719–730.

Weber, M. 1922. *Wirtschaft und Gesellschaft.* Tübingen: Mohr. Available at https://archive.org/stream/wirtschaftundges00webeuoft?ref=ol#page/n5/mode/2up

Weber, M. 1978. *Economy and Society.* Ed. by Roth, G., and Wittich, C. Berkeley: University of California. Available at https://archive.org/details/MaxWeberEconomyAndSociety

Wenar, L. 2012. "John Rawls." *Stanford Encyclopedia of Philosophy.* Available at https://plato.stanford.edu/entries/rawls/.

White, M. 2012. *Political Philosophy: An Historical Introduction*, 2nd edn. Oxford: Oxford University Press.

Williams, M. 1992. "Marxists on money, value and labour-power: a response to Cartelier." *Cambridge Journal of Economics* 16(4): 439–445.

Wolff, R. P. 1981. "A Critique and Reinterpretation of Marx's Labor Theory of Value." *Philosophy and Public Affairs* 11: 89–120.

Wolff, R. P. 1982. Reply to Roemer." *Philosophy and Public Affairs* 12(1): 84–88.

World Bank. 2015–2017. For income share held by highest 20%: <http://data. worldbank.org/indicator/SI.DST.05TH.20/countries>; for income share held by lowest 20%: <http://data.worldbank.org/indicator/SI.DST.FRST.20>; for GDP per capita: <http://databank.worldbank.org/data/reports.aspx?source=2&coun try=&series=NY.GDP.PCAP.KD&period=>. Data was downloaded as follows: Quintile data: for Germany, Russia, Ukraine, Iran: 3 April 2016; for Cambodia, Mali, and Thailand: 15 Sept 2017; for all other countries (exc. USA): 7 Aug 2015; GDP per capita data: 3 March 2016.

World Bank. 2016b. Email communications with World Bank research staff.

World Trade Organization (WTO). 2013. "Tariff Analysis Online facility." Chap. 87. Heading 8701: Tractors, for rates of export tariffs. *Available at* <http://tariffanalysis. wto.org/report/ExportMarket.aspx>.

Index of passages

This index lists references to chapters as well as passages. Passages are listed by Stephanus page number or Bekker number. For multiple references to a passage on a book page, a "(n)" follows the page number, where n is the number of references on that page.

Greek index

Name index

Archytas of Tarentum 142
Aristides 32, 73n20

Cambodia 183, 189, 190
de las Casas, B. 69, 73n22
Comecon 192, 193

Delian League 32, 36n101, 37n102

Easterlin, R. 179
Ecuador 183, 184, 189, 190, 192

Finley, M. 4n1, 87n30, 96, 127n8,
    152n105, 153
Fleurbaey, M. 165

Germany 184, 186, 188, 189, 190, 191

Hayek, L. v. 26
Hegel, G. 7, 15n40
Hungary 192

Iran 168, 183, 185, 189, 190, 192, 193

Jefferson, T. xii
Jevons, W.S. 124, 130n84, 171

Kant, I. 3, 25, 38–40, 167
Konstan, D. xii, xv, 3

Leontief, W. 124, 126, 130n82
Levitt, K.P. 33
Lithuania 192
Lysias 98, 100, 104, 108n87

Mali 183, 189, 190
Marx, K. xii, xiv, 2–4, 16, 17, 22, 33,
    51n1, 54, 75, 94; antithesis between
    use-value and exchange-value 11–12;
Capital 7; *Contribution to the Critique of
    Political Economy* 7; criticisms of Aristotle
    121–127, 171, 179, 198; develops
    theory of contradiction in capitalism
    from Aristotle 7–10; relation to Aristotle
    7–15; his use of Aristotle's metaphysics
    12–13
Meikle, S. xv, 2, 4n1, 8, 84, 117, 118,
    150n67, 153
Mill, J.S. 64n35, 124, 130n84, 171

Natali, C. 8, 9, 14n13, 14n18, 35n45, 93,
    94, 107n63
New Deal 16, 20, 33, 40
Nussbaum, M. xii, 2, 54, 63, 165–167,
    171, 198; capabilities and Aristotle's
    human function argument 70–71;
    criticisms of Mulgan, Wallach and others
    refuted 67–69; distributive conception
    66–67; relation to Aristotle 66–72

Peloponnesian War 32, 73n20
Penteconteitia 32
Pericles 32, 40
Persia 32, 69n20
Piketty, T. 179, 181, 188, 191, 192, 194
Plato 62, 68, 89, 135; *Gorgias* 155; on how
    people differ in nature 197; Rawls on
    52n34; *Republic* 44, 49, 77, 170
Poland 192
Polanyi, K. 2, 3, 8, 46, 98, 100, 103, 144,
    153, 198; on living well as normative
    principle 21–22; on *oikonomia* and self-
    sufficiency 16–21; on reciprocity and
    redistribution 30–33; role of status
    29–30; his theories and relation to
    Aristotle 16–34; two meanings of
    economic 26–29; on wealth not in
    accord with nature 22–26

Subject index

ability 41–44, 46, 92, 147, 159; innate 41–42; *see also* capacity
action 2, 12, 21, 28, 55, 58, 60, 84; in accordance with reason 70–71, 82; based on group loyalty 58; economic 28; rational 27, 28, 32–33; social 26
adaptive preferences 166
advantage 31, 43, 45, 60, 62–63, 119, 120, 136, 142, 155; less 21, 40, 43, 45–50, 85, 161, 172, 181; more 43–50, 53, 85, 172–173, 180; social 62; social disadvantage 68
aesthetic 38–39, 41
aggregate 79, 165–166
alteration 83–84; has forms 84; through work 12, 84, 116
analogy 82, 132, 142; proportions derivable by 82, 115
antinomy 112, 117; in Marx 127, 131
anxiety 22, 75, 89, 96, 101–103
appetites 89, 136; gratification of 89
argument of this book, 2–4
Aristotelian Principle 38, 40–43, 45, 198
artifact 12, 79, 84, 116–117, 127, 171
artisan 81, 100, 115, 119, 146
assets: common 44–45, 113, 135; comparable 113; natural 38, 40, 42–45, 49, 60, 62
asymmetric 155, 157, 171

beneficence 50, 158
beneficiaries 145, 158–159
benefit xii, 11, 43–50, 71, 74, 92, 96, 106, 133, 136, 137, 140, 142–143, 145–146, 150, 154, 156–159, 170, 172–174, 184, 190, 192, 194, 197
bilateral 157
boundary 18, 95; *see also* limit
bureaucracy 21, 27

calculability 26
capabilities 3, 54–6, 59–61, 63, 66–70, 165–168, 169, 180; and citizenship 67; and human function argument 70–71, 74; list of 167, 169; as set of vectors of functionings 61–62; and social welfare 165–169, 198; and theory of goods 62–3
capacity 81–82, 85, 116, 157; deliberative 68, 102–103, 105, 108; differing 156, 159; for growth 180; of humans xii, 41, 42, 68, 101, 105, 126, 167; to live well 21, 63; natural 42–44; of reciprocity 31; *see also* power
capital xii, 7–11, 20, 33, 101, 125, 127, 171, 191
capitalism 11, 16–17, 23–25, 27, 33, 46, 51, 191, 192; social market 191
capitalist 7, 8, 11, 25, 27, 33, 39, 46, 190, 194
change 83; and Aristotelian principle 41; comparability of 83–84; of form 12; in income 48; of materials into product 132; in relative income 179; rate of change in social welfare 181, 183; in utility 60; in value 10
chrematistics 7–9, 10, 12–13, 101
circulation 7–11, 13, 26, 101; Marx's model of developed from Aristotle 8
class: as *genos* 67, 82; social 23, 30, 46, 57–58, 98, 125, 159, 188, 192
classical studies 68
commensurability 83, 110, 114, 117, 145; strict 122–124, 146, 150, 151, 198; sufficient 117, 146
commerce 3, 10, 19, 23, 25–26, 104; in Aristotle 24, 57, 97–99, 136, 157
common(s) 9, 20, 31, 44–45, 93, 157; make money from the 100; meals 43, 69; perception 92, 100, 102; *see also* factor

community 3, 9, 12–13, 16, 18–21, 25, 29–31, 33, 44, 46–48, 50, 165, 170, 173, 174, 197; Aristotle on 55, 62, 75, 77–85, 89–93, 96–97, 100–104, 110–120, 132–148, 153–159; in Europe vs. USA 191–192; of interest in Rawls 43, 49; Rawls' rejection of 38–40, 45; in Sen 58, 61–62
comparability 83–84, 87, 145
composite 12, 79, 126, 165
constitution: Nussbaum's best 66, 72n3
contradiction 7–11, 13, 101, 143
cooperation 133, 148n2, 181; in Rawls' theory 43, 45–46, 48
corporation 27
cottage 18, 20, 24
counter-movement 21
craft 22, 32, 132–133; of commerce 98; of money-making or wealth accumulation 8–9, 12, 22–23, 35n45, 97; of *oikonomia*? 93; as part of city-state 98; of property acquisition 9, 95
craving: for money 21–23, 103
currency 98, 113, 124, 145, 171, 172; as part of *polis* 78; represents need 114, 145; *see also* money

deliberation 103; civic 22, 31, 56, 67–68, 93; deficient in capacity for 68, 102, 103; inability to 90, 196; legislative 72n9
desert 146–147; *see also* merit
diagonal pairing 111, 145–146; and *charis* 157; definition 137–140; and proportional exchange 140–144
difference: between unity and heap 78–79; in *eîdos* 79, 86n13; essential xiii; in form 126; formal 84; functional 59, 84, 120, 159, 197; Marx on 126; metaphysical 77; in models of circulation 7; in kind 156; in natural assets 49; in nature 77–78; qualitative 81, 112, 126, 147–148; principle of Rawls 3, 38, 43–50, 60, 172–173, 198; Sen on 59–62; and social 85, 125; in social welfare 191; in worth 115
disadvantage 68
disposition (psychological) 22, 96, 102, 156
distribution 7, 50, 139; Aristotle on 113; from common assets 109, 120, 135, 143; in form 118; by function 83, 115; of "life's chances" 68–69; of natural assets 38, 42, 44–46, 60; Nussbaum on 66; in Rawls 172–173; in USA 194

diversity: of ends 166–167; Sen on 59–60, 63
dominance: ranking in Sen 61
double movement 21

efficiency: in German system 191; Polanyi on 21; Sen on 56
end(s) (purpose, *telos*) 22, 25, 27–28, 56, 96, 100, 167; of circulation 10; diverse 167; of exchange 8, 9; of "the good for man" 56; in her- or him-self 25, 49, 173; of household 91; living well as 22, 96; money as 22, 96, 100–101, 103; of *oikonomikē* 93; *prakton* good as 93; of production 11; second-order 166; *see also* purpose
Enlightenment 2, 43, 44, 45, 85, 126, 197–198
equality 2, 26, 85, 126; vs. difference 147–148; in exchange 114, 117; and growth 180; reciprocal 80, 83, 85, 140–141
equalize 141
exchange xii, xiii, xiv, 1–3, 7–11, 19, 101–102, 123, 197; in accordance with nature 97; Aristotle's theory 48, 110–111, 125, 127, 163, 198; asymmetrical 171;and benefit 136, 146, 173; between unequal parties 50, 80, 83, 110, 112–113, 118–119, 124, 134–137, 139–141, 147, 173; and *charis* 75, 133, 153–159; and civic friendship 50, 70, 138; commercial and merchandising 24, 35, 94, 97–101; and commensurability 117, 122; communities of 132, 135; and comparability 111; and diagonal pairing 137–140; of equivalents or non-equivalents 102; fair 111; and exploitation 113, 136, 139; to fill lack in a self-sufficiency 85, 97, 99; form of e. contrary to nature 89, 98–102; just 112, 137, 141; of labour for wages, 46; market 17, 19, 24, 28; models of 1, 7–11, 124–125, 130n84; necessary 14, 18–19, 24, 94, 98; and need 111, 114, 123; need for equality in 114; not proper use 99; proportional 137, 140–141; ratios 26, 120–121, 124, 136–137, 170, 171; and reciprocity 31, 80, 170; and social conditions, relations 113, 115, 119–120, 139, 170; as status transaction 17, 29–30, 45, 47, 113, 173; terms of 137; -token 145; and value 126n80; voluntary 134–135; vs. use 127n102